Christians in the City of Lagos

CHRISTIANS IN THE CITY: STUDIES IN CONTEMPORARY GLOBAL CHRISTIANITY

Series Editor: Dyron Daughrity

Christians in the City looks carefully at Christianity in many of the world's great cities. It draws on interdisciplinary methods including anthropology, ethnography, sociology, phenomenology, and history. The series marks a significant contribution to the growing body of scholarship on world Christianity, lived religion, material religion, urban studies, and globalization as it engages people on the ground, in their local setting. The cities covered are drawn from around the world: North America, Latin America, Africa, Asia, Europe, the Middle East, and Oceania.

Books highlight how Christianity is changing particular metro areas, as well as how those areas are impacting the Christian religion. Most major forms of Christianity are discussed: Pentecostalism, Roman Catholic, mainline Protestant, non-denominational megachurches, Eastern Orthodox, immigrant forms, and house churches. The net is cast wide in order to understand what is happening with Christianity as it engages the great urban centers of the world.

Christians in the City of Hong Kong, Tobias Brandner
Christians in the City of Shanghai, Susangeline Y. Patrick
Christians in the City of Nairobi, Kyama Mugambi and Mark Shaw
Christians in the Cities of Johannesburg and Pretoria, Stéphan de Beer
Christians in the City of Montréal, Glenn Smith

Christians in the City of Lagos

CALEB O. OLADIPO

BLOOMSBURY ACADEMIC
LONDON · NEW YORK · OXFORD · NEW DELHI · SYDNEY

BLOOMSBURY ACADEMIC
Bloomsbury Publishing Plc, 50 Bedford Square, London, WC1B 3DP, UK
Bloomsbury Publishing Inc, 1385 Broadway, New York, NY 10018, USA
Bloomsbury Publishing Ireland, 29 Earlsfort Terrace, Dublin 2, D02 AY28, Ireland

BLOOMSBURY, BLOOMSBURY ACADEMIC and the Diana logo are trademarks of
Bloomsbury Publishing Plc

First published in Great Britain 2025

Series design by Rebecca Heselton
Cover image © Kehinde Temitope Odutayo / Fela Sanu / Getty Images

A catalogue record for this book is available from the British Library.

A catalogue record for this book is available from the Library of Congress.

ISBN: HB: 978-1-3504-0126-6
PB: 978-1-3504-0127-3
ePDF: 978-1-3504-0128-0
eBook: 978-1-3504-0124-2

Series: Christians in the City

Typeset by Deanta Global Publishing Services, Chennai, India
Printed and bound in Great Britain

For product safety related questions contact productsafety@bloomsbury.com.

To find out more about our authors and books visit www.bloomsbury.com
and sign up for our newsletters.

Dedicated in Memoriam

Benjamin A. Oladipo
(1921–94)

and

Josiah A. Oladipo
(1925–2007)

My two fathers who showed me the love of God and the enduring values of unity.
It was my greatest life fortune and happiest height to walk in spirit with such men.

Affectionately dedicated to:

Rosie Corona and Christopher Taiwo Oladipo
True global citizens and a constant reminder of the confluence of the
African and the Latin American cultures

Luka Teniayo Pupić
First best grandson who will live to bring joy to future generations

Petar Pupić and Caroline Kehinde Oladipo
Tender and joyful human beings with inner strength and integrationist
nature and identity

Clement Olu-Ayo Oladipo
An independent thinker with a remarkable sense of justice and an active
gatekeeper of our shared African roots

Contents

PART THREE Christians in the City of Lagos:
Stories of Love 95

A personal preface

The story of Christianity in the modern world is incomplete without a knowledge of how followers of Christ function in some of the largest cities of the world. This book chronicles the life and work of Christians in one of those cities – Lagos, Nigeria. It recounts their journey of faith, doubt, transgression, forgiveness, uncertainty, vulnerability, poverty, redemption, hope, despair, charity and wisdom. Each chapter is a record of the life story of a selected Christian whom I interviewed in Lagos between 2022 and 2023. Readers will experience these stories in all their naked power as they were told to me – stories relating how these individuals became Christians and their challenges of living as Christ-followers in modern-day Lagos.

Readers will learn that believers have not only come to God but have also been brought to God. The book is about Christian authenticity and aims to lead readers to understand the idiosyncratic characteristics of the lives of believers and the non-binary nature of Christianity itself. It will also offer a window onto the works and activities of God among God's peoples in one of the most populous cities of the world.

It is a story about the enduring values of Christians who are relating God's story as believers living in harmony with diverse ethnic groups – both Christian and non-Christian – in Lagos.

I flew to Lagos in December 2022 and returned there in August 2023 to conduct ethnographic research from which the fabric of this book is woven. The people I interviewed were from diverse Christian traditions and demography. They were of different ethnic groups, a microcosm of Nigeria itself, representing the character and natural depths of how followers of Jesus Christ function in contemporary Lagos.

While this book is a portrait of my experience with these followers of Christ in Lagos (where I grew up), it is also about how Christians live and work in that vibrant, bustling Nigerian hub. The vulnerabilities of these believers are not concealed but revealed with veracity. When wounds as well as joyful moments are shared, it leads to the creation of true community and fellowship.

In many ways, it can be said that there could be no Nigeria without Lagos, its commercial and industrial capital. Similarly, there could be no Lagos without its Christians. The Christians who populate the city have transformed it into a centre of excellence like no other in Nigeria. The people in Lagos are a part of a distinct Nigerian economic engine that propels its growth; and with over 20 million population Lagos remains one of the fastest-growing cities in Africa.

Most Christians in Lagos understand that not all those who migrate there from rural areas can be successful. A popular oracle for newcomers to the city offers wise counsel: *One must have the fortitude of a warrior and the patience of an angel to be successful in Lagos.* Or as one elder told me 'Living in Lagos requires the wisdom of a serpent and the gentility of a dove'. Another added that 'one must labor like a devil and pray like an angel' to make it in Lagos. It is not a city for everyone; only for those newcomers who are imaginative, scrupulous, serious-minded and determined. An octogenarian interviewee who had come to Lagos in 1947 said that he would not have been successful even in building his own house had not his God and his destiny from his native village accompanied him. With no relatives or network of friends in Lagos, he ventured into the transportation business, succeeding because of his God-given talents and destiny, he believed.

These pages are an account of how ordinary Christians who are janitors, filmmakers, accountants, attorneys, farmers, businessmen, traders, bus conductors, pastors, priests, teachers and university professors have been transformed and enriched by living in Lagos. We shall also see how living in Lagos has helped its citizens gain a new appreciation for their Christian identity. This book, rather than being a theological treatise, is about confession, absolution and the perspectives of Christian experience for ordinary Christians in Lagos – how they live, what they eat, how they spend their leisure time and some of the challenges they face in Lagos.

We will see how citizens of Lagos experience normal life – getting married, having children, having naming ceremonies for their newborn babies, graduating from college, having their first car, building their house, being recognized as a minister, attending non-traditional Pentecostal churches, getting their first job, changing careers and returning in their old age to their villages to benefit the people who sent them to Lagos.

Many have reached a stage in their walk with God that leads me to conclude that it is one thing for a Christian to say, 'I believe God', but quite another to aspire a life of such discipline and dedication that would want God to say to Christians 'I believe them'.

Naturally, travelling gives people a peculiar sense of serendipity. Along the way, the Lagos Christians have faltered but were not destroyed. During this journey, Christians in Lagos have not only turned the city to a Pentecostal centre of Africa but have also made it a multi-religious environment where Christians and members of other faith traditions live amicably, despite sporadic conflicts fuelled by political fragility and ethnic rivalries. Thus, Christians in Lagos may sometimes bleed, but are never mortally wounded, always rising from adversity. Members of all faith traditions continue in their struggle for self-discovery. If it is the nature of humanity to migrate from one place to another throughout life, then travelling provides a window to see other people in new ways. Thus, newcomers to Lagos tend to become more receptive to learning, to love, to challenges and to life itself.

The Lagos experience transforms Christian lives, helping believers to have convictions as well as challenging them in a spirit of becoming. But coming to Lagos also gives Christians the opportunity to experience important moments of unexpected happiness. Life, most Christians in Lagos recognize, is based on giving thanks to God. Christians receive and give by God's grace. If 'thank you, God' were the only prayer believers uttered, it would be enough to satisfy Jesus Christ, the saviour who has brought them to God. Thanksgiving is based on an inner attitude towards life. Christians in Lagos experience this fully by travelling from the rural areas, migrating to Lagos as pilgrims within their own land.

Life in Lagos, as everywhere, has both a dark side and a bright side. Christians in Lagos often describe their personal experiences and encounters with God in detail. They taught me that those who emphasize only the positive to the exclusion of the negative aspects of life are doomed to irrational optimism and arrogance. Those who emphasize only the negative sides are condemned to despair, self-pity and fear – the opposite of faith.

The people who shared with me their stories of faith in God expressed to me that life is simple, yet its profound complexities are inescapably real. The difference is between saying: 'Good! It is morning O Lord' and 'O Good Lord! It is morning'. The grapes and oranges, the fruits of human existence, are found in unexpected places. Some people are happy because the fruits are sweet, but others are sad because the fruits have seeds. Life is a terrain of unlimited and varied landscapes. It can be a territory either of disappointed expectations or fulfilled promises. The beauty of roses includes a lovely fragrance; but because there are also thorns, we must be prepared to overcome challenges along the way. This is the life of Christians in Lagos and, perhaps, in other places in the Global South.

This book was written in the part of the world that has seen a modernity that is ending even as it unfolds. A new world order that is relatively free of cultural particularity and political imperialism is slowly emerging, its contours relatively unknown. Perhaps one can get a sight of this future through a journey of faith with people who are totally different. Living with people from different historical and cultural backgrounds can help us become fully human and stretch us in shaping our own primary identities. Lagos is an indicator of how Christians live and work in the Global South.

In his poem *The Meaning of Africa* (1963), Abioseh Nicol described Africa perfectly when he wrote: "You are not a country, Africa, you are a concept, fashioned in our minds, each to each, to hide our separate fears, to dream our separate dreams." Davidson Sylvester Hector Willoughby Nicol (1924–1994) also known by his pen name, Abioseh Nicol, was a Sierra Leonean physician, academic, diplomat and poet. Nicol was the first black African to graduate with first-class honours from the University of Cambridge and he was also the first black African elected as a fellow of a college of Cambridge University. His works, *Africa, A Subjective View* and *Two African Tales* were published in 1964 and 1965 respectively. In these works, Nicol expressed his views that Africa is more than a continent, Africa is a concept.

The African Christian experience is a glimpse of infinity of an abiding faith in God demonstrated by Christians in Lagos. As they can face some existential challenges, it is irrefutable that the church is triumphant because Christians there do not hide their lamps under a bushel.

But this book is also about our attitude towards Christians from other cultures. Sometimes we wonder how the Christian experience is received or responded to in the Global South. What have we learned from their experience that can enrich or transform our own lives? What is our attitude towards Christians in the non-Western world? Have we listened to their songs, their vulnerabilities, their longings for God and their joyful celebrations? What is our attitude towards what may seem like their illogical faith in God? After my own experience of the people I interviewed in Lagos, it would be difficult for me to ever see Christians the same way.

As the church moves towards a more perfect union and the fullness of divine truth, the indigenous definitions of Christianity in Lagos have led me to one conclusion: the early European missionaries did not only lead the nationals to discover the Christian religion, but the indigenous people themselves discovered Christianity and transformed it with their own cultural idioms and spiritual lenses. Therefore, Christians in the Global South, one could argue, represent a transitional light of the Gospel and of the Christian faith in our generation.

It is not my intent to provide a town hall of information or a clearing house of Christian ideas and perspectives in Lagos. I debated whether I should write to a specific audience or adhere to a particular Christian school of thought or community as I did in my previous works. This book, however, portrays different Christians in the city of Lagos, and my imagined audience is diverse, cutting across multiple academic disciplines and socio-cultural boundaries. For example, cultural anthropologists and sociologists, as well as demographers and scholars with interests in migration of people from rural to urban centres, would benefit from reading the book.

I also envision those who desire evidence of the work of the Holy Spirit in how the lives of Christians are transformed by their faith, hope and charity. Above all, it is the stories of those who live and work in Lagos, and how the invisible hands of God have guided them through life circumstances. The book will be of interest to a wide variety of people interested in the spiritual well-being, social lives and works of others.

The book is divided into three parts. Part I of the book includes four stories of Christians whom I interviewed, whose experiences are unified by their enduring faith in God. Part II is not dissimilar, but the stories recounted there are a demonstration of the hopes of the people. Part III of the book tells the stories of Christians who are doing something new to carry the experience of their faith forward. We will see in part three that while the Christian faith is returning to its roots to test the youth of modernity, it is simultaneously moving forward to challenge the claims of Christian fundamentalism as well as secularism that still threatens to suffocate the life of the church. The church in Lagos operates between the past and the future.

These stories are only the tip of the iceberg, but they represent a path towards understanding what it means to live and work as Christians in Lagos. While some of the stories can be read as testimonies, the storytellers themselves perceive them as offerings, viewing their faith journeys as opportunities for service and the fulfillment of the promises of God.

When we are surrounded by abject poverty, we see our source of sustenance and redemption more clearly. Growing up in Lagos, I experienced such poverty. While a life of destitution can tarnish our image of God, it also builds and strengthens human character. Poverty does not destroy but rather brings into focus and elevates or reveals the other innovative, dormant 'gears' within us we didn't know we possessed that enable us to tap into the resources in the depth of our humanity. This ingenuity is within us, and poverty can awaken it. The poverty of the people of Lagos works to make them mature and insightful into their human condition, helping them develop new initiatives for living within their means.

In the process of drafting the manuscript, I initially thought I was merely relating the stories of Christians whom I interviewed in Lagos. But later, I realized it had also become a dialogue and conversation with myself about my own faith and the Spirit of God in me. The selected stories are also the stories that are most personal to me. They deserve to be shared with the diversity of people I have projected as my audience – both Christian and non-Christian. Their stories are the stories I, too, have lived. I have lived in a world of uncertainty, poverty and marginalization, experiencing emotional pain and political persecution. They have not dehumanized me, but their acceptance by the church has put a stain on Christianity itself. However, I have also experienced victories from unexpected places. I have been the beneficiary of kindness, generosity, and a strong sense of community among Christians in Lagos.

So, having known both poverty and affluence in Lagos taught me to depend on God completely and unashamedly, knowing that my victories or the blessings I have received in life have not come from any source or power other than God. And they have come through the community of ordinary people who are like me. It is through my Christian experience that I have seen God at work. Any ideas I have of the sufficiency of God are the cumulative effect of my own journey along with my fellow pilgrims and sojourners in Lagos.

We do not come to God alone and by our own initiative; we have been brought to God, and we climb the mountains of faith, hope and charity together. When I was living in Lagos in the 1970s, my relationship with God and others was deepened by attending Bible studies and prayer meetings where church leaders naturally emerged. I also learned to live with little and profited from the insights that come from knowing a non-materialistic environment. I saw fellow Christians exercising faith, never taking for granted such daily wonders as the gift of life, protection, provision, health and job promotion, as well as the miracles of new births into the family.

I lived in the popular borough of Itire-Surulere. Some Good Samaritans there often took me to Tinubu Square, where I was a junior clerk at Union Bank. During the rainy season, our house at Itire-Surulere was often flooded. The capacity to jettison professional success and embrace God in faith through poverty opened new possibilities for me and allowed me to expand my future. God does not do for us that which we can do for ourselves and for others. By working hard and praying with fellow Christians fervently, I learned that praying and labouring are an integral part of the Christian life. I was surrounded by Christians who were not casual about their faith and who took prayers as the oxygen of their Christian experience.

It is my hope that the reading community would embrace this book as an important stage in their own journey of faith and understanding of God, seeing why it is often important in faith to trade life's certainties for what we have not yet seen.

I would hope that this book can be of value to the church globally and to the glory of God. Some Christians I interviewed in Lagos did not disclaim or discard their indigenous African spiritual beliefs and practices as inferior or inauthentic. Rather, they perceived their prior experiential existence as incubators which prepared them for the arrival of a new way of being spiritual through Christianity. In the same manner, the early Christians followed Jesus Christ, practising their new faith without sacrificing their primary Jewish religious identity.

It is acknowledged that others believe in the concept of 'new wine in new wineskins' with little room for indigenous religions and the world views that accompany them. As we consider these two different pillars of understanding Christianity from the Christian missionary points of view, we can state without qualification or exaggeration that Christian mission is the opportunity to lead others to choose the God who has already chosen them, and to assist local people in finding the divine initiatives at the root of their faith in Christ through their own frameworks and spiritual wealth.

These stories of Christian experience are the stories of hope, which is a defining characteristic of the Christian religion and of the Christians in Lagos. The search for hope as demonstrated in the life and resurrection of Jesus of Nazareth is one of humanity's greatest longings. Especially in the stories recounted in Part Two, we see this hope constantly demonstrated in the rhythms of how Christians live. Through the practice of faith and hope, we become stronger in our relationship with the Divine.

Part Three celebrates stories of Christians in Lagos who are passionate about improving the quality of their lives and the lives of others. Their stories raise questions about the basis for their endurance and hope in Christ. Some shared with me that their faith in God is not transactional but covenantal. Christians serve God because God deserves their devotion and not because they want to gain material rewards. Their devotion to God has intrinsic value. For them, there is nothing they can do or offer unto God or to their fellow believers that would make God love them any more or less or add to the sovereignty of God who gave them life. I was often surprised at their responses to my questions and their joyful disposition because we live in an age of the prosperity Gospel, with materialistic goals and relentless greed.

It is true that some church leaders have abused their positions by amassing or acquiring wealth by taking advantage of church members. These avaricious leaders are often privately criticized by their members; but it does not stop them from flocking into their churches to worship God. There are no toolboxes for correcting or criticizing fallible church leaders because they are seen by many Lagosian Christians as the 'shepherds of the sheep' to be loved and respected, not employees to be summoned or paid with salaries and supervised. Their faith in God transcends the blemishes they perceive in their charismatic leaders. Christians understand that in God's Garden of grace, crooked trees can bear good and edible fruits. Faith flows in the rhythm of life and its struggles, giving rise to deeper questions of why we are created and what the purpose of our existence might be.

I also perceive that the Christian faith is returning to its earlier roots, with the spread of Christianity through personal stories and testimonies of what God has done for Christians, healing their maladies, safeguarding them from danger and awakening them from a slumber that tells them they do not belong to this world. What is certain in Lagos is that even as Christians are surrounded by menacing circumstances and afflicted by doubt, they continue practising their faith.

These miracles occur every day, seen only with the eyes of faith. The poor look at these miracles and marvel, while the affluent see them with suspicion and incredulous scepticism. Our own Christian stories are not complete until we become wounded and vulnerable in need of help from the Divine. Ours is a story that has no beginning or ending. It is a story of forgiveness, redemption, love, faith and hope – even when they all seem impossible.

Each generation is obligated to tell its own story that is unique to its own context. I am accountable to tell my own story, examining and supporting it through the stories of other pilgrims. The Christian story is ever extending into the lives of others. My purpose in this book is to find a space to showcase the Christian experience of others, helping them find their own voices, make their own mistakes and continue their own pilgrimages.

Simply put, I wish to share my thoughts and insights through the stories that Christians in Lagos have told me about the God they experience in their day-to-day life. One of the greatest lessons they taught me was that when the storms of life were raging, God stood by them and aided them in unexpected ways and places. The light of faith in them continues to shine brighter even amid the battle that darkness continues to wage; for the battle and the victory are the Lord's and not theirs. In addition, I learned from Christians in Lagos that the level at which we communicate with God in prayers is proportionate to the level at which we live for God's glory in the world.

The unique universes of the Christians I interviewed are extensive and not limited to the physical world. They see their ancestors in their dreams, instructing them to be faithful and to not leave the battlefield. They interpret their earthly conditions with spiritual contentment, seeing mundane things with spiritual interpretation. Their physical and spiritual spheres are connected; they never separate them to please others or placate those who are sceptical. Like the disciples of Christ, they are willing to die rather than deny their resurrected Lord. They see themselves as but instruments of God's gracious overture, knowing that in the long journey to their ultimate destination of eternal freedom, they are only incidentals in the overarching plans of God.

This book is different in the sense that it is not a construction project but a retelling of the stories of the journey and destination of the Nigerian Christians in Lagos. It is an expression of the breath of God for the people of God, and a spiritual offering of Christians in Lagos which calls for a response.

What is our attitude towards these Christians in Lagos? Do we ignore them because we do not live as they do or belong to their categorical expressions of Christianity? Alternatively, do we assimilate their stories or spiritualize them as being congruent with our own Christian stories?

As I listened to the Lagosian Christians and recalled my own experience when I lived there in my twenties, it occurred to me that we are all beggars listening to other beggars telling us where to find the daily bread with the help of the invisible hands of God.

It is an incontrovertible fact that Christians have a great impact in Lagos, and we should be drawn to their lives. They are praised by company and business executives who employ them for punctuality and loyalty. They work hard and pray for the success of their business, for their co-workers and for the people who employ them.

In a different context, Charles Swindoll wrote that

attitude is more important than facts or skills or intelligence. It is more important than education, wealth, and power. Attitude is more important than success or failures. It is more important than the circumstances. Attitude can make or break a home, a company, a church, a mosque, a synagogue, a nation, or the world. Life is approximately five percent what happens to us and ninety five percent how we react to it.

This book is a story about human attitudes and the discovery of our common humanity and our walk with God. It is about a journey whose destination has been revealed to the Christians in Lagos.

Caleb O. Oladipo
Buies Creek, North Carolina
7 November 2024

Foreword

Conceptual discourses and their chronological recounting – based not on anthropological overview and information but on raw ethnographic stories of people who have first engaged with the ideas being explored – serve as the best form of knowledge transmission. This is because concepts are usually interpreted and presented in abstract, theoretical terms, which may obscure their core meanings and impede understanding.

However, the elusive characters of such abstract considerations can be brought to the forefront of readers' understanding when an author chooses to portray them via a more concrete and relatable representation, such as can be achieved inductively, through stories of real-life experiences, followed by a more generalized discussion of the real concepts. This is what the author of this book manages to accomplish, allowing the reader and learner to reflect on their own life and experience as they see the lives and experiences of others, as told in their stories. It is only after a story is told that the reader realizes it has illustrated some complex and profound aspect of faith.

Whether fictional or non-fictional, the story-telling and narrative approaches to history, exemplified in this book, are one of the most effective pedagogical approaches, despite their inherent difficulties, including time-consuming attention to details and methodological accuracy. It is this compelling approach that first attracted me to *Christians in the City of Lagos*; I cannot but commend the author's writing style that stands out in this brilliant work. He presents the demographic and geographical development and conceptualization of Christianity in Lagos through the eyes of individual Christians who have had different experiences in the city, with the resulting perceptions of life truly immersed in religion and faith convictions.

The author, Dr Caleb O. Oladipo, discusses the multifaceted Christian concepts of transgression, forgiveness, poverty, redemption, hope, conversion, charity, wisdom, vulnerability and, most importantly, faith, from the vantage point of individuals whose life experiences in Lagos reflected them in specific and practical ways. This gives the reader a direct understanding of how Christianity has been changing in the city and how the fold of the religion there is distinguishable from others because of the unique characteristics of Lagos itself.

In this effort, Professor Oladipo carefully examines his own interactions with Christianity, relating them to the stories of people from different social standings and walks of life, thus painting a robust and comprehensive picture of the incredibly rich and diverse character of Christianity in Lagos. Viewing different aspects of Christianity from the experience-based viewpoints of professors, pastors, bus conductors, farmers, lawyers, priests, traders, janitors, teachers and many others offers the reader a nuanced understanding of the religion and its key concepts as practised by the people of Lagos. The author explains how these Christians interact with society at various stages of their lives, always prioritizing religion in their own idiosyncratic ways.

The very phenomenon of faith can shape an individual's perspectives and hone their abilities, making it possible for them to accomplish greater things in life. It offers a scale upon which successes and failures can be measured and rationalized. The importance of religion, and especially Christianity, to worshippers, transcends habitual, conventional gatherings to perform rituals together. Instead, it serves as a compass by which the path of life and survival is determined. The readers of this book can clearly see this notion in the way Dr Oladipo relates the first-hand experiences of the many people he interviewed in Lagos.

In Part I of the book, an overview of the Christian faith is presented using different dynamics and perceptions. The story of Rotimi Aborishade's experience with God as a thankful soul whom God deliberately found and led showcases one of the principles of the school of predestination concerning the nature of life and the ultimate fashioning of human existence by the Almighty. It further shows the approach to faith as a privileged opportunity afforded by the Almighty to humans. This is also clear from Segun and Modupe Adodo's perception of faith as a submission to the absolutism of God and the infinite capacity to do all things, with the only invocation being intentional faith in his ability. The accounts of these two experiences are illustrative of the transformation of contemporary Christianity in Nigeria and the nation's perception of what is considered to be faith.

The author also discusses the understanding of faith, which stems from the age-old natural and local perceptions of God, established through traditional and ancient African world views and spirituality. When Professor Oladipo highlights the beliefs of Charles Anyiam-Osigwe, he establishes the somewhat syncretic transformation of Christianity into a distinct category of faith that some scholars believe to be 'African Christianity'. Here, we are able to see both the conscious and unconscious conflation of African belief systems into the practice of Christianity in Nigeria, especially in Lagos. Furthermore, the lives of Michael and Mary Adunola express a reliance on faith as a boost of confidence in the face of adversity. (At this point, I am reminded of the factors and inspiration behind the formation, development and transformation of the

Aladura churches, as well as the denominations that have found their roots in them.)

The book's second part deals with the void filled by Christian consecration and belief. Christianity is a religion of hope regarding things on earth and things beyond. This hope became a 'selling point' for the religion as it brought comfort to the people during the early stage of its proliferation. The belief that religion concretizes hope is not one realized by abstract commendations but by hearing the direct recounting of first-hand encounters. The reverberation of the belief that God could save one under challenging situations, as faced by Joseph Dickson and Oluwafunmilayo Udoh and others, either showcases the highlight of hope or reiterates the ability of the faith to provide one. Using social media as a tool with the hope to reach millions in Lagos, Tobi Oreoluwa, the founder of the Street Church, employed pidgin English creatively to convey simple yet profound biblical teachings to Christians and non-Christians alike.

In a transition from this theme of hope, Oladipo turns to the subject of love, looking at it from the perspective of the Christian faith, and views it with compassion and understanding. The stories of Okandiji Babajide Lawal, Edwin and Christianah Nwaeze, Toyin Sylvester Sawyerr, and Samson Abolade Alabi and his wife, Victoria Oluwabunmi Alabi, emphasize the two-way interchange of love between God and God's subjects. The author relays the expression of love for God within the Lagos setting and complements it by demonstrating how God had expressed his love for different Lagosian Christians in so many diverse ways.

The main hallmark of Oladipo's book is the empirical discussion of an abstract concept of religion through the experience of individuals from the city of Lagos. The book provides practical evidence of the theoretical appreciation of Christian ideas and beliefs. It encompasses profound theological, narrative and expository discussion conducted for multiple purposes. Professor Caleb O. Oladipo has put a human face to what is usually discussed in abstract terms. We might well hope a scriptwriter in the Nigerian movie industry will convert this book into a Nollywood film, highlighting all its personal stories and their dramatic implications.

Toyin Falola
University Distinguished Teaching Professor
The University of Texas, Austin

Acknowledgements

This book is made possible by the generosity of Campbell University Divinity School, where I am serving as the Snellings Chair of Christian Evangelism and Mission. The school granted me a sabbatical leave in the fall of 2023, and I spent that semester at Kabarak University near Nakuru, Kenya, where I met some of the most dedicated Christians in the Global South. Professor John Ochola, the deputy vice-chancellor for research and academics, guided me and introduced me to the vice-chancellor, Professor Henry Kiplangat, who welcomed me to Kabarak with enthusiasm. Professor Frederick Ngala, the dean at the school of Education, Social Sciences and Arts, also received me gladly to serve on the faculty. Dr Elkanah Kiprop Cheboi, the head of the department of Theology and Biblical Studies, received me well and introduced me to the academic culture at Kabarak University, where education is offered in biblical perspectives. I enjoyed the exchange of ideas with brilliant undergraduate and doctoral students across the university, and I will always be grateful to Mrs Patricia Chebet, the University Librarian, who provided the resources that guided me throughout my stay. Ritaclare Ashley Omweri was very resourceful and rendered practical assistance that surpassed all my expectations.

I am grateful to Clarissa Strickland and Magdalena Rostron for their special editorial assistance in this book and in my previous publications. These two remarkable ladies provided far-reaching insights, and their suggestions have projected illumination.

It would be difficult to express my appreciation to my graduate assistants: Summer Caniglia Rice, Katrina Renee Tatum, Zachary D. Parks, Adrienne Aiken Morgan and Jill M. Haram. I am truly grateful for their fidelity and pleasant disposition throughout the process of my writing. Even when I was away, they encouraged me, and I will always owe them a debt of gratitude.

My colleagues are some of the best scholars and teachers I know in theological schools. Michael Gogdill, Alicia Myers, Larry Dickens, Lydia Hoyle, Cameron Jorgenson, Barry Jones, Derek Hogan, Sarah Boberg and Andrew H. Wakefield have no equals as servant-leaders. Campbell University Divinity School offers a Christ-Centred, Bible-based and Ministry-focused theological education to women and men who have felt called by God to serve in this and future generations. It is my greatest professional fortune and happiest height to serve at Campbell University with such men and women of integrity.

This book is dedicated to the glory of God and to my wife by the grace of God, Tylia Dideoluwafunmi Oladipo, my constant helper in my teaching and writing ministries, while she empowers others through the Sisters of Mercy to be the best they can possibly be for God's glory.

Series Introduction

Dyron B. Daughrity, Series Editor

Christians in the City is a fascinating and cutting-edge series that looks carefully at Christians in many of the world's greatest urban centers. It draws on interdisciplinary methods including anthropology, ethnography, sociology, phenomenology, and history. The series marks a significant contribution to the growing body of scholarship on world Christianity, lived religion, material religion, urban studies, and globalization as it engages people on the ground, in their local setting. The cities are drawn from around the world: North America, Asia, Africa, Europe, Latin America, and Oceania.

The Series' books highlight how Christianity is changing particular metro areas, as well as how those areas are impacting the Christian religion. Many different although often overlapping forms of Christianity are discussed in the volumes: Pentecostal, Roman Catholic, mainline Protestant, non-denominational, Eastern Orthodox, immigrant churches, megachurches, charismatic, evangelical, independent, and house churches. The net is cast wide in order to understand better what is happening with Christianity as it engages the great urban centers of the world. Christian organizations in the city – universities, private schools, and faith-based charities – will be explored as well.

The Series features established as well as rising scholars. We choose authors who live in the cities under consideration, or at least have lived in those cities. There is an intimacy that comes through in these volumes, and readers from those cities will recognize the streets, the sounds, the vibe, and the cultural accents that make cities unique. The volumes are written with crossover appeal – for audiences both inside and outside the academy.

Each volume contains interviews with leading figures from the city under consideration – as well as a broad array of laypeople – in order to gain a well-rounded perspective. There will be no shortage of material, as Christianity is not only the largest world religion in terms of adherents, but is also extremely widespread geographically, making it a diverse and complex religion that takes root in the soil of the cities it has been planted in.

The Series will consist of monographs on 25 of the world's great cities, with carefully chosen, exceptional authors who have an intimate understanding of the city they write about. As the list of books in the series expands, a global balance will be maintained. The current list of cities/volumes that have either been published, contracted, or are under consideration are:

- *In North America*: Los Angeles,* Houston,* Montreal+

- *In Asia*: Shanghai,+ Hong Kong,+

- *In Africa*: Cairo,* Kinshasa,* Lagos,+ Johannesburg,+ Nairobi+

- *In Europe*: Athens,* Berlin

- *In Latin America*: Sao Paulo,* Rio de Janeiro*

- *In Oceania*: Sydney*

- ***Books already contracted.**

- **+Books already published.**

This series has been several years in the making, and we are excited to see some of the books now coming to light. Over half of the books are contracted, but the search continues for authors for the remaining volumes. We are eager to receive proposals of cities from potential authors.

Over half of the world's population already lives in cities, and in coming years the number of people leaving the countryside for the city will continue to increase. Since its earliest days, Christianity was a religion of the city: Jerusalem, Alexandria, Antioch, Damascus, Corinth, Thessaloniki, and Rome. Established by the apostles themselves, that pattern continued. As Christianity expanded further, it gravitated towards cities: Aleppo, Edessa, Seleucia-Ctesiphon, Aksum, Etchmiadzin, and Constantinople.

The pattern continued, as the energy of cities attracted Christian missionaries, scholars, and laypeople in search of opportunity. As cities developed, Christians established bishoprics, cathedrals, monasteries, and institutions of learning. Today, the great centers of Christian thought and influence are located chiefly in cities: Seoul, Addis Ababa, Rio de Janeiro, Dallas, Athens, Rome, and Moscow.

A series on Christians in the cities is timely, and promises to break new ground.

For more information about this series, contact the Series Editor:
Dyron B. Daughrity, PhD
Divisional Dean of Religion and Philosophy
William S. Banowsky Chair in Religion
Professor of Religion
Pepperdine University
dyron.daughrity@pepperdine.edu

Introduction

The city of Lagos is located on the Gulf of Guinea in Nigeria, the most populous African nation state. With over 20 million people, Lagos, one of the largest cities in the world, is the epicentre of many cultural activities and a seat of spiritual knowledge in Nigeria. It continues to grow exponentially – not only in terms of population but also in terms of geographical territory by acquiring the surrounding towns and outskirt boroughs. In the past two decades, ethnographers have estimated that Lagos has grown faster than many other large cities in the world, including the US cities of New York City and Los Angeles.[1]

Sociopolitical and commercial life

Lagos is the commercial and industrial hub of Africa with a gross domestic product (GDP) that surpasses that of many other urban centres in Africa. It is strategically located adjacent to the oil-rich Niger Delta, a centre of crude oil refining, extraction and export. In the early 1970s, Nigeria was the third-largest oil-producing nation in the world, following Saudi Arabia and Venezuela. As a leading commercial base in Africa, Lagos is tied to the rise and fall of oil prices, creating a cycle of extreme poverty and wealth. An astounding oil refinery is now being built in Lagos by one of the richest businessmen in Africa, Aliko Dangote. It is the headquarters for many large business corporations and reputable educational institutions of higher learning, such as King's College, Eko Boys High School, Methodist Girls High School, Yaba College of Technology, Lagos State University and the University of Lagos at Akoka.

In addition, Lagos is the home of great religious and ethnic diversity among its peoples, including Hausa, Yoruba, Igbo, Fulani, Kanuri, Edo, Tiv, Nupe, Ibibio, Ijaw, Tsekiri, to name a few.[2] Diversity remains a source of both strength and political vulnerability in Nigeria, bearing the scars of political controversies and instabilities, and enduring many military coups d'état, some successful and others foiled.

Lagos (meaning 'lagoon') was named by Portuguese explorers around 1515 CE, although indigenous people had named it 'Eko' before 300 BCE.[3] The British retained Lagos as their colonial capital city because of the abundance of water that surrounds it, allowing water transportation of raw materials for European industries. Lagos became a major seaport under colonial occupation in the late nineteenth century and remains the capital of North and South Nigeria, amalgamated by the British in 1914.[4] The amalgamation of North and South was considered fraudulence by the peoples of Nigeria, especially by politicians in the South who deemed the mixing of the ethnic groups to be beneficial only to the British government, keen on reducing administrative costs. The construction of railroads from the interior Nigeria mainland to Lagos also expedited the transportation of agricultural products such as cocoa, soybeans, kola nuts and rubber to Lagos.

Before its political independence from Great Britain on 1 October 1960, Lagos was the political and commercial capital of Nigeria. In 1991, however, the Nigerian military government abruptly and surprisingly relocated the federal capital to Abuja, a more central location, to modernize and improve the Nigerian public image in the world. Still, Lagos remains the commercial capital and economic powerhouse of Nigeria; it tests one's limits but rewards hard work and endurance, while Abuja is the federal government capital with the three branches of the Nigerian constitutional democracy located there.

Ethnographers and some cultural anthropologists in Nigeria would consider Lagos both 'porous' and 'frozen': porous because of the freedoms that Lagos citizens and outsiders often enjoy, and frozen due to the existence of different ethnic groups in the boroughs of the city, who celebrate their idiosyncrasies and ethnocentricity amid social and religious diversity.

Lagos remains the preferred location for Nigerian politicians and business tycoons with their mansions built for their 'side chicks' (young girlfriends), earning them the dubious label of 'sugar daddies'. Lagos remains an inclusive and diverse city, as illustrated in a Yoruba saying, 'Ekó gbolè ó gbòle' (literally meaning 'Lagos accommodates the thieves and the indolent'). It is almost impossible not to find representatives of the more than 250 Nigerian ethnic groups represented in Lagos, with tumultuous relationships not uncommon, and sometimes exacerbated by opportunistic politicians.

There are more traders and merchants in Lagos than any other city in Nigeria, except Kano, an ancient northern commercial trade route in the pre-colonial era. Trading in Lagos promotes greater economic and business opportunities with profitable commercial and social interactions for the outside world, especially European countries. The city remains the trade route from the outside world to Nigeria, partly because European countries have informally adopted Lagos as a key commercial trading post in Africa. In the 1970s, when Nigeria graduated more university students than any other country in Africa, many of these graduates took advantage of the economic and business opportunities there to boost their business and entrepreneurial skills, particularly in the oil sector.

There are more than 170 accredited universities in the 36 states of Nigeria and in the federal capital of Abuja. More than half of the Nigerian universities are in the southern states surrounding Lagos. Nigeria has federal, state and private universities, and Osun State has the most universities with 16, including the most popular in Nigeria – Obafemi Awolowo University at Ile-Ife.

The skills of university graduates elevated the public image of Nigerians worldwide, and Nigeria became 'the giant of Africa', highlighting its high-quality education. It is important to note that most parents in Lagos value the education of their children and desire their intellectual and professional advancement. Most Nigerians view college education not just as an option, but as an expectation, making the socio-cultural environment highly literate and Lagos – a centre of excellence. Thus, the uniqueness of Lagos is rooted in its economic resources and educational opportunities. This has made the disintegration of the city impossible or impractical. The citizens of Lagos are like pilgrims in their own land.

In recent years, retired military generals and politicians have called for political and economic restructuring of Nigeria to boost unity and promote the autonomy of the three major regions of the country – northern, western and eastern regions. They argue that restructuring or decentralization of the federal government will lead to equity and fairness, unlike the current political lopsidedness imposed by the military government in the late 1990s. Such an approach to governance will result in a resounding maximization of Nigeria's abundant natural resources. It is further argued that a future decentralization in the restructuring of political configuration as envisioned by elderly statesmen and women in the country will be the bedrock of a united Nigeria. However, whether this will lead to a more economically prosperous Nigeria in the future and propel the country to the 'Promised Land' that the citizens desire and deserve remains uncertain.

Christianity and pioneering Christians in Lagos

Lagos has always been a fertile ground for Western missionaries, the propagation of the Gospel having been more successful there than in the strongholds of Islam in the northern cities, such as Sokoto, Maiduguri, Kano and Kaduna, and others. The approach of the European and American missionaries was also favourable towards Lagos, resulting in highly Western-educated Christians there. Ironically, the indigenous church leaders in mission schools were some of the earliest to oppose colonialism. In mission schools, they were trained to use the vocabularies of their Christian faith creatively to win civil liberty and political independence from European countries.[5]

It is also important to note the importance of Lagos for another reason. Established in 1976, the Christian Association of Nigeria (CAN) was founded to foster harmonious relationships between Christians and Muslims across the country. However, when interreligious dialogue became difficult politically, CAN leadership shifted to the promotion of Christian values in Nigeria. This shift was to forestall the entry of Muslim elites into the Nigerian government and to prevent Muslims from gaining an unfair advantage in their attempt to promote the inclusion of Shari'ah (Islamic law) in the penal code in the country.[6]

It is not by accident that Christianity entered Nigeria through Lagos when the Portuguese seamen and explorers, as well as the early Catholic missionaries, arrived in Lagos around 1472.[7] By 1515, several Catholic churches and mission schools had been established there. Some of the earliest church leaders in Lagos, however, were former slaves who had escaped from Brazil or gained freedom in the mid-nineteenth century and were determined to Christianize Lagos. One of the most celebrated pioneering church leaders in Lagos was Bishop Samuel Ajayi Crowther (c. 1807–91).[8] The slave ship that was taking him to the Americas was intercepted by a British anti-slave patrol ship on the Atlantic, and he was later sent to Fourah Bay College in Freetown, Sierra Leone, where he excelled as a foundation student in 1827.[9] He studied the Greek and Hebrew languages and rose to become the first post-Medieval bishop in Africa. He spoke thirteen languages and translated the Bible from English into his native Yoruba language. Translating the book of Leviticus quite early in the process, Crowther claimed that the 'instruction manual' in the book and the wealth of information about religious practice were enriching and consistent with the existing Yoruba spiritual beliefs. Therefore, the Yoruba people, he opined, would not need to walk very far before they entered familiar religious territory. By reading the book of Leviticus, his native Yoruba people would gain access to the kernel of the biblical religious tradition that was like their own. Samuel Ajayi Crowther was also the leader of the 1857 Missionary Niger Expedition, and Andrew F. Walls stated that '[Crowther] became convinced that the evangelization of inland Africa must be carried out by Africans'.[10] A fundamental question that probably occupied Crowther's mind was: 'How can the Christian faith be presented and reinterpreted so that the Yoruba people can hear God in Jesus Christ addressing them directly and immediately in their own particular context and circumstances without going through the intermediary of non-African acculturation?' The assumption behind this question was that Africans in general, and the Yoruba people in particular, would not achieve the full depth of their spiritual maturity unless it was directed by the eloquence and genius of their own existential realities, because European Christians who exercised final judgement and decisions over ecclesiastical and theological matters were Christians from different cultural and ancestral backgrounds. Crowther's achievements as a pioneering leader of the indigenous definition of Christianity in Nigeria and his impact on West African Christians are unequalled. Churches of all denominations continue to grow under the stimulus of vibrant indigenous spirituality and cultural idioms which Crowther had originally envisioned.

In looking at the development of Christianity in Lagos around 1841, the pioneering work of both J. F. Schön and Samuel Ajayi Crowther brought tremendous results.[11] In 2014, the Church of England belatedly and retrospectively recognized the monumental contributions of Bishop Crowther, and the Rt. Reverend Justin Welby, the archbishop of Canterbury, apologized on behalf of the Church of England for betraying Crowther 150 years after his consecration in 1864, saying: 'We in the Church of England need to say "sorry" that someone was properly and rightly consecrated bishop and then betrayed and let down and undermined. It was wrong.' A university named after him, Samuel Ajayi Crowther University, now honours his legacy in his native Yorubaland, and one of seventeen dioceses within the Anglican Province of Ibadan, itself one of fourteen provinces in the Nigerian Anglican Communion, bears Crowther's name. The works of Crowther also led to the founding of indigenous churches in Lagos and nearby towns, including Epe, Abeokuta and Badagry.

As the Christian faith was introduced in Nigeria by European missionaries, the indigenous people and the freed slaves were the first converts to Christianity. The already existing African spirituality served as an incubator for Christianity, leading to what could be called a 'second conversion'. The African Inland Church (or AIC) and churches like the Christ Apostolic Church founded by Joseph Ayo Babalola (1904–59) in the 1930s, as well as the Cherubim and Seraphim Church or the Aladura movement by Moses Orimolade in the 1920s, stopped attracting younger followers, as they had in the 1930s and 1940s – the burgeoning and miraculous years. The Celestial Church of Christ (Ijo Kristi l'ati Orun wa) had been significant in Lagos as one of the latest additional expressions of an indigenous definition of Christianity in Lagos, wearing white garments during worship.

The flowering of Pentecostal churches in Lagos was a new development in the growth of Christianity in the 1970s, with continued exponential growth at the expense of both the Catholic and Protestant churches. Except on only a few occasions in congregational life, the wearing of Western-style clothing during worship has not supplanted the traditional agbada among Yoruba Christians in Lagos. Most pastors, however, often wear Western clothes with colourful neckties. It is through Christianity that Nigerians have been most successful in the preservation of their idiosyncratic spiritual and cultural way of life. Christianity did not eradicate the Igbo or Yoruba cultures and spiritual beliefs but were simply absorbed into the practice of Christianity in Lagos. The lure of Western lifestyle and values has not been successful in turning

Nigerians away from their cultures and traditions, making Lagos the El Dorado of Africa with matchless opportunities for success and prosperity.

The Church in Lagos has become 'Yorubanized', with European missionaries increasingly regarded as co-workers rather than leaders, relegated to positions that were secondary in the life of the Church and replaced by indigenous actors. This has resulted in Christians in Lagos volunteering as missionaries in the neighbouring countries of the Republic of Benin, Togo, Ghana, Burkina Faso, Sierra Leone, Senegal, Liberia, Côte d'Ivoire and Cameroon.

Thus, this indigenization of the practice and principles of Christianity[12] in Lagos has made it possible for new church leaders and actors to emerge in these once-traditional missionary-initiated churches and take on new roles, including politics. For example, the Reverend Anthony Okogie, the Catholic archbishop of Lagos since 1973, gained national fame in the 1990s for his fearless opposition to the Nigerian authority for human rights violations and corruption.

Contrary to popular belief, many African Indigenous churches in Lagos are neither Pentecostal nor traditional in their views of spirituality and Christian doctrines. They are autonomous, often stirring up controversies by criticizing the consumption of alcohol, cigarettes or tobacco products, as well as the prevalence of sexual promiscuity. Smoking is prohibited in many AIC congregations because it is seen as contaminating the body as the temple of the Holy Spirit. AIC members also reject abortion, homosexuality and artificial insemination, which they view as unnatural means of exercising God's gifts of intimacy and procreation. The use of condoms to prevent pregnancies is also unacceptable, with their preachers often preaching strict abstinence instead.

In the modern era, Christians in Lagos call the earliest assembly of Christians in Lagos *Ijo Aguda*, and later did the indigenous people named the re-introduction of Christianity in Lagos by the Catholic missionaries the Catholic church.

Another remarkable characteristic of Christians in Lagos is their unique approach to the Bible. While many may see the Bible as a book of *reference*, I encountered numerous Christians in Lagos who use it as a book of *remembrance*. For instance, they often recite certain portions of the book of Psalms as suitable for healing or read Psalm 91 when they feel anxious. Thus, the Bible is seen as more than just a religious document suitable for academic studies; it is also viewed as a 'healing' Scripture that ensures one's well-being and provides direction during life's treacherous medical paths or difficult times. The books of Psalms remain a reliable companion and the first line of defence and intervention during moments of emergency or when they feel distant or disconnected from God. For miraculous healing and God's providence, Christians go to Psalm 30, 32, 34, 41, 66, 67, 92, 107, 116, 118, 124 or 138.

Psalms 46, 48, 76, 84, 87 and 122 are popular when they desire to feel the presence of God or long for the house of worship. On special Saturday nights, the Cherubim and Seraphim church members in Lagos congregate all night to invoke God's presence. When they feel rejected or neglected by earthly kings or rulers, they often read Psalms 47, 93, 96, 97, 98 or 99. When faced with criticism, Christians in Lagos often put their trust in God and they read Psalms 4, 11, 16, 23, 27, 62, 91 or 131. The largest group of Psalms that Christians use in Lagos, however, are associated with God's appellation or praiseworthiness. God is to be praised because of God's attributes as the creator of heaven and earth. The Psalms included in God's praiseworthiness are the following: 8, 19, 24, 29, 33, 65, 68, 100, 103–105, 111, 113–115, 117, 134–136, 139, 145–150. These Psalms are not directed to God for supplication, but for adoration in that God is worthy to be praised. The nature of God and God's holiness connote glory. For deliverance, divine intervention or when Christians feel perplexed or confused, they want to be reminded of God's unchanging love and sovereignty and they go to Psalms 9, 10, 57, 77 and 108. During times of difficulties when they need words of assurance from God, they often read Psalms 15, 36, 50, 75, 78, 81, 82, 95, 121, 125 and 129. When they suffer persecution, emotionally and spiritually or when they feel that life is treating them harshly due to their shortcomings, real or imagined, Christians feel remorseful and go to the following Psalms, pleading for God's help. They also consult with the following Psalms to lament, to heal emotional wounds and to seek God's presence, hope and vindication: Psalm 3, 5–7, 13, 17, 22, 25, 26, 28, 31, 35, 38, 39, 40, 42, 43, 51, 52, 54, 55, 56, 59, 61, 63, 64, 69, 70, 71, 86, 88, 94, 102, 109, 120, 130, 140 and 141–143.

When there is scarcity of rains during the rainy seasons, it is a bad omen, regarded as a collective punishment for God's people. Therefore, they pray for God's faithfulness and for God to remember his reputation that he will not forsake them when they languish or are in a state of decreasing vitality. There are numerous times in Lagos when heavy rains also cause flooding and the innocent suffer. A call for God's intervention often leads to the reading of the following Psalms: 12, 14, 44, 53, 58, 60, 74, 79, 80, 83, 85, 90, 106, 123, 126 and 137.

There are also Psalms that display royalty and wisdom. They inform Christians about how to live under the majesty of God. The earthly monarchical institutions and authorities are the direct result of God's providence. They show us the right way to live. They indirectly encourage Christians to not live in a certain way because it leads to perdition and could suffocate their longing for God and the life of the church. These Psalms include: 1, 2, 18, 20, 21, 37, 45, 49, 72, 73, 89, 101, 110, 112, 119, 127, 128, 132, 133, 144.

The Christians are aware of the historical contexts of the book of Psalms, but they also situate their minds that the God who led the ancient Israelites out of bondage is dependable, and his presence abides with them through their own existential condition. The book of Psalms represents a fundamental movement in the rhythm of the lives of Christians in Lagos. Those who love God and desire to follow the will of God cultivate the enduring habit of reading psalms as an instructional manual for how to live through the challenges of life. What I found quite instructive is that while Christians in Lagos make a distinction between the Old Testament and the New Testament, they do not make a similar distinction between the Hebrew Bible and their own life circumstances. They show appreciation for the Bible and cherish the Scriptures as being applicable to them in their day-to-day circumstances. Therefore, the Bible is more than a document to be studied as a reference book. Through the window of the book of Psalms, one sees God 'face-to-face' addressing those who desire to follow God. The Bible, therefore, is not only the *Word* of God but also the *acts* of God to those who trust God.[13]

Whether the vision of the Christians in Lagos to depend totally on God for sustenance is a result of political persecution, economic stalemate, poor governance or lack of adequate medical facilities, we are not certain. What is clear to me, however, is that everything they do reflects the God within that is near and dear to them. Life is treacherous but God is sustaining, and they feel the presence of God who abides with them in all circumstances.

A personal experience with
John I. Durham in 1985

In 1985, John I. Durham (1933–2022) was one of my Old Testament professors at Southeastern Baptist Theological Seminary in Wake Forest, North Carolina. He came to class one day with an analysis of the book of Psalms he had compiled and asked the students to examine the categories. We concluded that the book of Psalms included: (1) Hymns and Psalms of praise, (2) Laments, (3) the Royal Psalms and (4) the Wisdom Psalms. On my first visit to Lagos in December 2022 to conduct ethnographic research among Christians, I was impressed to see that Christians in Lagos concretize what we learned theoretically in class in 1985. Christians in Lagos put into practice what we learned in John Durham's Old Testament class as an ancient guide to understanding the book of Psalms. The psalms can be categorized broadly as psalms of adoration, confession, thanksgiving, supplication as well as intercession. Faith in God guides everything Christians in Lagos do, and the psalms are an indispensable source of strength when Christians feel that the world has turned against them; God alone is sufficient to cater for their existential needs, heal their emotional wounds and attend to their day-today needs.[14] The book of Psalms represents the fundamental movements of humanity and his relationship with the God of love in the rhythm of his life tapestry that is most basic.[15]

How Christians in Lagos see the rest of the Bible

Most Christians in Lagos view the Bible as God's love letter to humanity. Christians I interviewed stated that the Bible, like any love letter, is not flawless historically or linguistically. Many are not unfamiliar with contemporary archaeological research findings and understand that the Bible is often not factual archaeologically or scientifically. The biblical stories are not always harmonious or congruous when one compares one story of the life of Jesus with a similar story side-by-side in the synoptic gospels. While the stories in the Bible are not flawless, the imperfections in the stories do not matter once Christians begin to see the Bible as a unique channel through which God's love letter is communicated to humanity. Regardless of what one is reading with imperfect eyes and minds,[16] once the Bible is seen as the medium of God's perfect revelation, that God created the world and Jesus as Saviour came to redeem it, the stories have a new meaning beyond scientific analysis with believers becoming dedicated to its complete redemptive purpose. It is perhaps this view of plenitude that makes Christians in Lagos overlook the inaccuracies associated with biblical stories, with the redemptive message of God's love for the world transcending human claims of its apparent errors. While not scientifically perfect, the Bible is worthy of human reception as a revelation of God. The reader may not often be mature enough to comprehend the immediate contexts as God's letter of love. If readers attempt to demythologize aspects of the Bible that appear to be mythical, it will put the reader above the text; therefore, it is the reader that needs to be remythologized into the biblical environment for understanding, and not the Bible that must be demythologized.[17]

Human reasoning must be bracketed or suspended to create room by faith for God's love letter to reach the human hearts. Therefore, one's state of mind needs spiritual overhauling, and a devotional life is a sine qua non for an accurate interpretation of the Bible as God's love letter. The oft-repeated statement of Christians in Lagos is that a life of devotion is necessary for the right relationship with God and for the right understanding and interpretation of the Word of God. When an individual accepts the Bible as the authentic medium of God's revelation and that the God that Jesus of Nazareth incarnated is the true lover of the world, human doubts about the factual archaeological, scientific and historical accuracies of the biblical stories become minimal.

Many Christians in Lagos speak with surpassing clarity and enthusiasm about their devotion to the Bible as the most reliable revelation of God to humanity.

Seeing the Bible as the rock of God's revelatory character, and by using the analogy of the rock to depict the Bible, they often sing a song to show their fidelity and devotion to the Word and acts of God:

> Ol'ogbon k'ole sori apata
> Ol'ogbon k'ole sori apata
> Ojo ro ikun omi si de
> Ile Ol'ogbon duro.

> The wise man built his house on the rock.
> The wise man built his house on the rock.
> The rain came and floodings came.
> The house of a wise man stands.

It is an incontrovertible fact that the message of the Bible as God's revelation is to comfort those who are afflicted and afflict those who are comforted.

The transformation of faith in Lagos

Beginning in 1868, the Catholic missionaries in Lagos started working more collaboratively with the Yoruba people in Lagos and the Igbo Christians in the eastern region of Nigeria. These two ethnic groups helped the missionaries come to terms with the idea of indigenous Christian truth. It is not impossible to claim that indigenous preachers are the very ones who advanced and adapted the practice of Christianity for their peoples more than the European missionaries.

The healing of the centurion's servant in Capernaum, recorded in Matthew 8, is a good example of how this can happen. The Gentile general came to Jesus saying, 'Lord, my servant is lying at home paralyzed, in terrible distress.' When Jesus told him he would come and heal the man, the centurion answered,

> Lord, I am not worthy to have you come under my roof; but only speak the word, and my servant will be healed. For I also am a man under authority, with soldiers under me; and I say to one, 'Go,' and he goes, and to another, 'Come' and he comes, and to my slave, 'Do this,' and the slave does it. When Jesus heard him, he was amazed and said to those who followed him, 'Truly I tell you, in no one in Israel have I found such faith. I tell you,

many will come from east and west and will eat with Abraham and Isaac and Jacob in the kingdom of heaven, while the heirs of the kingdom will be thrown into the outer darkness, where there will be weeping and gnashing of teeth.' And to the centurion Jesus said, 'Go; let it be done for you according to your faith.' And the servant was healed in that hour. (Mt. 8.6-13 NRSV)

In a parallel fashion, it is the Yoruba and the Igbo who showed the missionaries that the truth of the Christian faith could also be delivered indirectly. Thus, it is the indigenous people themselves who have the potential to discover the practice of faith in God as Jesus of Nazareth proclaimed, and not only the missionaries assisting the discovery of Christianity for the indigenous people.

In today's era, many of those indigenous Pentecostal churches in Lagos are criticized by some Christians as 'prosperity' churches because of the theme of material wealth emphasized through the preaching of their leaders. But if one concentrates on the negative aspects of the church life of Pentecostalism, it is easy to miss the fervour of the preaching styles and its positive biblical teachings. The most common of these churches in Lagos include Deeper Life Ministries, founded by W. F. Kumuyi (b. 1941), Redeemed Church of God, Living Church Chapel, Mountain of Fire Ministry and New Covenant Church.

The challenges facing modern Lagos

The unregulated growth and the teeming population of Lagos create a sprawling and chaotic urban landscape. Immigrants from rural areas across Nigeria looking for a better life and new economic opportunities have flooded the city. It is a densely populated city of contrasts, with overcrowded residential zones such as Maroko, Ikeja, Oshodi, Ajegunle and Surulere, where there are sometimes six adults living in one room, while Victoria Island and some parts of the Lekki peninsula are inhabited by business tycoons and politicians who enjoy opulent lifestyles. Slum communities are proliferating in uninhabitable areas close to nearby lagoons and lakes.

Lagos continues to suffer from various problems such as water shortages and weak infrastructure. Poor sanitation services and heavy traffic, known locally as 'go slow' or 'traffic jam', have affected productivity extensively.

Also, government bodies and developers continue to find it difficult to keep up with Lagos' rapid, uncontrolled growth. Still, the people are resilient and creative, and the youths of the city are resourceful with entrepreneurial spirit and versatility.

In my own Lagos experience, one question always preoccupies my mind: 'What God do we worship in Lagos?' I have seen the vulnerabilities of the God of the ancestors as well as the God imported by the European and American missionaries. Both custom-based and federal courts are well supplied with the Bible and the Qur'an, the two holy books of over two-thirds of the world's population. But the gods proclaimed in and through them seem ineffective and are not universally revered. For example, the common people of Lagos who migrated there from the surrounding rural areas continue secretly to venerate the deities of their ancestors. Although a man on the street might be quick to swear in the name of the Christian deity or in the name of Allah, he is more cautious about cursing in the name of the god of his ancestors who led him to Lagos. The mental construct and potency associated with the god of one region cannot be transferred so easily to another location.

The localization of a god and its territoriality is not a new phenomenon in either Jewish or Christian context. If we recall the biblical story of a general in the Syrian army in 2 Kings 5:1-19, for instance, we see that the general, Naaman, was averse to taking a bath in the River Jordan to cure his endemic skin disease, thinking his leprosy was incurable. But Elisha, the mighty prophet of God in Israel, convinced him that he could be cured supernaturally and asked Naaman to take a bath in the river seven times, and he obeyed. When he was cured of his skin disease, Naaman exclaimed, 'There is no God, but the God of Israel.'

Christians in Lagos affirm the uniqueness of Jesus Christ, but they also hold sacred the belief that God has been dealing with humanity in all parts of the world. The quality of God's self-disclosure through Jesus Christ has never been lost in their conviction, yet they view this self-disclosure through the prism of their traditional spiritual beliefs and existential realities, which have never been lost. Still, it is because of this revelation through Jesus Christ that they discern what is true of God in their pre-Christian heritage in modern life. This is because the reality of God as expressed by early missionaries was not totally incongruent with their own African spirituality. The missionaries, however, missed early opportunities to link their preaching and proclamation of the death and resurrection of Jesus Christ with traditional African spiritual beliefs. In *The Many Faces of Jesus Christ*, Volker Küster restated best the views of Bengt Sundkler (1909–95) that 'the missionaries "missed the open gate for Christianization" when they did not connect the preaching of the death and descent of Jesus Christ with African belief in ancestors'.[18] It is not far-fetched, as some Christians in Lagos have told me, to claim that if Christian beliefs cannot be seen as congruent with the indigenous belief, the Christian faith must at least be seen as an extension of the traditional African spiritual beliefs, not a departure from it. It has been one of the more advanced evolutions of Christianity in Africa in general, and Lagos particularly, that there is now a willingness to incorporate elements of the African ethos and spiritual heritage into the preaching of God's gracious redemptive work.

Christians in Lagos have incorporated non-institutional and non-traditional faith practices into worship. It is not impossible to see a person who grew up as Muslim, Anglican or Presbyterian attending the Redeemed Church of God, or Winners' Chapel, or Deeper Life Ministries, or any of the Pentecostal churches. Their religious backgrounds served as incubators, preparing them for this new-found faith in Christ. Institutional religions were a preparatory road for their new-found faith in Christ. The ticket to heaven is not the institutional religion, but a personal encounter with Jesus Christ. The faith of their past is not useless, and need not be discarded, but is often renewed and transformed. Most Christians in Lagos have not accepted the imported understanding of Christianity without their own modification.

In the biblical post-resurrection story of 'doubting Thomas', we see his unbelief in Christ's resurrection throughout that week. The disciples were telling him that they had seen Jesus and eaten with him. They tried to convince Thomas that Jesus was alive; but Thomas insisted on seeing Jesus for himself before believing. When he did see Jesus's scarred hands and feet face-to-face in his resurrected body, he exclaimed, 'My Lord and my God.' Jesus responded to Thomas, 'You believed because you saw me, but blessed are those who have not seen me, and yet believed.' Thomas's personal encounter with Jesus was necessary for him to have true faith in Christ. In the end, Thomas was not a 'doubting Thomas' but a 'believing Thomas' who saw and encountered his Lord face-to-face (Jn 20. 24-29).

Where do Lagosian Christians go to eat on Sundays?

Lagosian Christians know where all the good restaurants are located, often taking their children, family members and friends to them. Some of these restaurants include the Bungalow Restaurant, the Lagoon Restaurant, the White House Restaurant, Salam's Authentic Lebanese Cuisine, Debonaire Pizza, the Ocean Basket, B. L. Restaurant Bar and Café and the Hard Rock Café. Several lesser-known restaurants have chains in Lagos. Examples include La Veranda Italian Cuisine, Vanilla Moon Orchid House Thai Restaurant, Taliedo Steak House, R.S.V.P Restaurant, Shiro Lagos, Z Kitchen, Yellow Chili, Izanagi Japanese Cuisine and Guppy's Restaurant and Bar.

Family prayer and daily routine in Christian homes

Most Christians in Lagos hold the view that the level at which followers of Christ communicate with God in prayers is proportionate to the level at which they live for God through Jesus Christ in the world. Early in the morning, when the muezzins in Lagos begin to call the attention of Muslims to pray, Christians also gather at the family altar to pray. I attended some family prayer meetings led by either the mother or the father in the home. Immediately following, mothers would instruct the older siblings to take care of the younger brothers and sisters, while they prepared breakfast for the family. In some cases, the females assist the younger sisters below the age of three to take baths and get ready for the day. Everyone takes part in family chores, which include sweeping rooms with locally made brooms, boiling water, running errands in the neighbourhood, and doing the dishes. Almost always, the morning prayers begin by singing a chorus or a hymn and sharing dreams. The more popular choruses are:

(1) Wa Wa Wa Emi mimo
Wa Wa Wa alagbara
Wa O Wa O Wa O
Come Come Come Holy Spirit Come
Come Come Come the Mighty One
Come! Come! Come!
(2) I am so glad I belong to Jesus.
I belong to Jesus; I belong to my Lord.
I am so glad I belong to Jesus; I belong to my Lord.

The family prayers often focus on adoration, thanksgiving for the gift of life, daily provision and safety. I observed fifteen patterns of morning devotion and noticed that many began with the phrase: 'Li oruko Jesu' (in the name of Jesus). Unlike family prayers, however, congregational prayers at revival meetings are collective and attendees often pray audibly and simultaneously.

Summary

Showcasing the life and experiences of Christians in Lagos has led me to certain fundamental beliefs about the Christian faith and how it is expressed there. The nature and character of Christianity in Lagos are unique. The reading of the Bible and daily prayers remain fundamentals for all Christians. Therefore, regular Bible studies and prayer meetings remain the glue that unites the different ethnic Christian groups in Lagos. While there is diversity of people, their narratives continue to unlock the grand vision of God for believers everywhere – the life of the church and participating communities of faith must reflect their own creativity and understanding of God.

Christianity has been most fundamental to the identity formation of the peoples in Lagos, and one must explore more deeply the hypothesis that while the Gospel cannot be domesticated, the Church in Lagos is there to stay. It continues to grow, spurred on by the stimulus of traditional African beliefs, and more significant to me, with Christians rediscovering their faith in God through the lens of their own spiritual beliefs. Church leaders in Lagos are the primary actors who are advancing the practice of Christianity for their own peoples.

Since the time I was growing up in Lagos, after spending time there in 2022 and 2023, my questions have now evolved to include addressing how Christianity can be presented and interpreted in such a way that Lagosians hear God in Jesus Christ in their own contexts without going through the agency of non-African enculturation. I feel that Lagosian Christians are reaching the full depth of their spiritual maturity, with the destiny of that maturity being the product of their own existential reality and traditional spiritual beliefs, representing in our generation a transitional light of the Gospel. It is an incontrovertible fact that the evolution of Christian development in Africa is evidenced by the willingness of Christians to incorporate elements of the African ethos and spiritual heritage into Christian identity. This is, perhaps, one of the resounding successful developments of the Christian faith in contemporary Africa.

PART I

Stories of faith

1

'I didn't go to God; I was brought to God'

Introduction

How Rotimi Aborishade came to Lagos as a Christian

Many Christians in Lagos exercise their faith with a deep sense of some specific historical event that brought them to the city. I met Rotimi Aborishade on 24 December 2022. His story demonstrates the all-consuming power of God in his life. Aborishade is affectionately and fondly called 'Papa Rott' by his close friends and colleagues in Lagos. In his fifties, he is quiet and respectful with a humble disposition. He has a persuasive personality, and I felt very comfortable at his home because of his winsome personality and his Christian hospitality.

Aborishade mentioned to me that God had chosen him and had sent Christians along his way to prepare him for a life of commitment to the church. He knew God's plan for him was secure, and it was this same God who surrounded him with the people that helped shape his Christian identity. People along Aborishade's path inspired him to strive to be righteous and continued to nurture him once he was in Lagos. Although Aborishade was fifty-two at the time I met him, it was clear that his journey had begun almost four decades earlier when he was attending Lagelu Grammar School in Ibadan, the Oyo State capital. During his student days at the grammar school, the Christian faith across Nigeria was like a new flower, blooming through the presence of a young generation of students across the country. They were some of the most committed and vibrant Christians of the time.

Aborishade met Christians who inspired him during these formative years. Most notably, they included Yinka Osunlalu Osuolale, Sunday Oladejo and

Omololu Adegoke, a prominent leader of the Lord Reigned Ministry (T. L. R.) in the 1980s.

Emancipation declaration of Christians in Lagos

The 1970s and 1980s were the two decades immediately following the end of the British colonial occupation in Nigeria. It was also at this time that Christianity began to gain a foothold among the indigenous peoples with corresponding church growth. Among the young people in Nigeria, especially at the Polytechnic of Ibadan, that growth was explosive. At the same time, it was also threatening the traditional church life of the Anglican Church Communion. The sacrament of baptism that had always preceded church confirmation was ignored, and youth in all the tertiary schools began to craft their own paths to follow Jesus Christ. The imported 'missionary Christianity', not being rooted in African cultures or the traditional African religions, was tied to literacy and had no organic linkage to the spiritual environment of the younger generation. University students in the 1980s found alternatives to what had been the prior imperial imposition of the Gospel message by missionaries. As independent people, they began to champion a faith in Christ where their understanding of Christianity could coexist with their indigenous spiritual environment and background. The path they took was in opposition to both the time-honoured traditional understanding of Christianity brought by European missionaries and the African traditional religions of their parents. It resulted in a totally different infrastructure of Christianity, if one can call it that, with a life of its own altogether. The establishment of the Student Union dominated Christian culture across the country, with the new phenomenon often discussed by university authorities. The tide could not be stopped by any ecclesiastical institution in Nigeria or abroad.

It was a rebirth of Christian identity with virtually all students in Nigerian universities knowing that Christian culture in Nigeria would never be the same. It was also an irreversible revival with even Muslim students 'on fire for Christ'. This revival threatened existing church institutions, especially the Anglican Church Communion. The catchphrase or watchword among Nigerian university students in the 1980s was 'Are you a born-again Christian?' This 'born-again-ism' was expected to lead to church growth outside the university environment. The result was both positive and negative. On the one hand, there was an exponential church growth; but on the other hand, it led to the idea that the missionary-pioneered institutions in Nigeria might not survive the takeover of Christianity by indigenous young university students.

These indigenous young people redrew the established ecclesiastical map of Christianity and its recognized authority, crafting their own understanding without benefit (or impediment) of the agency of either European missionaries or the traditional interpretation of Christianity by first-generation church leaders in Nigeria. This rebirth of Christianity or spiritual renaissance, fostered by young university students in the 1980s, shaped the faith of the people in Nigeria today. Many of these students migrated to Lagos following their graduation.

Aborishade was a direct product of this Christian revival of the 1980s, sharing with me that more than 90 per cent of the university students who became Christians through the revival are still committed Christians today. When he moved to Lagos in 1988, the spirit of the Christian revival migrated with him, remaining fundamental to his commitment to Christ.

Upon his arrival in Lagos, Aborishade's aunt accommodated him for a while as he became exposed to the new realities of living in the city. He was acquainted with other Christians who shaped him and inspired him, such as Kole Akinboboye and Chaplain Olasehinde, as well as Christian programmes such as River State youth camps, pastors' fellowship, National Youth Service Corps fellowship, and Rivers of Joy and Victory. These Christian groups and their leaders provided a new understanding for Aborishade of what it means to follow Christ, inspiring him in his Christian journey. Thus, God chose Aborishade and kept sending new Christians who nurtured him along the way.[1] These included Steve Akinola, Ayo Odunayo and Dr Akinboboye. These are some of the people who inspired Aborishade. Even when he was attending government schools and lived in far-away places, such as Sokoto State or Adamawa or Maiduguri in Northern Nigeria, God ordered Aborishade's life and sent dedicated Christians along the way.

Aborishade received degrees in electronics, telecommunications and geophysics. The Elf Company employed him, and wherever he worked, he received unhindered assistance. The good Samaritans he met awarded him contracts; he worked with the Shell Company in 1997, where he was offered numerous opportunities to interact with privileged and wealthy Nigerians. With all Aborishade's success, God kept his heart pure and unadulterated by the lures of unethical behaviour that would be inconsistent with his Christian values or principles. He shared with me that he had never indulged in drinking alcohol or smoking tobacco products because, with his Christian conversion, his body had become the temple where the Spirit of God abided, and he would not contaminate it with alcohol or tobacco products.

A life of devotion is needed for the right interpretation of the Word of God

It was a part of his being born again, raising an important theological question that cannot possibly be answered in one breath. Does a life of devotion lead Christians to the right interpretations of the words of God? In other words, what is the relationship between living an upright life and correctly interpreting the Christian faith? In Mark's Gospel, when Jesus told his disciples that casting out the devil could not be done without fasting and prayer, was Jesus Christ asking his disciples to live a life of devotion to perform righteous and miraculous deeds? Or was Jesus challenging his followers to live a life worthy of their calling? In other words, does a life of devotion have intrinsic or pragmatic value?

For Aborishade, life in Lagos was a Christian experiment in many ways. In 2001, he was in the telecommunication business when an engineer named Lawrence introduced him to Stocks. God continued to direct his path in Lagos, keeping his heart pure and simple. In one of the most profound statements during our time together in Lagos, he said: 'God chose me to be a Christian; I did not choose God; I did not go to God, I was brought to God.'

With his humble, respectful and gentle spirit, Aborishade had a profound and lasting impact on me. Because his mother's side of the family was wealthy, he could have benefited from the privilege of his family ties. But God was preparing him for more, surrounding him with important people who supported and shaped him.

In a city where the prosperity Gospel is so pronounced, more philosophers and theologians are needed for the proper interpretation of the Good News. Aborishade told me that he was full of gratitude because God had chosen him, and he had dedicated his life to influencing others in a positive way, directing them towards Christianity. He was convinced that if God had given a person power and influence, it was merely a test. In his native Yoruba tongue, he emphatically stated, 'O fi se adanwo ni.' He lamented that the networking of non-Christians in Lagos was stronger and more successful than that of Christians. He believed that one cannot 'speak' progress into existence but must work at it. Christians are good at 'putting their money where their mouths is', but they must also put their mouths where their money is. Especially in Lagos, Christians needed community leaders who would lend their influence through their social networks. Talk without action is empty. Lagosian Christians needed to realize their belonging to different groups could provide influence and the oxygen required for the societal transformation needed in a beloved community. Awareness of the tremendous needs of the people in Lagos can only be known and addressed when we socialize with others, sharing their pains and struggles.

'In as much as you did it for one of these, you have done it unto me.'
Rotimi Aborishade believes strongly that the church of the twenty-first century must be the church on the street, mending lives that have been broken and damaged. With so many lives twisted by oppression, both mental and physical, the Christian mission should be about reaching out to others so that we are truly our brothers' keepers. Aborishade believed if we looked carefully in the dark corners of Lagos, we would find there both heaven and hell, because we would see people living in both. It was his belief that we must, however, strive to create the heaven we believe is possible here and now for the glory of God. This is the story of the challenges that Christians in Lagos face.

Aborishade noted that while many Christians pray fervently and worship God devotedly, they do not participate in building their own communities both politically and economically. He stated that praying without working did not lead any community forward and a Gospel of prosperity was a hindrance to the full emancipation of Christians all over Lagos. Fervent prayer must be accompanied by the hard work required to build communities. We must work as if every bit of progress depends on us and pray as if all depends upon God. We must pray fervently as if all depends upon God's gracious overture and initiative.

The degree of wonder in each experience of my time in Lagos was superseded by the next. It is as if God were writing the stories of every Christian in Lagos if followers of Christ were there – just to live out the God-stories in their lives. For example, Aborishade shared with me how, over the past thirty-eight years, God had been guiding him, grooming him and helping him live out his own 'God-story' through his life and work. He described the challenges the established institutions in Nigeria had with the 'born-again-ism' of the 1980s. He named some who were passionate about telling their stories of how they had been born again. The movement spearheaded by young university students in the 1980s had resulted in a broad-based indigenous definition of what it meant to be a Christian. The net effect of this movement reverberated across Lagos, leading to a passionate devotional character of the Christian faith. It was as if a devotional life became totally necessary for a deeper understanding of the Word of God and its practical application.

The leaders of the movement were unstoppable, starting their own churches in Lagos and ushering in a new dispensation of faith in all the boroughs of the city. The leaders of the movement became church leaders and Bible teachers not just in Lagos, but all over Nigeria.

This revival movement, as Aborishade labelled it, lighted and ignited the fire of Christianity across all tertiary campuses of Lagos. When the history and destiny of the movement are written, it will cite leaders such as Yinka Osuolale and Sunday Oladejo, who both shaped and inspired the movement as young

Christians started to pray on the street corners and inside public transportation in Lagos. Although not confined to Lagos, in no other city in Nigeria was the movement felt with greater intensity and constancy. Aborishade stated that the movement reverberated as far as the University of Ibadan, the premier Nigerian university, about 200 kilometres north of Lagos. At this university, commonly known as UI, the Lord Reigneth Ministry or T. L. R. was founded, Omololu Adegoke being a prominent leader.

Aborishade, talking about the fervour of the revival movement, remarked that when he was at the University of Akure to study physics and electronics, it was clear to him that Christianity and Christians would never be the same in Nigeria.

When I asked him what he was most grateful for as a Lagosian Christian, he told me it was that he had not chosen God, but God had chosen him. He had become aware of this when he was serving as a student union president at the University of Akure, where he acquired great skill as a student leader. Even before then, as a student at the Polytechnic of Ibadan, his faith had been cemented. With this Christian background, he moved to Lagos in 1988 – a move he believed to have been ordained by God.

The life and work of Rotimi Aborishade as a Christian in Lagos

In Lagos, Aborishade came face-to-face with life's challenging realities. 'Living and working in Lagos as a Christian is difficult. It is to test our fidelity and faithfulness to God', he told me. It was there he was influenced by the ministries of church leaders as Pastor Tunde Bakare, a Muslim who had converted to Christianity. Aborishade was struck by how pastors in Lagos challenged their congregations to make their lives meaningful in their own communities. He had come to know the significance of making one's life count for a cause greater than and beyond one's own personal ambition. He enjoyed this privileged consciousness when he was in Port Harcourt working for the National Youth Service Corps, or NYSC. This programme was designed by the government in the 1970s under the military administration with the goal of fostering unity among the diverse ethnicities in Nigeria. It is rather like the 'gap-year' in Britain, in which every university student serves for a year in some part of the country – either where they grew up or in a less familiar part.

Aborishade's transition to Lagos was an eye-opening experience, where he was involved in diverse Christian fellowship groups with opportunities to meet some of the influential Christians who had transformed him.

The emerging Christian movement in Lagos did not see as binding the Anglican or Catholic traditional sacraments, which had been introduced by the Western world. Sacraments such as baptism, confirmation and the Eucharist, as well as the sacraments of healing, such as penance and the anointing of the sick, as well as marriage and the conferring of holy orders, had all been common practice elsewhere. Nowadays, Christians within the new movement observe naming ceremonies for new babies, practise celebrations on the purchase of a new car, or the building of a new house. They congregate to thank God for these God-given additions to their families. Faith is expressed in the daily rhythms of their existence with non-Christians often invited to celebrate with them. This non-binary understanding of their faith in God fosters cohesion between Christians and non-Christians in Lagos. Although opportunistic politicians have created or exacerbated division between Christians and non-Christians in Lagos, they have been unsuccessful in triggering any impenetrable division among devotees, who continue to place high value on their relationship with God and their fellow human beings.

Rabbi Jonathan Sacks points out in *Not in God's Name: Confronting Religious Violence* that the contemporary West is 'the most individualistic era of all times'.[2] According to Sacks, "Its central values are in ethics, autonomy; in politics, individual rights; in culture, post-modernism; and in religion, "spirituality." Its idol is the self, its icon the "selfie" and its operating systems the free market and the post-ideological, managerial liberal democratic state. In place of national identities, we have global cosmopolitanism. In place of communities, we have flash-mobs. We are no longer pilgrims but tourists. We no longer know who we are or why."[3] What Rabbi Jonathan Sacks describes about the West is not a common phenomenon from my experience in Lagos, and the social cohesion among Lagosian Christians continues to remain visibly strong. While life in Lagos has its social and economic challenges, Aborishade was surprised by the almost clannish loyalty of non-Christians to each other – a kind of fidelity he felt Christians should also show to each other.

Aborishade believes that his Christian witness in Lagos gives him the opportunity to choose the God who had already chosen him through Jesus Christ. He has rediscovered a divine initiative at the root of his faith in God. Now, his primary mission in Lagos is to lead others to choose the God who has already chosen them, helping them discover the divine initiative at the root of their faith in God as he has done.

Before I left his house, Aborishade showed me his orchard, where he had planted mangoes, tomatoes, pawpaw (papaya), plantains and pineapples. He told me that most people in Lagos raise rabbits and have fishponds to supplement their protein diets or their income. It is also common for Lagosian Christians to plant yams, cassava, peppers and onions. Many also devote a plot of land in their backyards for maize (corn), sugarcane and melons. It is obvious that most of the population in Lagos have diverse and multiple means of income.

Aborishade is a member of social networks such as the Rotary Club. Such social organizations draw local people in the community into positive actions such as building schools and keeping local roads maintained for easy passage and transportation. Before we left, I asked him to share the principal factors that guided his steps in Lagos. He bellowed with laughter, saying he never defrauded anyone, never stole from anyone and was not in the business of playing God. An ethical modus operandi guides Aborishade's personal Christian philosophy. When in a position of authority, greater responsibility and more action are needed, since success is in many ways more difficult to handle if you are a child of God than failure. How one handles success can be a test of the practice of one's faith. Christians are to stretch themselves for one another; living for the good of others is the very essence of being a true follower of Christ. Aborishade stated that Jesus is a man for others and, as his followers in Lagos, the best action we can take is to emulate the Master. 'Christian Sufism does not exist anywhere', Aborishade stated, 'because we cannot live spiritually in isolation.' He added that Christians could complain from Lagos to Jericho; but if one does not act, one could not claim to be a true Christian.

Summary

The time I spent with Aborishade that afternoon left a lasting impression on me, which could be summarized as a principle of 'ora et labora' – prayer and labour. After all, this is the example Jesus Christ gave us through his life and ministry. One of the Christian experiences in the Christian life is that of God's grace. An analogy that comes to mind is that of fish in the Atlantic. While one may state that the fish are in the ocean swimming, it is also true to say that fish do not swim but are carried by the ocean water. This seems to illustrate the experience of Aborishade when describing how he encountered the grace of God in Lagos. Sometimes, Christians are unaware of the metaphorical water of grace that carries and sustains them.

2

'My faith looks up to thee'

Introduction

Lagos is a unique city where Christians freely affirm their faith on the streets, taking seriously Jesus's statement in Matthew's Gospel that 'Everyone therefore who acknowledges me before others, I also will acknowledge before my Father in heaven; but whoever denies me before others, I also will deny before my Father in heaven.'[1] It is not unusual to see people handing out Christian tracts that teach lessons about Jesus Christ, even when unsolicited. Lagosian Christians are believers with a strong appetite for God and the redeeming love of Jesus Christ, and they want to share it with others. Their understanding of faith is that one cannot periodically 'perform' as a Christian, but that faith must be lived in the rhythm of everyday life experience.

In the atmosphere of such intensity, I was handed a tract about the second coming of Jesus. In the pamphlet, a priest cited the example of three football (soccer) players practising on the pitch and what they would do should the second coming of Christ take place unexpectedly as they played the sport they loved. The first player responded that he would stop playing and run to the nearest Catholic church to pray. When the priest asked about the reason for that response, the player answered that he wanted to witness the second coming of Christ on his knees praying. The second player, when asked the same question, responded differently, stating that he would kneel on the soccer field and begin to pray as there might not be enough time to look for a church. The priest asked the third player, who responded that he would continue playing soccer, stating that the Christian faith is not about performance but a way of life. The words of the tract added that knowing whose hands we are holding in life, whether through our leisure or in our moments of struggles, is the meaning of Christianity.[2]

Segun and Modupe Adodo: The overcomers through fidelity to Christ

Segun and Modupe Adodo were the first couple I interviewed in Lagos. Their story reminded me of the response of the third soccer player as they told me about their journey and experience of faith as Christians in Lagos. Segun, the husband, was clear about what living in Lagos meant to him and his family. He was passionate about his involvement with the 'Bible-believing church ministries', quoting the Holy Scriptures frequently in our conversation, especially Phil. 4.19 and Jn 5.13.[3]

According to Adodo, it is the unity among Christians in Lagos that distinguishes them from non-Christians. Additionally, their relationship with other Christians is a major factor in the life of the couple. When I asked them about living in Lagos as Christians, they were clear that their faith in God is what sustains them. They said that they looked up to Jesus, the Lamb of Calvary. It was clear from their response that they understand the incredible benefits resulting from social networking and cooperating with other Christians.

What struck me most about their stories is the view that the invisible God is more real in their lives than even the physical world, visible to the human eye. They have seen first hand the work of God in their lives which they live according to the guidelines given in God's precepts. Segun explained that the very existence of Christians in Lagos is a catalyst that holds the city together, regardless of the different ethnicities present in the city.[4] He sees that existence as a unifying factor and one which has possibly reverberated across Nigeria. In his view, one's ethnic identity carries less importance than one's identity as a Christian, which is primary, and which defines who one is. Once a person belongs to Christ, their identity as a Christian becomes dominant. Becoming a child of God and a follower of Jesus Christ means that ethnic differences begin to disappear.

Segun Adodo was excited to tell me of an incident showing Christian unity in Lagos. His community had participated in assisting a fellow Christian during a difficult crisis. Members of the community had selflessly given donations and aided that person without judgement or conditions. It is his firm conviction that this is exactly what Christians should do and that it illustrates their unity in need.

The couple are active members of the organization of Bible Believing Church Ministries in Lagos, where they are community leaders. Adodo is a construction engineer, whose main means of income comes from building houses. He shared with me an experience he had while studying at the Federal Polytechnic at Nasarawa near the current federal Nigerian capital of Abuja, before he had migrated to Lagos. Through that experience, God showed him that Modupe was to be his wife.

When he was a student at the Federal Polytechnic, he noticed that many faculty and staff members were not married. He wondered whether their lives could be pleasing to God while they were adults and yet remained unmarried. At the school, he observed ladies in their early 50s who were still single. And highly intelligent male academicians with impressive careers were also single. Concerned that he did not want his own life to be like those he observed among the single faculty and staff at the Federal Polytechnic, he prayed to God. Then one Sunday morning, he saw Modupe as an usher at the church he was attending. He felt that God was revealing to him that she would be his wife.

Prayer for healing as a part of living for God in lagos

In the course of my conversation with the couple, Modupe (now Adodo's wife) also shared a powerful testimony with me. Having been unable to sleep for an extended period and seeking help for her insomnia, she was diagnosed with clinical depression. Not wanting to resort to antidepressant medications, she and Adodo both prayed for victory over her sleeplessness. A few days following their prayers to God, her insomnia was gone – a victory they attributed to God and knew was God-given.

The couple made it clear that they saw their lives and the lives of other Christians as an 'investment' in God's plan for transforming the world. Their 'kingdom investment' includes regular tithing and paying offerings at their church. As I visited them in their elegant two-story home one Sunday evening, I could feel the presence of God there. My impression was that they feel God has blessed them because of their faithfulness. Contrary to my experience elsewhere in Lagos, Segun and Modupe helped me realize the difference between 'high religion' and 'folks' religions'.[5]

While it is difficult to define the relationship between the two, high religion emphasizes the precepts of one's faith, including what one believes according to the teachings of the religion. This approach tends to exclude individuals without those beliefs, labelling them as unbelievers, heretics or unorthodox. Those who espouse what can be called folks' religion, on the other hand, tend to take concrete, but faith-based, steps to ameliorate the conditions of the poor and the marginalized. The major religions of the world, such as Judaism, Christianity, Islam, Hinduism and Buddhism, have instructions that most devoted followers see as their respective fundamental teachings. Quite often, we cannot say that a religion is either high or folks' religion because the relationship between the two can be blurred, for example, when it comes to separating the fruits (folks' religion elements) from the roots (high religion elements). However, these two approaches do differ in terms of their more (or less) practical versus theoretical understandings of specific religious teachings.

All major religions of the world such as Christianity, Islam and Hinduism can be said to have elements of high and folks' religions. Some have described folks' religion in the following manner: 'People don't care how much you know, until they know how much you care.' The expression of this kind of religion in the modern world can result in a richer fellowship as its devotees emphasize mending lives that have been broken by oppression, drought, misfortunes, calamities or death in the family. The relationships between these two different ways of expressing one's religious faith are complex, with no easy roads to understanding their complexities. What is called folks' religion is not above or superior to high religion and vice versa; they often complement each other. One of the ways to understand this intractable relationship is to see it in the context of the life of Jesus Christ. He was who he was because of what he did, just as he did what he did because of who he was. In a similar manner, we might say a Christian is as a Christian does.

'High' religions deal with doctrinal belief and essential categories of Christianity such as Christology, pneumatology, ecclesiology or eschatology and so on. Folks' religions, by contrast, serve the lives of the people and their existential needs and conditions. While high religions are very important in teaching the rudiments of Christianity, it is in the healing of lives that have been twisted by oppression that Christ's teachings are most effective and enduring.[6] We can say, therefore, that the most powerful manifestation of Jesus Christ in the world today will not be only in words, but also and always in deeds.

In the story of Segun and Modupe Adodo, with their uncompromising desire to please God by investing in God's Kingdom, we see that it is the attributes of folks' religion that take centre stage and are most consistent with the ministry of Jesus Christ and of early Christianity. Jesus Christ being human himself, understood humanity and loved people unconditionally.

Segun Adodo was clear in his belief that the Lord, whom he worshipped, was constantly giving love and redeeming lives broken or twisted by the daily trials people faced. It was apparent to me, in listening to the Adodo, that one cannot be identified with Jesus of Nazareth without practising a faith that nurtures and transforms the lives of others, not simply through Christian rhetoric, but by taking concrete steps to live for others as did Jesus. The distinctions between folk's religions and high religion were clearly defined in my discussion that evening with Segun and Modupe Adodo:

Folk's religion	High religion
In folk's religion, the emphasis is on a present God	In high religion, the emphasis is on a transcendent God.
Jesus is a close companion	Jesus is at the right hand of God.
Christians must address systemic oppression	Christians must seek forgiveness.
God suffers with us in our struggles and pains	God is the Ruler and Judge
Faith is presented as trust	Faith is presented as truth.
Personal meditation is crucial	Public worship is mandated
The body is the temple of the Holy Spirit	There is body-soul dichotomy
An awareness of God is in every believer	There is a religious duty to fulfil
Focus is on experiencing God	Focus is on believing the Gospel
Without us, God will not	Without God, we cannot
Fear is the opposite of faith	Doubt is the opposite of faith
Believers embrace God's wide mystery	Believers go through a narrow gate
Living for God is its own reward	Getting to heaven is the reward
Believers are possessed by the Truth now	Believers possess the Truth now
Human nature is good	Human nature is tainted with evil
Forgiveness is about the future	Forgiveness is about the past
Salvation is the flight of a butterfly	Salvation is the path of a bullet
Knowing that God is with us is salvation	Assent to doctrine is salvation
I must let God love me	I must love God
Concerned with protecting life	Concerned with protecting doctrines
Emphasis on *being/doing* Christian	Emphasis on *doing/being* Christian
Active about church membership	Passive about church membership
Asks: 'Can God trust me?'	Asks: 'Do I trust God?'
Church's function is to transform the world	Church's function is that the world doesn't change the church

Both I and my field coordinator, Samson Abolade Alabi, who accompanied me on my visit that evening, felt deeply inspired by this couple and their children who are living the life they were born to and destined to live. Christians in Lagos live in an enabling spiritual environment. While their Christian orientations may be highly diverse, they are open to the expansion of their faith and the promises of God. They live in a more spiritually oriented universe, moving seamlessly back and forth between the physical and the spiritual spheres. What had been discouraged or denigrated in their past spiritual approaches has now been incorporated into their Christian life without conflicting tensions, and the God of yesterday is the same God of today and tomorrow for Christians in Lagos.

Summary

In my experience with those Christians with whom I came into contact in Lagos, I have concluded they do not see the world the same way as the majority of us do in the Western world. They experience the world with an expectation of the expansion of the promises of God. My encounter with Segun and Modupe Adodo confirms my belief that the faith of Christian Africans is not unlike the faith of the early Christians about whom we read in the book of Acts.[7] Christianity now has a firm footing across the African continent. The example of Lagosian Christians provides a clear lens through which to see the faith of Africans in general. It is still a continent where people consult with oracles and talk to their ancestors; it is a continent where prophets ring bells in the morning on dusty streets to call the attention of their people to the need for prayer to God, as it had been in the biblical world. Africa is a continent where there are tonal languages resembling the biblical languages; it is a continent where one can encounter belief in spirit possession, where rituals and sacrifices have spiritual meanings, and where believers have dreams and see visions. It is a place where faith-healing and dreams are fundamental parts of believers' religious sensibilities. These are understood and interpreted to be God's revelation at critical junctures as in the biblical days of the prophets. We see contemporary Christian society in Africa exhibiting practices which might be parallel to the times of Jesus, including such seemingly insignificant details as believers wearing sandals without socks to church, as many early Christians did.

If we can look at the practice of Christianity in Lagos from the African perspective instead of seeing it exclusively with non-African eyes, we will see that Africans present their faith in Jesus Christ to the world in the way that no other Christians do. One of the challenges an African Christian presents to non-African Christians is in the form of anomaly, also found in cultural anthropology. It is common knowledge that human life originates in the Rift Valley, and the people that live today in Ethiopia and Eritrea carry the physical features of many people in the world, including Caucasoids with the pointed nose of Europeans, as well as the full lips characterizing the people of West

Africa. The Habeshas of Ethiopia have semitic origins and speak semitic languages such as Arabic, Hebrew and Amharic. Therefore, it would seem more accurate to say that the Europeans have features like the Habeshas than to say that the Habeshas have European features. If Leah is the mother of Rebecca, for example, it is more appropriate to say that Rebecca looks like her mother Leah, than to say the mother looks like her daughter.

Similarly, one can say that the faith of modern Africans predates that of European Christianity and is more likely to be in alignment with the original practice of the early church fathers and mothers we read about in the Bible. If we can trace the original practice of Christianity to Africa, would it not be more accurate to say that European and American practices of the Christian faith should mimic the African original?

It is ironic that the faith that was probably associated with the African people originally, and belongs to them in both teachings and practice, is now being proclaimed mainly by European and American missionaries as if Africans were foreigners to Christianity. This painful anthropological and missiological inconsistency led Kwame Bediako to insist that Europeans and Americans "did not bring God [to Africa]; rather, God brought them, so that by the proclamation of the Gospel through the missionary activity, Jesus Christ might be known, for 'without Him [Jesus Christ]' the meaning of our religiosity is incomplete."[8] Kwame Bediako further insisted that "the key to the Africa's future lay not in emulating European [Christian] habits, but in developing the skills and expertise which Africans already possessed."[9]

3

The God of our ancestors is my God

Faith in God can best be expressed only through concrete actions, and, in Lagos, Christians understand that 'faith is life in action', as affirmed by the respected Lagosian elder and London-educated Catholic leader, Charles Onyenochibebga Anyiam-Osigwe. Nothing prepared me at the outset of our meeting for the deep ontological discussion that would follow.

In my conversation with him, he asserts that the God of his ancestors is the same God who led him to Lagos from his town in Igboland. The name he knew for God when he was growing up is *Chineke*, translated as the God who creates everything. While human beings can be credited with making what is visible in the world, such as bicycles, motorcycles, cars, aeroplanes, typewriter, computers and so on, only God creates[1] and is the sole subject of all beings, seeing and unseeing. This God, he believes, followed him to Lagos and continues to guide his thoughts and actions. He has great conviction for the confluence of Christianity seen from the Western missionary's point of view and his own understanding of God, stemming from the awareness derived from his ancestral tradition as an Igbo man. He observes no contradiction, and his faith in God, he argues, is a recapitulation of what he believed as an Igbo man. He did not stop worshipping the God of his heritage when he became a Christian because true faith means binding together the old with the new.[2] His faith in God is cumulative, not transient or transitional and not even developmental.

It was on Christmas Day when I visited his home, where a lively party of family and friends was ongoing outside his commodious compound. Amid all the gaiety, Anyiam-Osigwe gave me his full attention. He repeatedly asserted that when we pray to God, the centrality of that prayer is for the goodness of the community to which we are connected. During the decades he has lived in Lagos, he has prayed for his community to thrive. He contended, 'We should never wish evil to befall our neighbours because every evil planned against our fellow human beings contains the seed of our own destruction.' He is confident that our faith in God is demonstrated through our actions in the rhythm of life. One of the best ways to know God and the will of God as well as the needs of our neighbours is by knowing them, and this is not by magic. He looks forward to a day in the future when the Catholic church will have room for a canonized saint in Igboland, and he suggested Saint Chukwuemeka.

I have never encountered a Christian in Lagos who would exude his ancestral identity with such joy and satisfaction as Charles Onyenochibebga Anyiam-Osigwe. Yet his open-mindedness was also remarkable. The foremost question in his mind when I interviewed him on Christmas Day, 2022, was 'who is the God of the other?'

He shared a story with me. When he was young and his father wanted to explore potential candidates for wives for his sons, the father's main concern was not about the girls' religion, whether they were Christians or not. He would not even ask whether the potential wife was educated or not. Those were not what he considered the essentials of a successful marriage. Marriage is not only about love but also about the suitability of the couple to nurture the future generation. It is about commitment to forgive, to understand and to treat the other person as more important than oneself. Therefore, his father would ask any potential marriage candidates for his boys whether they could be good mothers, calm, dexterous, nurturing and protective, capable of creating a safe home. Were they of the strong character necessary to be good mothers to his grandchildren? Could they entertain unexpected guests in their house joyfully with African cultural hospitality? He saw these traits as far more important than being a card-carrying Christian or a learned academic. 'Faith must be demonstrated through concrete actions', he reiterated. Our faith in God is also a gift from God.

We exercise that faith in God in the rhythm of our life. Our journey in life is never by our human power or might but solely by the grace of God. Thus, for Charles Onyenochibebga Anyiam-Osigwe, the Christian faith intersects with Igbo ontology, reminding me of what Heinrich Weinel and Alban G. Widgery affirmed in *Jesus in the Nineteenth Century and After*. Their words were quoted by the distinguished theologian Howard Thurman, in *Jesus and the Disinherited* (1996). The full quote is: 'To some, God and Jesus may appeal in a way other than to us: some may come to faith in God and to love, without a conscious attachment to Jesus. Both Nature and good men besides Jesus may lead us to God. They who seek God with all their hearts must, however, some day on their way meet Jesus.'[3]

Anyiam-Osigwe stated that the New Testament he read in his native Igbo language is the blueprint for living well, seeking first the Kingdom of God and loving one's neighbour. He stated that one's prayer for others is essentially also for one's benefit. When we pray for the well-being of others, we pray for ourselves. He reiterated that the essence of life, and of Igbo ontology, is that we should do unto others what we desire to be done unto us.

Anyiam-Osigwe's faith in God as a Christian in Lagos is a recapitulation of his belief as an Igbo man. His claim that when we pray, the centrality of that prayer is for the goodness of the community, has resonance in the teachings of Jesus Christ and in the prayer he taught his disciples in the Gospel of Luke.[4] All human beings are connected, and we should never wish evil to befall our neighbour because every evil fashioned on others contains the seeds of one's own destruction.

The true essence of his faith lies in his actions. He insisted that my coming to Lagos was a purposeful, God-directed action and that faith always required a corresponding action. He stated that one could have faith in desiring a clean house, but the house would never be clean until someone took a broom and swept it clean.

The communion of saints in Lagos

When Anyiam-Osigwe started talking about the communion of saints, I knew I was interviewing a respected Igbo Catholic theologian. He was expressing his deep affection for Christian thought from the depth of the Igbo ontology and their understanding of spirituality that has grounded his Christian consciousness. He mentioned that Christian understanding is an extension of his beliefs in the Igbo ontological traditions subsumed into Christian awareness. There was never a time he did not cherish the existence of his Igbo religious understanding formed long before the arrival of European missionaries to Igboland and to Lagos. An aspect of that understanding is the belief that one's prayer for the success of others is linked directly or indirectly to one's own success as life is ordered by God in such a way that one cannot injure others without hurting oneself. All human beings are sanguinely connected and related since there is only one God who created all humanity. Thus, for Anyiam-Osigwe, the communion of saints means that one's prayers for others are fundamentally prayers for one's own benefit. Traditionally, this is known as 'waka'; when you pray for others, you pray for yourself.

Although he studied in London, he never abandoned his Igbo roots or strayed from the ways of his ancestral homeland. When asked what he would like to share with me or communicate to the Western and the non-Western world about his faith, he responded with great excitement. He stated that: 'Blessed are those that are the poor in spirit.' Inspiration doesn't come from wealth or riches but by depending on God as the poor in spirit often do. He was nuanced and reflective, stating that Christians in the Western world need to 're-in-God' themselves because life without God or a life of materialism is not consistent with the life we were created by God to live. Those who are enslaved to money or wealth acquisition can never be happy because they become insatiable in their quest for more, and they become dishonest to gain more materials.

If a person is nurtured in a Christian home, the values taught there remain with him or her permanently. But material possessions could lead to human forgetfulness and incessant myopic demands for more that would never satisfy an insatiable longing for things. This can deter one from following Christ. The inevitable result is forgetting God, the source of every blessing.

This amazing church leader reminded me that all human blessings come not from the East or West, North or South. Everything that human beings need in life comes from God. When materialism and consumerism dominate human life, one tends to forget God and question not only the existence of God but also the miracle of the goodness of God and the abundance in nature that God provides for humanity.

It is life in community that reminds us God does not do for us that which we can do for ourselves and for each other. Lagos can be a good place to live, but excessive focus on material possessions comes with misery and loneliness, avarice and the fear of losing them. Life in Lagos and the requirements of the Christian life demand that people be helpful to the less privileged by being present in their lives and offering them assistance. This is because the true Christian life is a life together, a life of involvement in the life of others.

When I asked him to speak about one of the lessons living in Lagos has taught him, he was modest and down-to-earth about his experience, saying that Lagos is a cosmopolitan city and that his churchmanship is the centre of his life. It is also the centre of social life and activity in Lagos. 'It is unrealistic to try to find the boys and girls of my elementary school days', he reminded me. 'It is impossible for 20 boys to maintain a relationship together for 20 years. High school classmates are difficult to find as we become septuagenarians. It is even difficult to rekindle relationships made only two decades ago at the University of London. But 'I thank God that the church has become the centre of my social interactions; my sense of community is robust because I go to church in Lagos'. He added that members of the church parish are his closest friends and colleagues, providing social networks and support that require no qualifications or quantifications.

He describes Christians as his closest allies, who worship with him, providing emotional support and spiritual well-being. These Christian social networks are central to how Christians live in Lagos. It is true that the modern technological age has connected us to others and given us closer proximity – but only in digital ways. It is equally true, however, that it has also separated us from one another and diminished our capacity to be gregarious and social beings in real life. While we can use phones to communicate easily and conveniently, when we are not physically present to see what is communicated by gestures and body language, we miss out on the total picture. Technology has served humanity well, but it has also taken away the essence of humanity, ushering in a life of isolationism, causing us to become robotic in our interpersonal relationships.

Before I left his home at the Government Reserved Area (GRA) of Lagos, Anyiam-Osigwe reflected on the African proverb that 'it takes a village to raise a child'. He also led us in a traditional Igbo prayer celebrating the protection of God. The traditional name of God in the Igbo language comes across in the prayer like glowing volcanic lava carrying the heat of God's love: 'Chineke will protect his people from every danger of life.'

Anyiam-Osigwe's faith in God is deep and comprehensive. He was almost professorial in his insistence that if Africans were left to develop their Christian consciousness and identity as a product of their tradition, we would be celebrating African saints, referring to them today as Saint Chukwuemeka and others. He sees this as the true meaning of the communion of saints. Before we departed, he asked the ladies in attendance to give us jollof rice and soft drinks.

One of the most meaningful and longest-lasting gifts I received, however, was the traditional Igbo prayer he offers to God every day. It is a comprehensive prayer, reflecting the traditional Igbo cosmology. The Igbo cosmology cannot be eradicated, but was transported nearly intact into Christianity and is absorbed into the practice of the Christian faith. The prayer insists on the belief in the Supreme Being recognized well before the arrival of modern-day European and American missionaries. Chukwu, or Chineke, created both the physical and the invisible worlds, enlivened by the reality of the ancestors as living in spirits (now residing with Chineke who created them and gave them life), and existence of both good and evil spirits, belief in essential duality or the phenomenon of pairing. The hierarchical order of ranking is:

- The Supreme Being

- Deities and deputies to the Supreme Being

- Spiritual Forces

- Ancestors ranked higher than human beings.

According to this cosmological order, the elder in the family ranks closest to the ancestors and offers prayers through his forefathers, whom he believes to be closer to the Supreme Being, Chineke; he is now closer by way of his transitional crossing from the physical to the spiritual. The Igbos believe that their ancestors are now saints and can intercede for them effectively to the

Creator, Chineke (the God who created and continues to create the heavens and the earth incessantly). Accordingly, everyone, whether alive or dead, plays a role in God's magnificent drama of creation and sustenance.

The intercessory prayers of the ancestors through the forefathers do not, in any way, however, negate the responsibilities any individual has in reaching out to Chineke directly in his or her personal prayers of supplication, even while calling on the ancestors to add their voices to his or her own prayers.

Traditionally, a bowl of water is brought to an elder for him to wash his hands; a glass of water will be brought for him to rinse his mouth. He must be clean, and his ablution complete before he offers his prayers unto God. In addition, a plate of kola nuts and a hot drink are brought to him so that he can pour out libations to his forefathers immediately following his prayers. Following these sacred rituals, he breaks the kola nuts into pieces, throws some out to the heavens to acknowledge his ancestors and then pours out libations to Chineke and to his forefathers. He eats some of the kola nuts in solidarity with the ancestors and then passes the rest to those with him to eat in communion. All except children partake in chewing the kola nuts and in drinking some hot drinks.

When asked for a typical morning prayer an Igbo elder might offer whether in Lagos or in Igboland, Anyiam-Osigwe proposed the following:

Chineke kere elu igwe na ala
God who created the heavens and the earth

Anyi enyegi otito na ekelele na ututu ah
We praise and thank you this morning

Kele gi otu isiri me anyi ahu ubochi taa
We thank you for letting us see a new day

Ndi nna nna anyi
Our forefathers

Na ndi ikwu anyi
Our relations

Ndi isiri ibele kporo gina ha nnu ibeahu, anyi ekelele unu
Whom you have been called from this world and are still in our memories, we greet you.

Soro nu anyi na ayo Chineke ka ihe diri anyi ma taa ma gawa na ihu
Join us in pleading with God that all will be well with us today and going forward

Anyi na ayogi Chineke
We are pleading with you, God,

Ka inoyere anyi mgbe dum
That you be with us always.

Biko na echekwa anyi mgbe dum
Please look after us always.

Mee ka ihe gara anyi nke oma
Make things go well with us.

Biko mee ka ukwu hare ikpo anyi na njo
Please ensure that no evil befalls us.

Biko Chekwa anyi na opupu anyi na mbata anyi, na ebele ebe anyi nu
Preserve us in our going out and our coming in wherever we may be.

Ekewla ka ndiiro anyi mere anyi
Do not permit our enemies to triumph over us.

Mee ka ahu di anyi mma mgbe dum
Bless us with good health.

Nye anyi ahu ike nke onuahu na ke mpuru obi
Grant us strength of body and spirit.

Gozie aka oru anyi dum
Bless the works of our hands.

Anyi ekelele gi na ununa ekpere anyi, nakpute ya, mere anyi otu anyi siri
yoo gi. Isee
We thank you for listening to our prayers and granting them as pleaded.
Amen

Chineke, the name of God among the Igbo people, is more than a figment of imagination embedded in mythology or literary tradition. God is felt through the existential crises of the people. Chineke is not buried in the metaphysical principle of the ancient people or relegated to the background of human life. Chineke is beyond reproach and not consumed by the fire and fury of philosophy but walks and talks to the Igbo people in both Igboland and Lagos, where Chineke abides with the people. Anyiam-Osigwe shared many stories with me, proving the efficacy of prayers to Chineke for his children, their families, progress in their vocations and for safety in daily routines. He prays this prayer for his whole society and his immediate community in Lagos. In a profound way, 'Chineke, the God of the ancestors, is the same God we worship in Lagos and this God abides with us still.'

The prayer demonstrates the Igbo belief in the Supreme Being, their ancestors and various spiritual forces, as well as the importance of hierarchy and intercession in Igbo cosmology. This belief parallels what Osadolor Imasogie depicted as 'bureaucratic monotheism'.[5] Through their ancestors who are believed to be closer to the Supreme Being, the elders petition God in prayer and thanksgiving.

4

Michael and Mary Adunola

The opposite of faith is fear

Let us begin this chapter with an important subject among Christians in Lagos – faith. The opposite of faith is not simply doubting, as many Christians in Lagos maintain; the opposite of faith is in fact fear. This is one of the lessons I learned from Michael and Mary Adunola when I interviewed them.

Many Christians to whom I spoke on the streets of Lagos shared at random the story of Abraham *not* sacrificing Isaac.[1] To them, it is one of the most important stories in the Bible about faith, serving as a sort of benchmark for many Lagosian Christians who live by faith day in day out. They are familiar with the manifold interpretations of the story of Abraham's not sacrificing Isaac, whose significance is highlighted by the fact that it is recorded in all three Abrahamic faith traditions of Judaism, Christianity and Islam.

The Hebrew Bible is full of narratives common to these Abrahamic faith traditions. Perhaps this account, recorded in Gen. 22.1-19, is one of the best ever about faith. It remains a perplexing story in which a loving God asks Abraham to sacrifice his only son, Isaac. Isaac was born only after Abraham's barren wife, Sarah, finally became pregnant – through God's intervention – when she was 90 and Abraham was 100 years old.

The story raises ethical challenges and conundrums about the nature of God's love and demands. Critics have argued that a God who would command sacrificing one's only son to please him must be cruel. In today's world, people would turn away from worshipping such a God. But Søren Kierkegaard interprets the story as a supreme illustration that ethics is limited where faith in God is required. Accordingly, there is a higher law than that which guides humanity in society – the law of exercising faith in God. This law is not automatic or mechanical, but teleological and purposeful. One of the earliest examples demonstrating this kind of faith occurs in the Hebrew Bible, in the book of Daniel, Chapter 3, when three faithful Jews, Shadrach, Meshach and Abednego, defied the commands of King Nebuchadnezzar, declaring they would worship only God and not any idol of the state, stating:

> O Nebuchadnezzar, we have no need to present a defense to you in this matter. If our God whom we serve is able to deliver us from the furnace of blazing fire and out of your hand, O king, let him deliver us. But if not, be it known to you, O king, that we will not serve your gods and we will not worship the golden statue that you have set up.[2]

Godlessness and faithlessness

Godlessness is not always the same as faithlessness, but neither is possible for humanity. Godlessness can be viewed as the conviction that one can live without God – something hardly realistic because God does not withdraw from humanity to prove his existence. A human being can believe in God's existence and remain a non-believer if there is a lack of understanding of God's grace sustaining human life. There could be blood in adult tears, but godliness means that the presence of God is still enduring through human pain and suffering.

Faithlessness is a denial of the reality of faith in the orbit of human existence. Human beings are surrounded by experiences of the faith of others if not their own. Both godlessness and faithlessness are the conviction that neither God nor faith is dominant in one's life or has meaning in one's life. It is illogical to be godless or faithless, however, because these qualities of belief do not depend solely on acceptance by humanity. There are other factors involved that are independent of humanity, including the purposes of God. This is the foundation of the interpretation of Kierkegaard as he accounts for the story of Abraham's not sacrificing Isaac. But who was Søren Aabye Kierkegaard that we should attend to his understanding?

Søren Aabye Kierkegaard (1813–55)

Søren Aabye Kierkegaard was one of the most influential philosophers of the early nineteenth century. A Danish philosopher and a religious thinker, he was the youngest son of his parents, Mikaël Pederson and Anne Sørensdatter Lund. He was born when his father was fifty-six years old, and his mother was forty-four. From a very early age, he was a serious student with an unusual theological imagination, believing that the essence of life was a balance between intellectual life and piety. In the thinking of Kierkegaard, faith in God is an inward journey, both existential and emotional. Faith cannot be duplicated or transferred from one person or generation to the next, and it has little to do with religious or public display of piety through institutions, including ecclesiastical institutions. He saw faith as intensely personal. There is no single and consistent path to exercising faith in God because each one of us is unique in our relationship with God. Faith in God involves no exacting criteria because it is personal, always between God and the individual.[3]

In *Fear and Trembling* (1843), Kierkegaard offered his interpretation of the story of Abraham's not sacrificing his son, Isaac, on Mt. Moriah. His interpretation spread like wildfire at a young age, bringing him fame as one of the nineteenth-century existential philosophers. According to him, 'Whether a man has a right to make this affirmation [of faith in God], must be left to him; it is a question between him and the Eternal Being who is the object of faith whether in this respect he can hit upon an amicable compromise.'[4] He went on to state that 'what every man has not a right to do, is to make others believe that faith is something lowly, or that it is an easy thing, whereas it is the greatest and the hardest'.[5] It was clear in the mind of Kierkegaard that Abraham did the hardest thing by following God's command to sacrifice his son, Isaac. The faith of Abraham can be said to be non-mechanical but rather teleological and purposeful. Kierkegaard states, 'Let us then either consign Abraham to oblivion, or let us learn to be dismayed by the tremendous paradox which constitutes the significance of Abraham's life, that we may understand that our age, like every age, can be joyful if it has faith.'[6]

Kierkegaard understood that God's demand to sacrifice Isaac on Mt. Moriah was, from a purely human point of view, an unethical demand, but faith in God sometimes absorbs the unethical. Thus, Abraham had to take a 'leap of faith' and accept this seemingly unethical demand of God. One of the questions philosophers often ask is: 'Is it ethical to do something because God commands it, or God does command it because it is ethical?' For Kierkegaard, a more relevant question might be: 'What does God desire of me that would be pleasing unto him because of unrevealed purpose for the world?' God's plan for the world is often unknown and not clearly understood by humanity. But it should not be doubted. God shows mercy, but God is also prudent with the overall plans for human transformation which only few Christians see through the Bible. It is only by faith that we can breathe the plans of God for us, without the oxygen of reason.

Abraham suspended the responsibility of caring for and protecting his son, and, at this point, made what we might see as an unreasonable or impossible choice because he was transfixed by what he perceived to be above the ethical principles of his society. The bar of one's relationship with God is raised when one can say that he not only 'believes in God' but that 'he knows God'.

In his obedience, Abraham became aware of his own infinite distance from God. According to Kierkegaard, Christianity is not about feeling or believing in God, but about having God in the orbit of one's life through faith demonstrated in concrete action. And knowing God in action will be out of step with the ethical demand or principle of one's society.

Because of Abraham's long-standing relationship with God in the very rhythm of his life, he understood that it was God's will that he was to sacrifice Isaac. Abraham's teleological faith dictated that he was not to be guided by the ethical norm of his society. In other words, the opinion of others in his society could be forfeited by virtue of the unique relationship between God and Abraham. Kierkegaard believed that God's command was not absolute but based on the enduring covenantal relationship into which Abraham had entered with God. It was not out of some obligation that compelled Abraham to obey God's command; rather, it was as a loving son obeying the loving father whom he knew. Thus, Abraham's compliance in being willing to sacrifice Isaac was not justified by mindless obedience making him give up the most precious of his possessions for God's cruel pleasure and delight. While this may be the intermediate interpretation of the story, Kierkegaard advocated for an interpretation invoking the concept of teleological faith that could look beyond the sacrifice and see God's ultimate purpose in revealing the nature and purpose of God more completely, in contrast to the Canaanite deities with which Abraham was familiar.[7]

In the present day, Carol Lowery Delaney, an American cultural and social anthropologist at Stanford University, challenges Kierkegaard in her book, *Abraham on Trial: The Social Legacy of Biblical Myth* (1998). According to Delaney, the question one must ask about this story is: Why is faith in God not illustrated by a father's unwillingness to sacrifice his son as an alternative to a test of faith? The force of Delaney's argument is that it can still be a demonstration of faith when a father shows unwillingness to sacrifice his son, even when God demands it. After all, one of the paths we can take towards the destination of knowing God's will makes us become a spokesperson when conscience is wounded for doing what is wrong.[8] When we do the right thing, however, our conscience rejoices. Thus, it must be God's command if it is ethical, and not 'it must be ethical because God commands it'.

Emmanuel Levinas (1905–95)

Emmanuel Levinas was a Lithuanian French philosopher who interpreted this story of Abraham's not sacrificing Isaac. Levinas believed that ethics is the queen of philosophy,[9] with the deepest human obligation in life being to protect the lives of others. A true covenant between human beings and God is not made in a vacuum but between one person and another, in living and active society. We can hear God only through the lives of other human beings. The obligation to honour and protect life is sacred because every life is precious and irreplaceable. When God commands 'thou shall not kill' in the Hebrew Bible, it is a universal command to always place the lives of others above one's own. According to Levinas, an unforgettable moment in this story occurs when Isaac asks, 'Father! The fire and the wood are here, but where is the lamb for a burnt offering?' Isaac, therefore, calls the attention of his father, Abraham, to the truth of the sanctity of life and the demand of God for the preservation of life. Isaac draws his father's attention to responsible fatherhood. Thus, it was Isaac's own faith that intervened, believing that a true God would not allow a father to sacrifice his son. Levinas sees Kierkegaard's interpretation of the story as inconclusive since he notes Kierkegaard overlooking the call of Isaac to Abraham, his father, to obey God's command to protect life.

For Kierkegaard, the rigid 'ethical' rules of community must sometimes be violated to be righteous and be faithful to God. For Levinas, however, one's faith must be exercised within the community and cannot be exercised without it. One cannot leave the community behind to exercise faith in God esoterically, as God is the God of community. How can one love God unless that faith takes into consideration the vulnerability of individuals? All human beings are imbued with God's image, and we cannot pretend to love God we cannot see; we can only love the people created in God's image that are visible. In this way, Levinas turns the philosophical meaning of 'the love of wisdom' to 'the wisdom of loving'.

Could Abraham be testing God as God was testing Abraham?

With these various interpretations, one can imagine that even as God was testing Abraham, Abraham was simultaneously testing God. One of God's commands is 'thou shall not kill'. By going along with God's direct command, Abraham would be defining the kind of God he had been asked to follow; he was discovering the character and nature of God along the way. If the attributes of the God in whom Abraham trusted were not different from the immorality (exemplified by cannibalism) prominent in the Canaanite deities of his experience, then Abraham is deluded and his quest for the true God must continue. To obey such a God would not be an act of piety, but a retrogression of his faith. If Abraham had carried out the command of God to sacrifice Isaac, it would have been akin to following the same old pagan deities in the surrounding land of Canaan. How could Abraham make a distinction in his life between the Canaanite deities and the God of Israel? The act of God's testing Abraham must be for a good purpose. Likewise, Abraham's testing of the nature of God he was to follow must reveal the goodness of that God. Belief in a God that requires human sacrifice as an offering would be abhorrent and an anathema.

In this text, we do not see Abraham rushing to execute God's command. Abraham answers Isaac's question about where the lamb for the sacrifice would come from by stating in Gen. 22.8 'God himself will provide the lamb for a burnt offering, my son.' The response of Abraham was to assure Isaac that his life was not in danger, and there is a series of steps through which he moves:

> He gets up.
> He dresses his animals.
> He gets his attendants ready to escort him to Mt. Moriah.
> He cuts the firewood.
> He sets off.
> He sees Mt. Moriah.
> He instructs his attendants to wait.
> He takes the firewood.
> He places the firewood on the back of Isaac.
> He takes the fire.
> He takes the knife.
> He and Isaac do not run but walk toward Mt. Moriah.
> He and Isaac talk (not sing) on the way to Mt. Moriah.
> He makes various preparations getting the altar ready.
> He ties Isaac onto the altar.
> He stretches out his arm.
> He raises the knife.

One of the points in this story is that Abraham is able to rescue the hope of humanity for the true God who combines sovereignty with morality. In this way, God saves Jews, Christians and Muslims from historical religious embarrassment and discomfiture, proving God's ultimate nature is hope, love and justice.[10] Abraham endures what must have been his confused agony in acting in seeming obedience to God's command to the very point of sacrificing Isaac, with the faith that he would not allow the life of Isaac to be in danger. In this way, the religion of ethical monotheism was established in the Abrahamic faith traditions.

This story, known as *Akedah* in Judaism, establishes Judaism's unique insight among ancient religions, cults and cultures related to the danger inherent in having human beings submit to the orders of individuals claiming unique access to the wishes of 'the gods' or of any god. Thus, Christianity is ultimately based on a covenant between God and humanity. The Christian faith is like a multifaceted diamond, which must be seen from all sides to grasp its fullness. Even with the various sides, however, it is one faith – the faith of an individual before God. We are not saved vicariously by the faith of others. It is not the faith of Abraham or Isaac or Jacob or Joseph, but the personal faith of everyone.

Furthermore, the ability to quote the Bible verbatim does not make one a Christian. It is not to quote Abraham, Moses or Elijah but to emulate what they did in their exercise of faith. To be a Christian is not to practise the religion *of* Jesus but to practise religion *like* Jesus. The Christian faith is like an artichoke, its kernel hidden by many layers of leaves. While these layers can represent traditions followers have built around the truth, they sometimes stand in the way of encountering the actual truth of God in its naked power.

I have come to appreciate all the many Christian traditions for what they are, but I have also come to realize that they are not the truth in themselves, but interpretations of the truth layered upon the truth itself. I don't think that God is interested in policing the borders of human righteousness. Our relationship with God is guided by God's invitation and our response; it is not about God's expectations imposed on humanity. I think that God invites humanity to enter his tabernacle of righteousness through Jesus Christ, and even our response is a gift of the grace of God.

The truth of Christianity is the truth of Jesus of Nazareth – the Christ. It is the truth of his living, the truth of his dying and the truth of his rising again from the dead for the salvation of the world.

While in Lagos, I met a man who exercised this kind of teleological faith in God. His name is Michael Adunola.

Michael and Mary Adunola: *The opposite of faith is fear*

Michael is an automobile entrepreneur in Lagos. His wife, Mary, served for a long time as the vice principal of Magboro Community High School in Lagos. Mary has remained a practising Catholic while Michael, although raised Catholic and determined to continue to carry Catholic teachings with him, is a member of a Pentecostal church. He attends Day Star Church regularly and is a respected church leader there.

In 1999, Michael experienced something in Lagos that transformed his life. Feeling a deep sense of burnout, he resigned from his work early that year. Not knowing where his next means of livelihood would come from or how he was going to support his family, he became paralyzed with fear. In November of that year, he became increasingly uncomfortable and anxious because he could not fulfil his financial obligations to his family. As weeks turned into months, the heavy weight of his financial demands led to an overwhelming sense of restlessness.

One morning after taking a bath, he heard a voice saying to him, 'Is there anything too difficult for me?' It was like the voice of God to Abraham on Mount Moriah. He took this to be the voice of God, and buoyed up by his faith, he managed to shed his fear. Soon, he received a new and satisfying job. In a similar way, God provided a 'ram, caught in a thicket by its horns' for Abraham. Since then, Michael has remained free of worry, stating that if a Christian could do something about a particular hardship, he should do it; but if not, he should not worry. Christians should not worry or be anxious about tomorrow, because God is never daunted by hardships we go through in life. God holds tomorrow although we may never know what tomorrow holds.

Mary also experienced hardship but was able to overcome a debilitating health condition by praying. When she was sick, the couple prayed for her to overcome her illness. Although her sickness kept her in bed for days, Michael continued to pray for healing. One day when Mary awoke, she asked for a drink of water and health returned to her miraculously.

The couple insisted that their faith in God was unconditional because they have seen God's power and the activity of Jesus Christ in their lives. In the context of their stories, it is worth remembering that many people in the Global South still face abject poverty as well as a lack of adequate medical care. Healthcare providers are sometimes overwhelmed due to a lack of equipment and tools they need to mitigate the diseases that have already been eradicated in the Global North. Water-borne diseases, such as cholera and typhoid fever, are common. In Lagos, malaria, more than any other disease, still claims the lives of many children before they reach their fifth birthdays, and attempts to produce vaccines have been slowed or thwarted by many factors.

Summary

Søren Aabye Kierkegaard was a Lutheran philosopher with an understanding of the faith formed solely between God and an individual. Kierkegaard celebrated the Reformation era and endorsed the sentiment of the superiority of the relationship between an individual and God versus any institutional provisions of faith. While mindful of the slogan of *sola fidei* (faith alone) coined by Martin Luther, it is instructive also to see Kierkegaard's contributions in seeing the preeminence of faith as a celebration of the elevation of the individual's faith in God.

Emmanuel Levinas, on the other hand, influenced, no doubt, by his Jewish identity, was propelled by his focus on hope through a dialogical relationship with God that can lead to justice. He saw one's duty to another person as paramount because God is just.

It must be noted that Michael and Mary Adunola were strongly influenced by their strong Christian belief that nothing can be achieved in life if we are motivated by fear. Theirs is a faith that casts out fear and allows an individual to thrive, strengthened by their personal relationship with God.

PART II

Stories of hope

5

'I was in prison and you visited me'

His name is Joseph Dickson Udoh. He was originally from Akwa Ibom State before migrating to Lagos with his parents as an infant. He maintained that if God was not good to him and he did not obtain God's mercy in his life, there was no reason to believe in God or affirm the love of God in the world. He had held two things dear in his life: the Bible as a manual for living and the belief that nothing was new under the sun since the God who was alive and active yesterday was the same today and forever.[1]

On 19 December 2022, I visited him at his elegant photocopying and laminating business shop at Magboro, on the outskirts of Lagos. I asked him and his wife, Oluwafunmilayo Opeyemi, to tell me their story of what it meant for them as a young couple to be Christians in Lagos. Joseph was enthusiastic and eager to tell his story. He began by sharing his experience in a Lagos prison.

Udoh and two of his best friends, Charles and Ndubisi, used to swim in the Atlantic Ocean when they were teenagers. One day, the strong Atlantic currents carried Charles away from the shore and he drowned. His body was never to be found, but Udoh and Ndubisi made it back to shore safely. Once there, they faced unanticipated dramatic problems. They were both accused of jointly killing their friend, Charles, as a ritual to help them obtain wealth and fortune. Naturally, the family of Charles was devastated, insisting that these friends were evil and had only pretended to befriend him. The boys were blamed as wolves in sheep's clothing, and Charles's family insisted that they should be brought to court as criminals. The police arrested Udoh and Ndubisi, charging them with ritual killing.[2] When the boys appeared in court before a female judge with their hands and feet shackled, the judge summarily ordered the imprisonment of both Udoh and Ndubisi at the notorious federal prison for juveniles at Ikoyi, Lagos. The prison was often overcrowded and lacked adequate sanitation; any provision for medical care was minimal at best and not a priority of the prison administrators. In order to reduce the prison population, the government would periodically find draconian and unlawful ways to do so, including poisoning some of the inmates as unfit and undesirable for society. Such measures led to the boys' utter terror at the prospect of being in jail.

Concerned that Udoh could also be poisoned in prison, his mother took food to him every day and instructed him never to eat the food provided by the prison staff. After several months of his incarceration, some members of the Foursquare Gospel Church visited Udoh, bringing him toiletries, including soap, towels, toilet tissue, napkins and a copy of the Bible. The prison ministry of Foursquare Gospel Church also provided snacks, crackers, bread, groundnuts and garri (a popular Nigerian staple food).

For the first time in his adult life, Udoh started reading the Bible on a regular basis, which subsequently led to his becoming a Christian while still in prison. He recalled his mother telling him that when he was born, and she was attending a Christian evangelical event, the preacher had anointed the infant Udoh's head with oil and dedicated him to God. Remembering this, Udoh dedicated himself even more faithfully to reading the Bible.

A new beginning

One of the leaders of the Church that had reached out to him during such a prison visit informed Udoh that he would soon be released. So Udoh was confident that at the next court appearance, the judge would set him free.[3] When he appeared before the judge, he told the truth about his friend, Charles, stating that he had simply drowned. After hearing all the evidence, the new presiding judge, a male, ordered that the shackles on Udoh's feet must be removed because they did not belong on the feet of a teenager.

Before he walked out of the prison on the day he was released, Udoh gave away all his belongings to other prisoners – many of whom have been unkind to him during his incarceration – not expecting to ever return.

After his release, Udoh took a job as a bus conductor for a transportation company, collecting money from the passengers and giving accounts to the driver. During this time, the driver accused him of stealing the money collected from passengers; the accusation devastated him, casting doubt on his new-found faith and freedom in Christ. Although the evidence supported his innocence, the nagging of the accusers was so unbearable that he left the company that employed him. In the months and years that followed, he went back to school, obtaining his own driver's license and finally became a mature and responsible citizen. He once again was reading the Bible regularly and seeing it as a dependable manual of Christian living. He was introduced by a new friend to a church in Lagos, the Redeemed Pentecostal Church. It was here that his faith continued to mature, increasing the strength of his convictions.

He later decided to enrol at a school run by the Redeemed Church he had joined. The educational opportunities of which he availed himself there paved the way for him to start his own business.

Marriage to Oluwafunmilayo

He met and married his wife, Oluwafunmilayo Opeyemi, and soon afterwards the couple had a baby boy. Udoh was certain that God wanted him to name the baby Israel. When their second baby, a girl, was born, she was named Bethany. This was followed by the birth of twins, who were named Goodness and Mercy, a boy and a girl respectively.

When I asked the couple why they used such significant names for their children, especially the twins, Goodness and Mercy, Udoh was quick to respond that God had revealed to him that he would be good to him and would continue to show him mercy through Jesus Christ. Therefore, they had chosen names which were related to their Christian identity and faith rather than using the traditional names for twins, often preferred by the Yoruba people.

Udoh's wife, Oluwafunmilayo Opeyemi, shared her story that when she was born, her parents had rejected the doctor's medical advice that her mother have a Cesarean section delivery. Instead, her father prayed to God for a natural delivery. But the doctor was adamant, insisting on a forced epidural in preparation for the Cesarean. However, the syringe with the drug fell on the floor of the delivery room and shattered into dozens of pieces. The father started praying to God even more fervently, and the baby was delivered naturally. Oluwafunmilayo Opeyemi's deep Christian faith had its foundation in her birth, close to miraculous, thanks be to God.

Christians in Lagos live as a community. Any lines of distinction between one Christian denomination and another are blurred, if they exist at all. The stories of Udoh and his wife, Oluwafunmilayo, can inspire others to follow Jesus Christ as they are a living testimony of the grace of God. The stories of their personal encounters with God inspire others. Udoh told me that he gives 20 per cent of the family income to God's causes, believing that the path to God's blessings in life is through giving.[4]

Looking back on his experience at the notorious Ikoyi prison, where inmates are often targeted and can be randomly poisoned to control the prison population, Udoh feels that God sent his mother as a strong shield with her constant maternal presence in his life during this time. He told me that his life was given a new meaning because of the Foursquare Christians who had ministered to him with their gifts to meet his needs when he was in prison. He has dedicated his business to glorifying God and was determined to give back to those who have given him so much.

A catalyst for unity: The Christian character of Lagos

Isabel Wilkerson's book *Caste: The Origins of our Discontents* (2020) and an earlier work by James E. Cone, *The Cross and the Lynching Tree* (2011), were both songs of promise produced in a climate of racial injustice in the United States, meant to resurrect hope during the time of hopelessness infused with endemic apathy. At the same time, these two books are a powerful reminder that the ones who are perceived as innately undesirable because of the colour of their skin or their socio-economic background will continue to carry the burden of the structural ills and misfortunes of society. This is an indictment on society itself, and it is perplexing that some may still be blind to these fundamental injustices.

One might even consider racism and class inequality to be a part of the DNA of American society.[5] In the African context, the existing relative social unity is paradoxically undermined or even broken by the façade of democracy enforced by opportunistic politicians. At the grassroots level, people in Lagos are often united, but their political leaders often employ tribalistic measures which work against this unity. Certainly, this was the experience of Joseph Dickson Udoh. Like racism in most Western societies, tribalism and classism in other societies can be equally poisonous; but in Lagos, it is ameliorated by the faith of and its practice by the Christian there. Those who discriminate against others as inferior or as a lower class because of the colour of their skin do so not because the eyes of the discriminators are blind but their hearts.

Rather than a 'black and white' vision of life, a dream of a grey area of acceptance of those who are different is a beautiful symphonic and harmonious alternative to a clannish tribal life. Certainly, while racial discrimination persists in many parts of the world, with injustice not yet fully banished, the story of Udoh is a testimony that the Christian faith must not be wielded as a weapon of exclusion but should be a tool of harmonious relationship.

Summary

The Cross and the Lynching Tree reminds us that more needs to be done in a country where one's skin colour determines one's educational, economic and social status, and where a person ought to live and whom to marry. On the other hand, many African societies have been plagued by tribalism, which is a cause of corruption and favouritism among politicians. This has led to unending business regulations that are designed to exclude members of another tribe from starting a business, resulting in an economic stalemate and lack of national progress. If the hope of our collective future can reside in the opposition to racism and tribalism, I see a ray of light in the example of this couple and in Christianity in general.

It has been my discovery that among Christians in Lagos, there is a faith that seeks to minimize tribalism and remains a creative force for harmony among diverse ethnicities. Christianity as practised in Lagos is a messy and complicated religion with many layers and twists and turns, but that is also its uniqueness and the beauty of it in Lagos. In this story of Joseph and Oluwafunmilayo Udoh, the husband (Joseph) is originally from Akwa Ibom State in the East, while his wife (Oluwafunmilayo) is a Yoruba from the West. Although they are of different ethnic groups, faith is a catalyst that nurtures their unity, removing them from their respective tribal particularities. Lagosian Christians often worship together, entering the marriage covenant, as Joseph and Oluwafunmilayo Udoh have done, regardless of their ethnic and tribal origins. They have a faith in Christ that can transcend the tribal differences that characterize the Nigerian political climate.

6

The Street Church in Pidgin English

To live a meaningful life in Lagos, one must have some understanding of pidgin English. This form of language, which allows people of different language backgrounds to communicate, is a simplified form of English which does not require formal training to learn. In Lagos, its use permeates all aspects of social and economic discourse and interactions. It is a way of communicating that is acquired through day-to-day activities rather than learned in an academic setting. It is a dynamic language, evolving as new words enter its ever-growing and interminable vocabulary. It is the language of bus conductors, cobblers, tailors, attendants at petrol stations, entertainers, musicians, traders, market people, artists, janitors and white-collar workers in Lagos.

If a passenger wants to get off a bus at the next station, for example, he will not tell the driver that he wants to get off. Instead, he would say, 'I want to comot next.' It is probably derived from 'I want to come out next'. And saying 'na weiting dey worry you, my pickin'' conveys 'what is worrying you, my child'. One of my favourites is, 'My life in Lagos dey go better, na tey igo tey.' It means, 'My life in Lagos will improve, but it will take time'. God has a popular name in this language – 'Baba God'.

One Thursday in December of 2022, I interviewed a young man named Tobi Oreoluwa. He had creatively employed this street language to convey simple yet profound biblical teachings to Christians and non-Christians alike. It was his strong desire to communicate the teachings of Jesus to ordinary people, and he proceeded to do so in pidgin English. In this way, he started what is now called 'Street Church', which has attracted a lot of followers.

Oreoluwa's hope was to approach and inspire the 'unchurched'. As we talked, he emphasized he wanted to reach the people that would normally not associate with any church. He said, 'We want the church to be accessible to the unchurched. So, instead of asking for people to come to a church building, we take the church to them through social media.'

In less than a month after the Street Church emerged, it was already attracting hundreds, including non-Nigerians. It uses pidgin English to preach the Gospel and transmit its message through social media. The colours used on their social media platform are yellow and black. People who come across those yellow and black images on social media platforms find Bible passages in pidgin English and slang, both of which are clear and comprehensible to them.

History of Street Church in Lagos

Created in February of 2021, the motto of Street Church is 'The Gospel According to the Street'. African Christians are coming to it in droves on social media sites. Each morning upon rising, they start their day with Bible passages which are shared alongside expressions that are common among Nigerians, usually presented in pidgin English. When I visited Lagos in 2022, the most popular passage was Eph. 2.8-9, pointing out that God alone is the Saviour of humankind. It was expressed as follows: 'Na tree near tree, no be sey monkey sabi fly.' This is to say that even though monkeys cannot fly, when trees stand close to each other, monkeys can perform what is in their nature to do, that is jump from tree to tree. Or in other words, if one is to be saved, it can only be because of God's taking the initiative.

By the end of 2022, it was estimated that the Street Church had gathered over a million followers, with many Christians listening to the message by tuning on the radio on their way to work.

Tobi Oreoluwa first dreamed of such a venture in 2018. His father is a pastor of Christ Apostolic Church, founded by Joseph Babalola in the 1920s, making it one of the earliest African Inland Churches in Nigeria. The young Oreoluwa found that church attendance had become monotonous for him; he felt that it had exhausted the old ways of conducting worship. Although he was no longer interested in attending church services, he remained committed to the Christian nurture of his upbringing.

He began to explore alternatives. He felt strongly that God could still use him, and his faith remained steadfast. He determined that he could not just throw away everything connected with the church and its established ways of worshipping. It would be like throwing out the baby with the bath water. But just like scientific knowledge evolves, one's religious perspectives can evolve as well, even incorporating elements of pop cultures. Oreoluwa began working to include aspects of African culture and ways of life in his Christian understanding. His afrocentric thinking inspired him to explore new avenues in the production and dissemination of Christian awareness in Lagos.

In June 2018, in his private devotional reading, he read a verse in the second chapter of the book of Habakkuk (2:3).[1] *The message I give you waits for the time I have appointed. It speaks about what is going to happen. And all of it will come true. It might take a while. But wait for it. You can be sure it will come. It will happen when I want it to* (NIRV). He decided to make the verse available to others on Instagram. And that's how it all started. Soon, many young people were talking about it and making T-shirts prompting the emergence of Street Church.

In late 2019 and early 2020, Oreoluwa attended a crossover service[2] at a church in Oregun, a popular borough. A crossover service is one in which people gather on December 31, remaining there through January 1, as the old year 'crosses over' into the New Year. Crossover services are common among Christians across Nigeria with non-Christians often joining Christians to participate. Such services are usually jam-packed. After that particular service, the church at Oregun became Oreoluwa's church.

But in October of 2020, tragedy struck in the form of the Lekki Massacre, when many young people lost their lives because of police brutality. Lagosian police would indiscriminately stop young people, demanding to know how they had acquired their expensive and fashionable cellular phones or expensive clothes. If there were no satisfactory answers to such interrogation, police were at liberty to shoot 'suspects' with live ammunition. This led to subsequent protests against the police brutality on the part of the youth in Lagos, leading to the Lekki Massacre.

Oreoluwa, who was away during the protest, speculated that he could have been one of the youths who were killed during the massacre. He believed God saved him by making him travel out of the city at the time. He saw this 'salvation' as the ultimate sign from God that his purpose in life was to proclaim God's glory to others.

In February 2021, during Covid-19 pandemic, he began to share his own devotion and started promoting Street Church in pidgin English, through his Facebook, Twitter and Instagram accounts. This proved to be revolutionary for him. (In comparison, one might argue that Martin Luther [1483–1546], who spearheaded the Protestant Reformation of the sixteenth century, would not have been successful without the arrival of the printing press across Europe.)

The time was ripe for this kind of revolution since many followers of Oreoluwa were looking for new answers, seeing that their Church no longer filled the void in their lives and was no longer relevant. Many of this new generation rallied around Oreoluwa and he started building a vibrant community of followers. His focus was on the message. And he was overwhelmed with the enormity of the positive response across Nigeria, especially in Abuja, Ondo, Ife, Ibadan, Port Harcourt and Warri. Through his ministry in pidgin English, followers began to see the Bible as alive and speaking to the wellspring of their existence.

This Street Church has a dream

The Lagosian Street Church has been taking advantage of the entrepreneurial spirit of African youth to get the message of salvation across. Now, the dream of the founder of the Street Church is to have the Bible translated into pidgin English. Oreoluwa's parents live at Ikorodu, while the church is at Oregun, a distance of approximately ten kilometers away. The purpose of having a location at Oregun is to be able to give to the people that come to church. Oreoluwa felt strongly that the church is not to take from the people, but to give to them. He noted that in the traditional music industry, entertainment is given to people and people in return pay money. But the purpose of the kingdom's 'music' is to advance the message of God. The goal of the Street Church is not to draw the attention of God's seekers to their assembly, but to encourage each individual to first find God through the Bible which speaks directly to the core of their heart. And then in their relationship with God, they can join a local congregation of their choice. The philosophy of the Street Church is partly that Christianity is not only the social religion of a gathered congregation, but more fundamentally a private faith expressed publicly as believers honour their conviction by living lives which demonstrate and embody those convictions. God is first experienced personally privately through divine revelation. Once this is achieved, believers can appreciate and join with one another. It is not impossible, therefore, to assume that every Christian is a potential preacher and evangelist in expressing their private religious experiences and convictions to others.

The Street Church does not take offerings. Its sole goal is to make available the imperishable Word of God to the people on the street. While this may be a very different kind of approach to ministry, the effect is that Christianity is neither temporal nor transient in Lagos but has a very concrete expression and is there to stay. The ministry of Oreoluwa is unique in its dissemination of the Gospel, still contributing to the faith of the people.

Tobi Oreoluwa was thirty-two years old when we met in December 2022. I was impressed with the passion of this tall humble young man, the founder of Street Church, which made the Christian faith known and reborn in the hearts and minds of so many young people in Lagos. It was his dream for his Street Church that the faith of the people be not static or monotonous, but become lively, relevant and dynamic for every generation. Christians should never feel disillusioned, he told me, but become a part of the church again and again. People of faith should never be exhausted by outdated forms of religion and faith experience; they should never become as dead people in their faith in God. Rather, their faith should be the living faith of those who have passed on the baton of their faith to a new generation, making the Christian heritage an endless and everlasting relationship with God. We constantly witness innovative and inspirational thinking in areas such as medicine and technology. Why should the life of the Church in Lagos or anywhere else be any different? Our Christian faith is not something that should reside in archives, covered in mothballs. It must be something that has relevance for younger generations.

There are two major factors that led Oreoluwa to rethink his position on the role of the Christian church in Lagos: (1) his own 'Africanness' and (2) his abiding faith in Christ. He told me about his Afro-centrism and his passion for Christ and combined them with a deep understanding of pop culture. He insisted that one can be *in* the world, without being *of* the world. Pop culture can be a tool for the propagation of the faith for the new generation; one should perceive pop culture as being a vehicle for God's message for a new generation.

As an illustration, Oreoluwa cited the parable of the miniscule mustard seed, pointing out that many in Lagos could not relate to it as they had never seen a mustard seed. But they could understand the relevance of the ubiquitous *agbalumo* seed which is also very small. Following this way of thinking, he started using the familiar vocabulary of the people to transmit the message of salvation. The response was overwhelming. The essentials of the faith start to make sense when communicated through words that are familiar. Then people begin to relate positively to the Gospel. Their faith starts to have a new meaning because of its relevance, and the lens through which they see Christianity becomes their own.

The defining characteristics of Tobi Oreoluwa

When I recall images of Tobi Oreoluwa, I see him as tall, slender and bearded. But these are not the characteristics that define him. It is his humility, tenacity, fidelity to his African heritage and to his faith that make him who he is. It is his unrelenting passion for making the Bible accessible and the Gospel understandable to the common people on the streets of Lagos which sets him apart.

He was excited as he quoted Hab. 2:3 from memory: *'For there is still a vision for the appointed time; it speaks of the end, and does not lie. If it seems to tarry, wait for it; it will surely come, it will not delay'* (NRSV). The Aramaic Bible in the Plain English version reads: *'Because the vision has been for its time and the end comes and does not lie, and if it delays, you should not lose hope for yourselves, because it comes quickly and does not delay.'* Another passage that Oreoluwa likes to quote is Josh. 1:9: *'I hereby command you: Be strong and courageous; do not be frightened or dismayed, for the Lord your God is with you wherever you go.'* He abides by these messages and in their witness in his own life.

Oreoluwa's journey of destiny began in June 2018. The experience of avoiding death in the Lekki Massacre had a profound effect on him as it made him feel that God had saved him for a purpose. It gave him courage to start disseminating the Christian message in the language of the people. He is still doing this with the same strong conviction that led to the 2019 founding of the Street Church.

The Covid-19 pandemic also proved to be a blessing in disguise since it made him explore the social media accounts and their role in bringing the Bible to the people through presenting its message in the language familiar to them. The people were inevitably drawn to the language that was understandable to them, and often also dramatic and even humorous vocabulary of common people. But later many began to understand the depth of his interpretation of the Scriptures. A void was filled, and the Street Church became a preferred alternative to traditional congregational worship.

Throughout the rest of 2020, Oreoluwa's version of the Bible in pidgin English became for many Christians a credible hermeneutic or interpretation. Many started to say, 'This is what I need.' The young founder of the Street Church was surprised and even overwhelmed by the emotional and technical support of the youth of his generation, from people he had never met. His goal was that those who live on the streets of Lagos must benefit from the Living Word of God (Jesus Christ), as well as the written word of God (the Bible).

In the Gospel of Luke, chapter 15, Jesus tells the story of a loving father and his two sons.[3] The younger son asks for his share of the inheritance so he can be on his own. The father reluctantly agrees to his son's hasty, impatient and premature request. After squandering the share of his inheritance, and becoming destitute, the boy 'came to his senses' and returned to his loving father at home.

Had the father desired to convey to the people the value of the love, joy and forgiveness of a loving parent he would have most likely sent this same rebellious son out with the message. This is not only because the son had experienced the father's unconditional love, but also because he had known the streets of the world. He could speak the language; he would know where those who needed the message would congregate to feed swine; he would know the whole geography of the world outside. He would now be more tolerant and willing to forgive. He had experienced both – the world of a loving, forgiving father and the world that is consumed by the lures of secularism, violence, fundamentalism, selfishness, arrogance, impatience and sorrow. This story in Luke's Gospel further teaches us that one need not extinguish the candle of others to make his own candle shine brighter.

Tobi Oreoluwa has seen with clarity that the street language of the people is a suitable and effective medium to express the salvation story. There is no 'linguistic gatekeeper' to communicate the eternal message; if there were, every Christian would have to learn Aramaic or Hebrew or the Semitic languages to communicate with God. But Jesus is the Inaugurator of the inherent capability of the vernacular. One's culture needs not be abandoned and eradicated to communicate the message of the Gospel. God's own people can be the very medium which conveys the message, making any need for translatability superfluous. Even the very lives of Christians can be the Bible, because they do not only possess the truth of the Gospel, they are also the embodiment of the truth and they are possessed by it. It was in this way that Tobi Oreoluwa stoop down to conquer the message of the Bible and redemption for the people on the streets of Lagos.

In Lagos, the language of the street is a suitable vehicle to convey the Good News; it is the language of heaven and it is a part of the vernacular as inaugurated by Jesus who spoke Aramaic – the common language of the people of his days. The Street Church born in Lagos is now thriving there because it is a church which meets people where they are on the streets and follows the rhythm of their existence.

Examples of the Pidgin English usage of the Street Church in Lagos

Bible Text	Street Church Version	Pidgin English Devotional	Commentaries
Mt. 7. 7-11 'Ask, and it will be given to you; search, and you will find; knock, and the door will be opened for you. For everyone who asks receives, and everyone who searches finds, and for everyone who knocks, the door will be open. Is there anyone among you who, if your child asks for bread, will give a stone? Or if the child asks for a fish, will you give him a snake? If you then, who are evil, know how to give good gifts to your children, how much more will your Father in heaven give good things to those who ask him!'	Talk to me directly, don't go through the corners.	Today, open communication line again, ask God for wetin you need for your life, and he go direct you on the path to go. If you wan talk to God, talk to am direct and stop dey use middleman. You and God no get beef, God love us any how and E dey give am joy when him children talk to am direct.	Talk to God directly about your needs and do not go through empty intermediaries.
Ps. 128.2 You shall eat the fruit of the labor of your hands; you shall be happy, and it shall go well with you.	Things go soft on us!	This year 2023, you don put in the work like never before, you don try and Baba God say make we tell you say things go soon soft! You go enjoy the profit of your work, things go get for you and you go happy!	Have confidence in God that all your worries will soon be over, and you will become happy.
Rom. 8:28 We know that all things work together for good for those who love God, who are called according to his purpose.	Nothing spoiled!	Even when the matter never settles get the confidence say God get better plan for you. Tag your person and tell am 'nothing spoil'.	When things look apparently bad, be assured that God's plans for you are far richer and greater than your imagination. God will not let you suffer, and you will laugh at last.

Isa. 54.4 'Do not fear, for you will not be ashamed; do not be discouraged, for you will not suffer disgrace; for you will forget the shame of your youth, and the disgrace of your widow-hood you will remember no more.'	We no go cast in Jesus's name!	You no go cast, no worry! Jesus dey with you on dis one. Nothing go shame you on top that situation instead na laugh you go laugh comot! The dragging wey you dey expect go turn to dancing because God go fight your battle for you! You no go cast; God's got you!	Do not be afraid because God will not allow you to cry forever. Your destiny is in God's hands.
Rom. 8.1 There is therefore now no condemnation for those who are in Christ Jesus.	No evidence!	Dem go explain tire, no evidence for that old life o! You wey don stand kpomkpi with Bros. J, dem dey find as dem go take condemn you? Dem no go see shishi evidence! Because Jesus don carry all the evidence, he don troway am!	Those accusers will be ashamed because Jesus will fight your battle. Jesus is all that you need and he is your best defender. He will uphold justice for you.
I Cor. 8.6 Yet for us there is one God, the Father, from whom are all things and for whom we exist, and one Lord, Jesus Christ, through whom are all things and through whom we exist.	Na God be our source.	For us, na God be our source! No be just of riches alone according to Philippians 4:19 but na him also be the source of life, wisdom and every other thing to us. Na why that proverb wey we dey talk 'river wey forget im source go dry up' dey important.	God is the source and the ground of our being. Therefore, depend on God because God is the source of all things. Your future is doom and gloom if you forget that God created you and that Jesus loves you.
Prov. 21.13 If you close your ear to the cry of the poor, you will cry out and not be heard.	Who you Epp?	You wey no dey help when God put you for good space, how you wan receive help for days wey no good? Sometimes just overlook say some people dey always try do otherwise and just sincerely help the people wey dey needy around you.	Do not overlook those who are less privileged, because no condition is permanent. Chances are that the poor today may become wealthy tomorrow. Therefore, provide for the poor today because of tomorrow.

Bible Text	Street Church Version	Pidgin English Devotional	Commentaries
Prov. 18.24 Some friends play at friendship, but a true friend sticks closer than one's nearest kin.	My G for life!	Life sweet when we know say people dey wey get our back, e dey sweet belle when we know say people dey wey understand us and want the best for us. For dis days wey people like to cut others off at any small inconvenience, take time to appreciate d meaningful friendships for u life.	Be kind to everyone because in your midst are friends that will fight for you through thick and thin.
Prov. 10.19 When words are many, transgression is not lacking, but the prudent are restrained in speech.	Plenty talk no dey full basket.	My guy e better make you leave story for storybook, plenty shalaye na okoto you go start to talk. Your words are important and na in am your integrity lie. If you too day talk, e no get as you no go jam talk and when you jam talk, anything your eye jam na you come know that one.	Do not talk too much because you lose your respect as a child of God if you do not listen more than you talk. It is always better to look before you leap. There is wisdom in saying nothing unless what you want to say will make a difference.
Gal. 5.1 For freedom Christ has set us free. Stand firm, therefore, and do not submit again to the yoke of slavery.	Stand Gidigba!	Because say Bros J don free you, e don comot the tag of Devil boy boy from our neck and we no be slave to fear again, so make nobody worry you with these things, stand well well, make dem no try shake you.	Do not become a slave to anyone, because you are free as a child of God; if God has set you free, you are truly liberated from any form of enslavement. Therefore, stand firm and defend your freedom in Christ who has set you free.
Ps. 23.5 You prepare a table before me in the presence of my enemies; you anoint my head with oil; my cup overflows.	You go bellefull!	Dis month of September, your plate go full, your cup go overflow because God don prepare this month specially for you! You no go lack any good thing, you dey swim in abundance and anything wey your hand touch dey blessed!	You will not lack any good thing in life because God is your overflowing abundance. God will be good to you no matter what! You are blessed indeed.
2 Chron. 15.7 But you, take courage! Do not let your hands be weak, for your work shall be rewarded.	E never reach you no mean say your workings useless!	Because e never works no mean say e no go work, e never gel no mean say e no ge gel. If you dey find sign, make you for no give up, na the sign be this! Keep working because our Lord say your work go get reward soonest!	Do not ever give up; if you do not try, you have already failed; but if you try and you are persistent, success is just around the corner. So, take the next step and receive your crown.

Summary

Oreoluwa told me that the Street Church is about the message of the Bible, and he was pleasantly surprised to find that his message had reached Abuja, the Nigerian Federal Capital Territory, and all the major cities in Nigeria as fast as it did. Through his Street Church, the Bible is made alive and present in the lives of ordinary people. When asked where he wanted to go with the Street Church and the Bible, Oreoluwa was quick to say that the appeal of pop culture was important to him as a tool in the next step of his revolutionary journey. Christianity comes to humanity not as a whole, but in bits and pieces. Our faith comes not only from above to the privileged but also from below to the poor and the marginalized who have been ignored to the periphery. Oreoluwa wants the young generation to know God through the vernacular and the language stimulated by the vocabulary and culture of their generation. It is to these people that the good news of Jesus of Nazareth comes to bring joy.

For example, he wanted people to be talking about the Bible casually, and not while hearing and asking about it from the pulpit. It is when conversations about God saturate our lives and fill our day-to-day activities, that we are truly redeemed. Therefore, for Oreoluwa, Christianity is never meant to be locked away in dusty archives but rather, it is meant to promote righteousness of everyday life in every generation. His priority now is for the entire Holy Bible to be translated into pidgin English.

I was deeply moved by Oreoluwa's insistence that he was only a piece of the puzzle in the movement to make the Bible heard and understood by the people on the streets of Lagos. He has only lit the fire. Future generations will have to continue guarding it and make sure in the coming days that the glory of God reaches the people on the streets of Lagos.

One of the major tasks of Christians in any generation is to speak prophetically from within the cultural community of its own time and context. Christians are the resource for transformation and should grow new wings of proclamation from the stimulus of their own time and experience. This way, the Gospel will be relevant for each generation, crafting their own unique traditions. Lagosian Christians are innovative and culturally relevant; but at the same time, they are countercultural. They are saying 'yes' and 'no' simultaneously to pop culture and contemporary youth. They do not rebel against the language of the modern world but instead use the language to proclaim the Gospel in the spirit of authenticity. They are open to pop cultures without being exposed to it.

It is Oreoluwa's purpose to make the Gospel meaningful and relevant to his generation. While Christians may reinterpret the Bible from time to time, based on their experiences, the eternal truth of the Gospel and its relevance in every generation stand firm and immutable. The Gospel does not change. It is the challenge of every generation to craft the Gospel in the new language and vocabulary of contemporary society. The enduring nature of the Gospel comes with the authority for dynamic equivalence and reinterpretation. It is within societal consensus that the Gospel becomes liberated and born again in every new generation. Each Christian in the modern world must speak from the context and wellspring of their own generation.

7

Emmanuel Tenyon Hunye

A child shall lead them

Introduction

A few years ago, the associate dean at Campbell University Divinity School invited me to teach a course called 'Christianity in Africa', offered to our Master of Divinity degree-seeking students. Following this invitation, I read everything I could think of in my preparation, especially books and articles written by African scholars and church leaders.[1] When the time came for me to teach the course, I noticed that approximately 70 per cent of the students enrolled in the class were of African origin. They were eager to connect with the roots of the Christian faith from their ancestral homeland and to do so through that African lens.

Deciding to teach the course from a historical perspective, we began with the New Testament origins of Christianity in Africa and its connection to North Africa by examining the Gospel of Mark. I could not have anticipated the overwhelming response from those who enrolled. They were immediately enthralled and fascinated. In the course of the term, I was to experience many more surprises than I could have predicted when I was preparing to teach the course.

For example, many students began to experience a crisis of identity, with their discomfort resurrecting memories of the crisis I too had faced when I was in graduate school. Unlike theirs, my graduate studies in church history had often focused almost exclusively on the history of the church in Europe and North America. Let me explain.

As they listened to my lectures showing that John Mark, the writer of the first Gospel, had started the Church in North Africa, my students became incredulous! They were flabbergasted! This crucial piece of church history was conspicuously missing in my own academic training and pedagogical upbringing in Western classrooms – an omission that has not yet been sufficiently addressed in those classrooms. Yet it is absolutely essential to recognize that the roots of the Christian faith include the writers of the New Testament who were born and lived in North Africa, connecting the early life of the church to North Africa more intimately than to any other continent in the world. This fact of history has eluded Africans at home and abroad, divorcing people of African descent from their own historical Christian roots and identity. It is a painful irony that the faith that began in North Africa has had to be reintroduced to Africans by missionaries in European cultural trappings of the modern era as if it were a new faith.

Thankfully, scholars in the Western world have started to challenge the old notions, changing this biased trajectory of the history of the church. The history of how Christianity began cannot be fully understood without acknowledging the contributions of North African Jews and Gentiles during the embryonic stages of its development. So, who were the main actors and pioneers of Christianity in North Africa in biblical times?

John Mark

John Mark is a towering figure of Christianity in its embryonic state in Africa. One of the greatest ironies in the history of Christianity is that the infant Jesus Christ lived in Egypt as a refugee.[2] The writer of the Gospel, John Mark, was born in Cyrene, North Africa. Thomas Clark Oden, the director of the Center for Early African Christianity at Eastern University, St. Davids, Pennsylvania, is an authority on this important subject. In his *The African Memory of Mark: Reassessing Early Church Tradition* (2011), Oden reminds readers that John Mark should be remembered for his contributions to the origin of Christianity and that he was born and raised in North Africa before he became universally known as the first writer of the account of the life and ministry of Jesus of Nazareth.[3]

Mary, the mother of John Mark, of the tribe of Levi, was a wealthy woman who married Aristobulus, the elder brother of Barnabas, one of the disciples of Jesus of Nazareth. Mark's Jewish name was Ian or John, and the name Markus (Marcos), or Mark, is of Latin origin. The most popular destination of the Jews between 200 BCE and CE 150 was North Africa,[4] especially the Pentapolis, the five cities of Darnis, Apollonia, Cyrene, Ptolemais and Arsinoe/ Teuchira. All those cities were in the Cyrenaica province, with Jews often migrating there in the aftermath of anti-Jewish massacres in and around

Jerusalem. Oden states: 'The traditional African narrative of Mark begins with his birth in Cyrene (ca. C.E. 5—15), and from there tracks him to Jerusalem, to Rome, back to Cyrene in Africa and finally to his death in [Alexandria,] Egypt.'[5] The first ten years of Mark's life were probably spent in Cyrene,[6] with at least eight other facts about John Mark that continue to be of interest to African scholars:

(1) John Mark was born near modern-day Tripoli, Libya, called Ebryatolis (city of Jews).

(2) He was forced to flee from North Africa to Jerusalem when he was ten years old.

(3) Mark travelled extensively, returning to Alexandria, Egypt, in his old age.

(4) He started the embryonic form of early Christian catechesis in Alexandria and was the founding father of the African Church.[7]

(5) John Mark was drawn to the ministry of Jesus in Jerusalem around the age of ten, and never left, becoming 'the first among the disciples to write the good news of the coming of this incomparable person who changed his life entirely'.[8]

(6) John Mark wrote the first Gospel that bears his name.

(7) John Mark lived with his mother, Mary, and his father, Aristobulus, at a place called Zion Hill, near Jerusalem.

(8) John Mark was multilingual, with Jewish ancestry and African cultural identity.

These essential details of his life show Mark's historical connection to Africa. This connection has deep implications for contemporary Christians in Lagos and greater African Christians who continue to draw strength from the knowledge that Christianity is not a Western religion exported to Africa in the modern era but one of 'African traditional religions'. Perhaps, the pre-Christian identity of Africans has been exaggerated. Without undermining the influence of European missionary movements in Africa in the nineteenth and twentieth centuries, it is important to note that Africans did not accept Christianity as a *new* religion but as the resurrection of an *old* historical tradition started by John Mark in North Africa.[9] Therefore, it can be argued that Christianity is not so much a new religion across Africa, but a faith of remembrance. While the exact location of John Mark's birthplace is inferential and circumstantial, there is little doubt that he was born and raised in North Africa. As Oden further writes: 'Now Aristobulus has a son named John [Mark]. And after they had taken up their abode in the province of Palestine, near the city of Jerusalem, the child John grew and increased in status by the grace of the Holy Ghost.'[10]

John Mark and the great lesson he taught

John Mark's Gospel influenced the writings of the rest of the synoptic Gospels. There is no doubt that the ministry of Jesus inspired the young John Mark with its teachings of faith, hope, love, forgiveness, joy and peace. Those were the controlling dynamics that Jesus evoked and inspired in the life of John Mark. Thus, he began to breathe and thrive in a new atmosphere of love, forgiveness, hope and faith, emerging from an environment of hate that had his family flee Jerusalem to North Africa before Mark was even born, and then again leave hostile North Africa, returning to Jerusalem in Mark's preteen years. John Mark was led in a new direction as he observed the life and ministry of Jesus of Nazareth.

The religious movement Jesus started as a Semitic form of faith outgrew its original ecosystem boundaries, expanding into an organized propagation of faith for the world at large. It became a new appealing form of expression, even as its essence and vitality were initially interpreted by a variety of witnesses, personalities and different methods of recollection based on Jewish identity. It became an urgent task for Mark to recall Jesus as a charismatic Jewish rabbi, a sage and miracle worker, and the revolutionary religious leader of a new movement, drawing the hearts and minds of the people in Jerusalem to turn to God. The words and actions of Jesus became the rule of his life and were imprinted on his mind. For Mark, this new Jewish rabbi was more than an ordinary person; his message had eternal significance for all. Perhaps the defining moment for John Mark was the epiphany that while Jesus was human, he was the bearer of an eternal message from God. As a teenager, Mark realized that Jesus had created a new way of life, and the life of his followers would never be the same. So, Mark realized the transformation that the message of Jesus brought, and his Jewish identity became renewed as he continued to follow Jesus.[11] Perhaps he was one of the earliest followers of Jesus to be convinced that his relationship with God was being made anew and he was indebted to Jesus of Nazareth for it. John Mark knows that the ministry of Jesus transcends the fulfillment of Judaism and goes to the heart of a universal kerygma or proclamation from the heart of God. While Jesus rarely goes against the Bible, his mission is a manifestation of the spirit of God with his own authority, and Christians today will recall Jesus saying, 'you have heard it said, but I say unto you.' John Mark developed an indissoluble spiritual bond with Jesus and his ministry. He became tenacious and influential, with a deep oriental memory of Jesus and his ministry.

John Mark's memory of Jesus

The fidelity of Mark to Jesus was irrefutable, leading him to write down his experiences with the guidance of the Holy Spirit. As time went on, the new Palestinian Christians cherished more and more the oral recollections of events and sayings related to the life of Jesus. The community recalled vividly the sayings of Jesus, and the transitional light of the Gospel started to glow even brighter. In missiological terms, Jesus became recognized as the embodiment of the mission of God in the world through the oral circulation and collections of his sayings and the stories he told. He was not merely a charismatic leader, a sage or a miracle worker or the leader of the emerging Christian movement. For Mark, Jesus was much more. He was also the viceroy[12] of God and God's representative on earth, as some Christians in Lagos had asserted.

Perhaps, Mark wrote for the purpose of catechetical instruction in Alexandria, Egypt, to elicit more testimonies from the Hebrew Bible. Mark was young, and he based his work on Peter's memories of Jesus from whom he learned the rudiments of the new faith tradition and its movements. It should not escape readers that Mark's father, Aristobulus, was a relative of Simon Peter by marriage. Quoting Coptic scholar Samir Fawzy Girgis, Thomas C. Oden states, 'Peter was married to Strapola, a relative of Mark's father',[13] and the 'family lived together with Mark's [wealthy] mother and her brother Barnabas.'[14] This might explain the close relationship between Mark and Barnabas on the one hand, and between Mark and Peter on the other. This should also be illuminating for those Christian readers who have wondered why Mark was often called 'my son' by the elderly Peter.[15] The rapidly diminishing population of eyewitnesses to the life of Jesus gave Mark a sense of urgency to record an account, which he proceeded to write in Greek. Although he spoke Aramaic, it was a language becoming unintelligible outside Jewish family circles. Perhaps Mark had acquired a Berber language from North Africa as well.

Mark's Gospel is a vivid account of the life of Jesus from the beginning of his public ministry to his death.[16] It is a masterpiece of the oral reminiscence preserved by Peter, but it also shows remarkable signs of earlier written materials having been researched by the young author. He followed a specific outline: first, Jesus's Galilean ministry, then his Judean ministry and closing with a specifically detailed account of the Passion Week.

In our modern era of pop culture, Mark would be considered a good blogger. He sometimes wrote in incomplete sentences as if the audience knew or should know what he meant. Yet, he wrote for audiences outside his immediate circles of Palestinian readers. He wanted those more remote readers to know something about the technical terms associated with Judaism which Jesus reflected and embodied.

The escape of John Mark and his father from the jaws of lions

One day, when John Mark was in his teen years, he and his father Aristobulus were walking along the River Jordan. Suddenly, they were attacked by two ferocious lions. Aristobulus cried out to his son in desperation to escape and save himself, but Mark was surprisingly calm. The selfless cry of Aristobulus to his son has been documented but is not always acknowledged. Oden makes an important observation when he writes: 'The encounter with the lions is often discounted by Westerners, but not necessarily by the African mind.'[17] To this father's desperate cry, Mark answered, 'Christ, in whose hands our lives are committed, will not let them prey on us.'[18] The young Mark then prayed to God for life preservation. Oden concludes by writing that 'the lions were rendered harmless'[19] and this 'miracle' prompted Aristobulus to ask his son to explain to him more about the Lord Jesus Christ. This event was a turning point for Aristobulus, who then believed in the power of the Lord Jesus Christ to save. His son then baptized him.[20]

Upon hearing of this encounter with lions near the River Jordan, who would doubt the veracity of the new faith as recorded by Mark? It was an event not related to him by others, but one which he experienced first-hand. Thus, the power of Jesus became real to him.

Thomas C. Oden further observes that post-Enlightenment thinkers with their incessant desire for empirical knowledge and the path of 'dare to know' by experience would cast doubt on this story of the encounter with lions. But this is often the first step on the path to belief among African Christians, who often ask, 'What has Christ done for you?' At the core of the philosophy of Enlightenment is the desire to know by experiential knowledge, guided by one's conscience. One can say without exaggeration that the personal faith of Mark was no longer the faith of Peter passed on to him, but that he now owned his faith in the Lord Jesus Christ. This is what has also impressed me as I have talked to Christians on the streets of Lagos.

There remain those Christians in Lagos who, one can argue, are an adumbration or a foreshadowing of John Mark, not because they are pioneers in writing about the life of Jesus Christ and his ministry for their people in Africa but because through them, their fathers and mothers became Christians.

Emmanuel Tenyon Hunye:
A child shall lead them

I met Emmanuel Tenyon Hunye in December 2022 at a small school compound in Lagos. He is a member of the Deeper Life Ministry under the leadership of F. M. Kumuyi, who had been a brilliant student at the University of Ibadan and a mathematician in his early career. While he was in Lagos as a professor, Kumuyi was called into Christian ministry and has a large following now with his international ministry, Global Crusade with Kumuyi, G. C. K.

The first thing Emmanuel Hunye said to me was: 'Salvation is real; and God is real in my life.' To him, Jesus was to be experienced personally, and his anointing is secure. He became a 'born-again' Christian in 1982 and has never backed away from his faith in God. He recounted to me the passage in Acts 16.31 when the prison doors were miraculously opened for Paul and Silas to escape, but they remained calm in the presence of the jailer. The jailer then asked them, 'Sirs, what must I do to be saved?' They then responded, 'Believe in the Lord Jesus, and you will be saved, you and your household.' Although Hunye was somewhat reticent at our initial encounter, when I asked him to share with me what it meant for him to be a Christian in Lagos, it was as though I had lit a fire in his belly. This is his story.

Emmanuel Hunye has ancestral connections in both Nigeria and the Republic of Benin, the Francophone country bordering Nigeria to the West. His grandmother was from Lagos, but he was born and raised in Badagry, one of the slave trade coastal regions in the suburbs of Lagos. He likes to share how he became a Christian through a personal encounter with Jesus Christ in 1982 when he was at Abeokuta in Ogun State, approximately 100 kilometres northwest of Lagos. He had attended an Easter retreat at Abeokuta where he experienced conversion. This decision invited persecution and alienation from his family, particularly his father, who was a traditional religious occult worship leader. Emmanuel's persecution was even more pronounced given the leadership role that his father held in those non-Christian religious rituals. A popular leader, his father did not want Emmanuel to be associated with Christians as that would undermine or jeopardize his standing in the occult religious organization. Unable to win Emmanuel back to the occult traditions, his father persecuted him and was largely alienated from him.

One day, Emmanuel was with his father on the farm when a life-changing event took place. Emmanuel was bitten by a venomous scorpion, and his father stood by helplessly as Emmanuel prayed to God that the venom would not claim his life and that his life would be preserved for the glory of God. In disbelief, his father saw Emmanuel recover swiftly, unlike many others who had been bitten by poisonous scorpions, whose venom usually resulted in swollen arms and legs, sometimes even death. But seeing Emmanuel unhurt, he attributed the 'salvation' of Emmanuel to the power of Jesus Christ.

In the aftermath of the event, his father retreated completely from criticizing his son for being a Christian. His dramatic testimony reached Emmanuel's two older brothers, Gabriel and Elijah, who were also committed Christians. When their father observed their deep adherence to their new-found faith in Christ, he was overwhelmed. He witnessed the remarkable lives of his three sons and saw how the light of the Gospel could not be hidden within them. Seeing the authentic character of the lives of his sons, he too converted to Christianity. Inevitably, he faced enormous challenges as a leader of the occult movement, who abandoned his old way of life. He was persecuted severely, with threats to his very life if he did not return to the group and continue to abide by their rules as the leader.

During that time, Emmanuel's mother died. It was Emmanuel's duty to perform certain rituals in the process of giving his mother a decent burial. Some of these traditional rites were at variance with his Christian beliefs. His refusal to participate in the traditional spiritual burial rites further intensified the anger of the occult group members, who directed their fury at Emmanuel's father. The hard feelings were extreme, but every evil plotted against the sons and their father by the non-Christian surrounding them yielded no harmful consequences.

When Emmanuel's father experienced the results of the power of living out the Gospel through his personal encounter with Christ, he became a compelling proclaimer of the Gospel, spreading its words where he lived. The one who had once been a persecutor was now a promoter of the Gospel.

As we talked, I asked Emmanuel what challenges he was facing now as a Christian living in Lagos. He mentioned that he planned to start a 'Church in Your Home' ministry. He felt Christian denominationalism was a distraction and had become an obstacle for authentic proclamation and personal experience of a direct encounter with God. The differences implanted by Christian denominationalism in Lagos do not foster unity but create a spirit of competition that is not helpful to the body of Christ. This lack of unity has become the enemy of the Church of God in Lagos. The vision of a 'Church in Your Home' could help the church recapture the essence of a true life in Christ. Whether it is 'Paul or Apollo', Emmanuel argued, the main point of the Christian faith is to extend the love of God to all humanity by proving it through the way we live. For Christians in Lagos, to be biblical is to *do* what St. Mark did in his Gospel, not to quote Mark's Gospel verbatim. All who experience Christ first-hand are redeemed and have been anointed by God to proclaim the message through their own lived experience.[21] He added that when we call upon the name of God, we are saved and there can be no compromise with obedience to God when we are in Christ.

When Emmanuel's grandmother died, the funeral was to be conducted by a non-Christian group. However, Emmanuel refused, claiming that his grandmother belonged to God, who had created her and that she was now at home with that God. Although many in the community pressured Emmanuel to bury his grandmother according to non-Christian traditional rituals, Emmanuel prevailed. At that point, members of the entire family surrendered their lives to God, becoming bearers of the word of Christ to their communities, wherever they are, in Lagos and elsewhere.

Summary

Is Christianity returning to its original roots within a religious environment that is fundamentally hostile to it? What roles are Christians playing to foster Christian identity in Lagos? The crucial question that Christians must now answer is like the question that the early disciples faced in their milieu of Judaism – how to exist as an isolated, autonomous, culturally sensitive, religious entity in the Hellenistic world. Christians in Lagos today exist as the embodiment of the Spirit of Christ, amid a hostile, corrupt political world as well as one which espouses the old religious ways of life.

While the Christian faith must continue to return to its roots as it tests the untried faith of its youth, it must also be simultaneously moving forward to challenge the claims of Christian fundamentalism that still stand to suffocate the life of the Church. The Church of today's Lagos is in a liminal time between the past and the future.

8

My skills are useful tools in serving God

Olalekan Yusuf lives in Lagos, and he is a remarkable Christian pastor with a strong Muslim background. I was amazed at how well he knows the city of Lagos and its many boroughs. His life in Lagos began when he attended the prestigious King's College. After finishing high school, he attended the University of Lagos.

His background in another faith tradition is instrumental in the way in which he practises his Christianity. One can see among Christians in this city that faith transcends one's original religious identity. It is not impossible for the son or daughter of an Imam to become a Christian pastor. I have also encountered females who grew up in a devout Christian home, but then married a Muslim cleric, for example. This exogamous culture of Lagos is one in which people often marry outside of one's ethnic or identical religious group without being ostracized by their community.

As an example, the wife of the current Nigerian president, First Lady Madam Oluremi Tinubu, is a practising Christian pastor, although her husband, the Honourable Bola Ahmed Adekunle Tinubu, remains a Muslim. In the life of Olalekan Yusuf, we see how his Muslim background became an asset for serving as a pastor. Additionally, his skills and natural gifts became tools in Christian service.

How Olalekan Yusuf became a Christian

Olalekan Yusuf maintains that no one can become a Christian without the work of the Holy Spirit and the unseen influence of the intercessory prayers of other Christians. He has a deep appreciation for the understanding of the

Holy Spirit from his studies of the life of Saint Paul of Tarsus, who was a devout Jew and a Pharisee.

The well-educated Paul desired to become a rabbi and had studied under Gamaliel, a master of the Jewish law and a popular teacher. Tarsus, an influential city in Asia Minor during Paul's day, was a highly civilized city where Paul was influenced by both the Judaic and Hellenistic cultures. Yet some other forces must have been at play. Pastor Yusuf told me that he fully agreed with Paul's statement that 'no one could become a Christian, except by the Holy Spirit'. Therefore, the function of the Holy Spirit, he felt, is to bring to God those who have been chosen. They become Christians through Jesus Christ. Without the tugging of the Holy Spirit, no one can go to Christ on his own.

There was tangible evidence of this in the life of Pastor Yusuf himself. When he was a young Muslim, he fell into a trance and saw a girl praying for him. Having never seen anything like this, he felt his heart beating faster, with the resulting strange physical warmth all over him.

As a young adult in Lagos, he liked to participate in spirited political conversation and social discussions. As a college student, he enjoyed debating sensitive issues. He worked at becoming a very skilful debater, winning many competitions. At one such debate, he defended the 'pro' side that an evangelist was more important than a pastor, even while still a Muslim.

Yusuf later studied civil engineering, joining an engineering firm where he worked faithfully for years with only one token. Although poorly paid at the company, he saw his loyalty to the job as a test and kept praying for a breakthrough in his life. He felt that if he were faithful in small things, it was as unto God. In his Yoruba tongue, Yusuf stated: 'A maa dan e wo; a ko le dan e tan', meaning one would be tested but not cast out and destroyed. And Yusuf, like Job, although tested, emerged very much alive and stronger.

He finally left the engineering firm and went to Ifako, on the outskirts of Lagos, where he had the opportunity to speak to a congregation. The people there were so impressed with his eloquence in proclaiming the Good News of Jesus Christ that he was asked to serve as the pastor of the burgeoning Redeemed Church. At that time, the congregation was unhealthy and in disarray, without a strong minister to lead them. Yusuf's calm demeanour brought about a time of unity and fervour to the church, which led to a new life.

He related to me that another pastor, Enoch Adeboye, later anointed his head with oil, and that anointing gave him a lasting feeling, experienced even after several years.

Yusuf has served as a provisional pastor since 2017, providing leadership to more than twenty congregations in Lagos. With his calming presence and sense of mission, he has nurtured struggling congregations back to health and growth.

When Yusuf is not preaching or counselling leaders of the congregations he supervises, he enjoys watching entertaining Nollywood movies – innovative art and music productions by Nigerian artists and entertainers popular especially in the Global South – and reading e-books.

When asked about the challenges he faces as a provisional pastor overseeing over twenty churches, Yusuf is quick to say that pastors in Lagos are often tempted to embezzle money and neglect to teach their congregations that 'the love of money is the root of all evil'. His experience at the engineering firm earlier in his career, where he was poorly paid, taught him not to be consumed with the love of money. 'Money is a good servant but a bad master', he concluded. Due to the love of money, some of his close friends fell into occultism. He himself was tempted to pursue wealth and accumulate money as many of his friends did, but, in the end, he resisted the temptation and did not fall prey to the practice of occultism because God protected him and set his mind to telling the truth. His personal journey had led him to believe that prayer is the answer to all human needs and strengthens our relationship to Christ. He chose to be a Christian in the first place because of his personal encounter with Jesus Christ.

The principle of epistemological reciprocity between Muslims and Christians in Lagos

What interested me most in the life of Pastor Olalekan Yusuf is seeing how his background as a Muslim informs his Christian leadership awareness. The differences between Islam and Christianity among Lagosian Christians are strong and cannot easily be brought into harmony. However, there are some Christians and Muslims who believe it is possible to foster healthy relationships between the two religions. The cords that make up various religions, while often separating believers, can also unite them. Perhaps religion is more than a cultic activity. Human religious awareness is an indivisible entity unified by human efforts to grasp the totality of existence, and this awareness is one way the universe is rediscovering itself.

The principle of epistemological reciprocity[1] suggests that since devotees of any living non-Christian faith tradition are committed to their faiths due to the same kinds of internal reasons that Christians claim for their beliefs, Christians have no grounds for claiming any epistemological advantage over other believers. One of the most hopeful results of accepting the 'other' in religious differentiation is the mutual enrichment that such collaboration and acceptance can bring. Human beings are not created to be self-sufficient but are interdependent beings. We move in and out of each other's lives as mutually dependent beings, always needing one another. Life is ever-expanding as we grow into each other and learn what it means to be human through the lens around the orbit of another human being. In a similar manner, each religion provides certain truths about the essence of faith and human spiritual destiny. No one faith tradition has the whole truth about God and human spiritual destiny. The words from the great Jewish sage Abraham Joshua Heschel (1907–72) comes to mind. Heschel's point and his philosophy of comparative religion is that religions are a means to an end and that no one religion has a monopoly on holiness or spiritual completeness or conclusive insight.[2] God's self-disclosure is often incremental and comes in stages. Therefore, any conversation that provides enlightenment about other faith traditions is a credible way of proclaiming the authenticity of our own. Conversely, vilifying those we see as 'the other' can be destructive, having the opposite effect of being what Christians consider evangelistic. When there is an interaction between and among different faith traditions, various responses can emerge as a result:

First, when a follower of Christ is confronted by a Muslim, he can respond by referring to some traditional point he considers safe. He could say, for example, that Jesus is his Lord and Saviour, and he would never have anything to do with a Muslim. Likewise, a Muslim could encounter a Christian and respond in a like manner. Yet, I encountered many Christians and Muslims in Lagos and found there were very few who held exclusive views of their faith. A part of this is because many extended families have members of other faiths, and family ties transcend religious and doctrinal categories and affiliations. Therefore, family members would never ostracize those among them who are of another faith. Family ties 'trump' religious affiliations.

Second, a Muslim might respond by arguing with a Christian, trying to discredit any truth and goodness in the Christian faith tradition as entirely false or mistaken insofar as those beliefs differ from what he finds worthy in his own Islamic faith. This too, however, is not a demonstration of accepting faith in God, whose self-disclosure is ever dynamic. Most Christians in Lagos have Muslims in their extended families, and they are humble and generous in their assessments of the faith of others, understanding that they are finite beings.

Third, Christians and Muslims have together built schools and hospitals in Lagos, finding common ground in working together for the benefit of the community where they live. In my own experience in Lagos, I have observed that when a Muslim is impressed by what he learns from Christians, he does not desert his own faith to convert to Christianity totally and completely. He simply adds new religious information to the old.

Most Christians and Muslims view the interactions of one faith with the other as a way of binding together the old with the new. Christians demonstrate an openness to Muslims, as Muslims do towards Christians. This may be unique to Lagos, as opposed to the way Christians and Muslims relate to one another in Northern Nigeria, for instance. I encountered Muslims, like Pastor Yusuf, who allowed their Muslim backgrounds and identities to transport them into a new awareness in Jesus Christ. Yusuf has not allowed Christianity to nullify his Muslim background and identity; rather, he has permitted it to transform and enhance the old.[3] This seems to be a supreme demonstration of faith. 'For those who are not against us', Christ said, 'are with us.'

It is within this kind of dialogical and constructive framework that humanity can reclaim or recapture much of the inner strength and vitality of God and, therefore, enhance or contribute to the universal understanding of God within their God-given particularity. It is not a sign of enmity to the Christian heritage to embrace aspects of the Islamic faith, as demonstrated by the life and ministry of Pastor Yusuf. Past experiences of God are not exhaustive; the new future of our faith traditions often brings with it past religious rituals and traditions. Thus, it is not being disloyal to the Christian faith to believe that some of the positive aspects of Yusuf's ministry can be traced to his Muslim upbringing.

The best days of Christianity could be ahead when devotees of Christianity realize that the movement Christ inaugurated in the world is not intended to be defined by a canonical religious exclusivism but should be both inclusive and transformative. Only those values of forgiveness, grace, love, compassion and mercy are exclusive – no matter one's faith tradition. After all, the labels we have coined, such as Christianity and Islam, are our own artifices, speaking more about humanity than about God.

Perhaps disloyalty to the past in any religious tradition is the failure to communicate what is divine to the human consciousness. In the experience of Yusuf, whose Islamic background has not been completely erased or perceived as tainted, his past continues to inform and teach him its lessons that God is only one, and God's divine way binds us together with the chains of religious institutional forms and traditions. Yusuf's Islamic consciousness, therefore, prepared him for Christian vocation in a spirit of toleration and humility.[4] If the past does not make us ready for a more complete truth that leads us to the unity we see demonstrated in the life of Christ, the past has failed humanity.

Yusuf is aware that any 'religion' in the hands of humanity can be both a tool and a weapon, both inspirational and exploitative; both a fascination and a burden; both an adventure into the unknown and a calling into a life that is loving and fulfilling, providing opportunities to cross difficult barriers that separate us. Faith, on the other hand, sets humanity free from onerous religious restrictions and doctrinaire. That is why Yusuf converted to Christianity – an experience that, for him, was not simply a conversion but a divine transformation.

How Pastor Olalekan Yusuf sees the movement inaugurated by Jesus

In Lagos, Christians claim the uniqueness of Jesus Christ in ways that are consistent with the usual Bible and Christian faith traditions.

While the offices of Christ have special significance for all Christians, their interpretations vary from one denomination to another. The three offices of Christ among Christians in Lagos (and perhaps worldwide) are the biblical ones of prophet, priest and king. Most Christians in Lagos see the need to affirm the expressions of the indigenous spiritual paradigms while also affirming the traditional offices of Christ they inherited from the church in the Western world through missionaries and early church fathers. They would add these offices as well: liberator, healer and ancestor. Nigerian Christians like to see the face of Christ from their own unique perspectives, recognizing and finding an indigenous name for the Jesus of Nazareth they follow.

The claim that Jesus is a prophet from God is partly a matter of his historical identity, with specific Jewish origin. When believers state that Jesus is the prophet of God, they often mean that Jesus of Nazareth saw himself as God's spokesperson who came to proclaim repentance in anticipation of the coming Kingdom of God. Jesus is not only a spokesperson for God but also the eschatological prophet who came to announce the end of time and the need for repentance. This eschatological viewpoint is grounded in the claim that the Kingdom of God was at hand and is at the centre of the message of Jesus (John 1). In this sense, Christians also affirm that Jesus is the prophet-messiah.

Another central office of Christ is that he is a priest. Christians in the Majority World see Jesus as not only living in the world but is also concerned with its shape, meaning and direction. As a priest par excellence, Jesus criticized the world of disintegration and warned its leaders of the imminent consequences of their worldly paths if they did not turn towards God. Jesus crafted an alternative vision for the transformation of the world at large and pursued the transformation of his own social and political world. Yusuf affirmed that Christian pastors should proclaim the redemption decreed by Jesus, but also urge political leaders to turn to God. A Christian view of the redemption inspired by Jesus as a priest is not only about personal salvation after death, often the only theme highlighted in the Christian history of redemption, but also about the transformation of this world we live in here and now. It is an incontrovertible fact that an emphasis on the transformation of this world is one of the major contributions that pastors in Lagos could make today.

More recently, Christians in Africa have started to call the attention of believers in the Majority World to the office of Christ as their ancestor.

One of the first African theologians to articulate this view was Christian G. Baëtta (1908–94). According to him, 'For whatever others may do in their own countries, our people live with their dead.' Tanzanian theologian Charles Nyamiti (1931–2020) and Bénézet Bujo (1940–2023) from the Democratic Republic of Congo are other African Christian scholars who popularized the 'Christ is our ancestor' movement. This concept has its origin in the consistent enactment of the roles of ancestors in religious rituals across the African continent. Life, they have argued, flows from God through the ancestors to those who live now, and to subsequent generations. Yusuf affirmed that both African spiritual beliefs and Islamic contexts have influenced many pastors in Lagos, who perhaps see Jesus through the lens of this spiritual life that flows to the believers through Jesus Christ, the Proto Ancestor.

At the heart of the Christian concept that Christ is Prophet, Priest and Ancestor is that followers of Christ can directly and immediately address God in Jesus Christ through the believer's own spiritual circumstances and cultural contexts, without going through intermediaries and interpreters. But their assumptions go beyond the distinction of what is familiar and what is unknown. The heart of their argument is that one cannot achieve the full depth of one's spiritual maturity unless it is directed through the lens of his cultural and indigenous prism.

A paradox of the Christian faith relating to the offices of Christ is that every believer wants Jesus Christ to have indigenous titles which define the offices of prophet, priest, king, chief or ancestor. With such indigenous titles, faith becomes intimate and relevant, and the followership of Christ becomes more meaningful. At the same time, however, Christians recognize that their faith in God cannot be domesticated. Thus, it is within the bounds of our indigenous spirituality that we are also set free and inspired to articulate the essential categories of the offices of Christ.

Pastor Yusuf recognizes the ancestral and Islamic framework that contributes to his effectiveness as a Christian minister. He also knows that there is a difference between custom (what the Yoruba call *asa*) and religion (known as *esin* in the Yoruba tongue). Perhaps the effectiveness of Jesus of Nazareth as prophet and viceroy from God was in large measure due to his being and his works. Therefore, it is probably more life-giving to practise religion *like* Jesus than to practise his religion. Muslims would say it is better to practise religion like the Prophet Muhammad than to practise his religion. In the modern world, it is not necessary to jettison one's identity or to discard one's religious upbringing to be relevant. Yusuf, rather than discarding his religious upbringing and Islamic identity, embraced his background as a Muslim and as an engineer. They became factors that strengthened his capacity for effective ministry in the church.

The Christian faith has never been seen in a more favourable and fruitful condition as today in the Majority World. All statistical data point to the rapid expansion and interminable character of the Christian religion. For the first time in post-medieval history, the centre of gravity of Christianity has shifted from the Northern Hemisphere to the Southern Hemisphere. Thus, we will see Christians in the Southern Hemisphere and its large cities continue to nurture and redefine what is meant by Christianity, as well as the offices of Christ. The light shines in the darkness, and the darkness cannot overcome it (John 15). The light of the Christian Gospel in the world cannot be extinguished; its enduring value for all humanity cannot be domesticated by any one era or any one Christian denomination.

David the Shepherd, Jesus the Carpenter: Fulfilling destiny as Moses the God-chosen

When I migrated to the Western world in my early adulthood, I was surprised by the human obsession with external beauty. I grew up in an environment where such obsession was regarded as too extravagant and unnecessary. Whatever is natural is also beautiful, and the philosophy of beauty was associated with cleanliness. Before the modern era of multi-million cosmetic industry, most Africans paid minimal attention to external beauty but upheld the significance of internal beauty and its defining characteristics such as humility, fidelity, integrity, wisdom, bravery, truthfulness, diligence and selflessness, to name only a few. These are also the abstract nouns of inner beauty that I observed to a limited extent in Lagos. In the modern era, however, there are ferocious efforts to focus on external beauty such as facial appearance, the wristwatch we wear, the shape of our body, the colour of our skins and whether we are slender or heavy. This obsession has translated to an inferiority complex and name-calling for some, and, in extreme cases, to an incurable debt and overspending to protect what cannot endure for a day for millions of people in the modern era.

The most important characteristic of the Christian life is obedience nurtured and protected by faithfulness or righteousness. For example, David was not born to be a shepherd all his life. He was born to be a king of Israel. Throughout his teenage years, however, he was in the field tending to the sheep and protecting them from predators such as lions. This was a part of his preparation for his supernatural call to be king. It was through this mundane and transitory route that God prepared him for a supreme and supernatural service. God was preparing David through everyday routine fraught by obedience and attentiveness to the Spirit of God. This routine of everyday obedience and faithfulness was a part of the preparation ordained by God. The beauty of David as 'a man from God's heart' was characterized by humility without obsession to the external. Even David's father, Jesse, missed the inner strength of his son that only God could see. The internal beauty of a child of God is a divine beauty that is transparent only to God, and it does not fade with age.

In a like manner, Jesus of Nazareth was not born to be a carpenter. However, he was in Nazareth for almost thirty years making furniture with Joseph. God was preparing him through the routine of working with Joseph as a carpenter for the fulfilment of his supernatural call as the saviour of the world. God prepares us through the mundane things of life imperceptibly for our supernatural calls. The day-to-day responsibilities are the means to the supernatural end. God uses this routine of truthfulness and obedience that come in our day-to-day activities as a test for greater things we are being prepared to accomplish. There are no spectacular mountaintop preparations, and we are not often privileged to know this ahead of time because they are hidden in God's providence. God sees our potential, not our pitfalls, and we are always called by God before we are called by men or the church. The internal beauty that God sees in us was planted there by God and God is never surprised that we are qualified to serve him. Our internal beauty that God sees is not through cosmetic surgery, and God is not fooled by our artificial beauty pageant or contests. God sees our beauty, and he is not discouraged by our preparations as carpenters for his glory.

It is in this way that Jesus's ancestry is linked organically and symbiotically to the lineage of King David. They were born to be kings, and their identical preparations through the natural and insignificant routine of life are what sets them apart for God's glory. The only security that David and Jesus needed was provided by God and their faithfulness was confirmed through their obedience, and their destiny secured in God alone.

One of the most enigmatic leaders in ancient Israel was Moses. Although he was insecure and imperfect, Moses was iconic, and his relationship with God was unequalled, leading God's people through the most consequential period of history. He was meek and assertive, and when God called him to lead the Israelites out of bondage in Egypt, he responded to God to send somebody else. Apparently, he was not fully aware of *who* was calling him, but keenly cognizance of *what* God was calling him to do. The task of leading God's people out of captivity in Egypt was monumental.

Like Moses, most of the leaders who have been called by God to a specific task have also lived or were born in foreign lands. But in the end, the triumph of Moses was noticeable because God was with him and ahead of him. Accordingly, the fifth book of the Hebrew Bible said about Moses:

Never since has there arisen a prophet in Israel like Moses, whom the LORD knew face-to-face. He was unequaled for all the signs and wonders that the LORD sent him to perform in the land of Egypt, against Pharaoh and all his servants and his entire land, and for all the mighty deeds and all the terrifying displays of power that Moses performed in the sight of all Israel.[5]

Moses grew up in Egypt, but the land of Egypt did not assimilate him or his Jewish background. Without his experience in Egypt, however, it is doubtful that he would have been fully prepared or successful to lead God's people through a tumultuous period in their history. He was destined to lead God's people through the wilderness, and the preparation as a young Jew was a sine qua non for the liberation of God's people from slavery in Egypt.

One of the most courageous decisions Moses ever made in his long career as a leader is recorded in Num. 11.11-30. Following the complaints of the Israelites in the wilderness, Moses took their murmuring to God, who instructed Moses to select seventy elders to assist Moses in sharing the administrative management of the people. These seventy elders were instructed to stay outside the tent so that the Spirit of the LORD could flow through them as the Spirit did Moses himself. These seventy would then utter prophetic words as commanded by God as they remain outside the tent. There were two men, however, who remain inside the tent and did not follow the instructions of Moses to stay outside the tent. These two 'rebels', Eldad and Medad, were among the registered elders. Although they were inside the camp, Eldad and Medad also prophesied. A young man ran to report that Eldad and Medad were disobeying the rules yet prophesied. Joshua, apparently furious and frustrated, asked Moses: 'Eldad and Medad are prophesying in the camp . . . . My Lord Moses, stop them!' Moses, who had been blessed with broad shoulders through his relationship with God as a young Jew in Egypt, did not stop Eldad and Medad but responded: 'Are you jealous for my sake? Would that all the LORD's people were prophets, and that the LORD would put his spirit on them!' It goes without saying that Moses had the mind and Spirit of God and understood that the Spirit of God transcends the rules of 'tickets and receipts' of human understanding of the Divine.

Perhaps Heb. 11.29-40 best summarizes the characteristics of leaders of faith and what they endured as God's chosen. Some of them were tortured, others suffered mocking and flogging, and a few were in chains and imprisonment. Still others were stoned to death or subjected to death by sword. Majority were destitute and in the words of the writer of the book of Hebrews: 'of whom the world was not worthy. They wandered in deserts and mountains, and in caves and holes in the ground.'[6] It would have meant a different matter entirely if the writer of the book of Hebrews said, 'they were not worthy of the world'. Is it possible that the statement alludes to the resurrection of Jesus itself? Is it possible that the world is unworthy of the life of sinlessness of Jesus and therefore resurrection of Jesus was a vindication of his earthly sinless life as he lived for others? No earthly grave would be able to hold back the Beloved Son of God who came to live for others in the world. Jesus, in the final analysis, is a refugee who belongs exclusively to God and who cannot be corrupted by the taint of the grave dug by humanity.

Summary

This chapter is the story of how a highly educated, quiet civil engineer with a strong Muslim background became an influential proclaimer of the Christian Good News in Lagos, overseeing more than twenty congregations and putting them on a solid footing to becoming missionary-producing congregations. Pastor Yusuf's story is also striking because of his robust understanding of the organic linkage of the physical with the spiritual world. The reality of the world of the spirit that our naked eyes cannot see is genuine to him and more tangible than even the physical world of flesh and blood. This reality became the path that ultimately drew him to Christ, and he desires to serve God faithfully because of what God has done in his own life and through him in the lives of many in Lagos.

PART III

Stories of love

9

The miracle of my father's birth led me to Christ

Okandiji Babajide Lawal is a good example of the philosophy of Horace Bushnell (1802–76), the North American theologian and congregational minister, who proposed in the 1800s the idea of Christian nurturing as essential to maintaining a Christian life from one generation to another. In the opening chapter of his book *Christian Nurture* (1847), Bushnell defined Christian nurture as being divine: 'There is then some kind of nurture which is of the Lord, deriving a quality and a power from Him, and communicating the same.' For Bushnell, it is not necessary that a Christian should know the details of his conversion experience if he is raised in a Christian environment. Christian conversion ought to be as simple and gradual a transition as the transition from childhood to adulthood.

Nurtured in a family of faith, Okandiji Babajide Lawal's own father was a devoted Christian who nourished Lawal with stories of his grandparents as committed Christians. Lawal's grandparents had no children for several years. When American Baptist missionaries arrived in Nigeria through Lagos, the infant mortality rate was high. The couple lost several children to stillbirth and became disheartened. Once Lawal's father was conceived, the missionaries adopted the pregnant mother, who was simultaneously suffering from glaucoma. The gradual loss of her vision due to the damage to the optic disc caused by increased pressure on the eyeball constituted double jeopardy. The missionaries cared for her in Lagos, helping her overcome the glaucoma and have a successful pregnancy. And now, Lawal's grandmother had a baby boy, who later fathered Okandiji Babajide Lawal.

As Lawal's father grew, the missionaries sent him to school, providing for his material and emotional needs. The story about how Lawal became a Christian, nurtured by his father and mother, portrays a typical journey of faith. His own father had become a Christian due to the influence of the missionaries. The fact that the missionaries were there to care for the needs of his grandmother and father, leading to his father's becoming a Christian, was seen as a divine mission.

As Lawal described it to me, he saw the security of his faith in Christ through the influence of his own parents as God's greatest gift. He stated repeatedly that, for him, Jesus Christ could be described by the phrase 'Jesus is a gift with a lift.'

As an electrical engineer, Lawal could be making a lot of money. But his Christian identity required of him a strong adherence to ethical standards that include integrity, love, honesty, compassion, fidelity and diligence. In life, God calls us to excel so that we can serve others and transform their lives. He sees one's Christianity as a path to transformation, meaning once a person becomes a Christian, there is a total life redirection. The Yoruba call this transformation *ironupiwada*, a complete turnaround of one's life. It connotes living a productive and responsible life for God.

When asked what Christ had done to make him live a transformed life, Lawal was quick to give me an example. He had worked for a particular man for about a year, but his employer ended up leaving Lagos. The mobility of the labour force could be devastating in some circumstances, even though companies headquartered in Lagos might have branches and distribution centres across the country. About seven years after the transfer of Lawal's senior associate, Lawal desperately needed two essential pieces of very expensive equipment for which he had no funds. He shared his urgent need with a friend, who advised him to travel outside Lagos where he could purchase the pieces at a more reasonable price. When he arrived at the suggested place, the first person he saw discouraged him because of his lack of funds. But he was sent to the managing director of the company anyway. As he was on the way to the office of the managing director, he saw someone who looked familiar to him. It turned out to be the previous boss. He asked Lawal, 'Are you the same Mr Lawal who worked with me about seven years ago? I remember you as a man of integrity and an amazing child of God. What can I do to help you?' He then took Lawal to the office of the general manager, introducing him to the manager as a man of integrity. As a result, Lawal was allowed to buy the pieces of equipment by making scheduled payments. His faithfulness in small things seven years earlier had rewarded him abundantly when he most needed it.

Lawal sees Lagos as a 'pressure-cooker' city, where one wrong step in the business sphere could ruin one financially. Building a secure financial life in Lagos can be achieved, but one small misstep can also damage what took decades to build. The temptations to step outside the bounds of what is right and honourable are many, and each one is very alluring.

Lawal spent many hours driving in Lagos because of the 'go slow' or heavy traffic in the city. He explained that being a child of God requires discipline because the hardship of 'go slow' may lead to the temptation of taking bribes in business to compensate for the hardship. For example, one may be working at the Nigerian Port Authority, and it is possible to make a great deal of money there by accepting bribes to clear the way for goods for Nigerian citizens. Taking a stance against corruption in Lagos is a challenge with great financial and emotional costs. Living in the city is very expensive, but Lawal believes that without the clear direction of life provided by Christ, one has no future as an honest person.

Lawal's story is also the story of many others in Lagos, affirming that godlessness is not the same as faithlessness. Neither godlessness nor faithlessness is possible because human beings live in a community and are gregarious, while often migrating from one place to another. Godlessness is the conviction that one can live without God, but one cannot compel God to withdraw from humanity. God does not retreat from humans to teach them a lesson about the existence of the Divine or to prove the reality of that existence. Faithlessness denies the reality of faith in the orbit of human existence. Humanity, however, is surrounded by the experience of others who are exercising faith in the Divine. The faith of other people is sustaining, even when one doubts the authenticity of his own faith in God. Neither godlessness nor faithlessness is practical in the orbit of human existence – one of the greatest lessons of being a Christian in Lagos.

Faithlessness and godlessness represent the conviction that neither God nor others exist to lift humanity from their condition, even when it is asserted that neither God nor others have meaning in one's life. It is illogical to live without God and others. Therefore, it is illogical to be godless or faithless. Making provision for God and faith in one's life is the path to authentic life and direction, and one cannot be truly happy in life unless one knows God and the creative empowerment of other human beings in the shared community.

Do Lagosian Christians worship the same God to which the missionaries led them?

One missionary in Lagos was delighted when he received a plot of land from a local tribal leader on which he could begin to build a mission hospital.[2] Once the work on the building began, he started each workday with Bible study and prayer for his working men and women. Before the hospital was completed and started full operations, all the crew members had accepted Christ as their Lord and Saviour, making the missionary very happy. The construction time itself had been a productive evangelistic success.

With their work completed, all the workmen returned to their respective homes and nearby villages on the outskirts of Lagos. The missionary began organizing a series of follow-up evangelistic visits. To his disappointment, he found that his new converts had remained comfortable tending to the shrines of their local deities. He confronted them with what seemed to him gross apostasy[3] and inconsistencies with their confession of faith as Christians. He chastised the converts for not being truly converted. But they expressed their surprise at the missionary's ignorance that at the construction site, they had been praying to the God in the locality of the hospital. Their name for God in the construction region is Olodumare.[4] Although that name had power there, that God was not in charge in their homes and villages. The gods in their homes and villages are quite specialized, depending on their existential needs. At home, they were compelled to build shrines for the deity that owned their land. They explained to the missionary, 'If we try to pray to your mission God here, the local deity would be very unhappy and make too much trouble for everybody.'

This is a situation many Western missionaries encounter on the mission field. They often find that for the indigenous people, God is very specialized, both geographically and functionally. This God is often different from the one that missionaries were there to proclaim, leading some to demand the eradication and abandonment of those localized deities. The 'localization' of God should not surprise contemporary missionaries. The idea of a territorial or localized God is one that is prevalent in the Bible.

The pages of the Bible are replete with stories of the territoriality and specialization of God. Jacob, dreaming at Bethel, said: 'Surely Yahweh is in this place. . . . This is none other than the house of God' (Gen. 28.16-17). Mount Zion on which King Solomon built the first temple is repeatedly referred to as the 'hill where God resides' (Ps. 9.11; 96.2; Isa. 8.18).

When the Syrian military general, Naaman, was suffering with leprosy, he disdainfully claimed that the waters of the Syrian rivers were as able to cure his leprosy as those of the Jordan River. However, when he was healed by bathing in the Jordan River (not in a Syrian river), he realized the power of the Yahweh of Israel and exclaimed: 'I know that there is not God in all the earth but in Israel.'

Yahweh is the tribal name for the God of the Hebrews; but another name for God is *Elohim*, the name associated with the God of the universe. In the first chapter of Genesis, it is Elohim who created the universe. This creator of the universe is also the creator of humanity, but frequently a more personalized or more tribally-related deity plays the secondary role – Yahweh. Thus, there is Elohim, and there is Yahweh. Often, the high God and the tribal God are one and the same, but not always so. In some cases, we see the High God creating the universe and the tribal God creating the people and their cultures. This can explain the two creation accounts in Genesis. One involves Elohim, 'the High God' (Gen. 1-2.4a), and the other entails Yahweh, 'the tribal God of the Hebrews' (Gen. 2.4aff).

Don Richardson wrote a book entitled *Eternity in Their Hearts* (1981) in which he retells the Genesis story but emphasizes the relationship between what he called the Melchizedek factor and the Abram factor. In his retelling, God instructs Abram to leave his homeland and go to a place God will show him. God promises to bless Abram if he does what God wants him to. 'I will make you into a great nation and I will bless those who bless you . . . ' (Gen. 12.2-3). This covenant with Abram dominates the pages of Genesis. Abram was not 'egotistical, arrogant, aloof, or self-centered', Richardson wrote.

When Abram reached the God-intended destination, he undoubtedly encountered the peoples of Canaan. They did not speak his language, and they did not eat or dress like Abram. Above all, Abram speculated that they did not worship Yahweh, the tribal God of the Hebrews, who had sent him. The first thirty-six chapters of Genesis mention more than forty different tribes who were different from Abram or the tribes he represented.

Abram probably thought that Yahweh (God) would make his ancestry line great, and all his progeny would receive God's blessing. After all, he had passed God's test by leaving his country as God had commanded.

According to Richardson, Abram learned that Sodom and Gomorrah were far from God, with many tribes following the examples of the immorality of Sodom and Gomorrah. God told Abram to go to Canaan and proclaim to the Canaanites the love of God. But a surprise awaited Abram! The Canaanites, whom he thought were not worshippers of God, introduced Abram to El Elyon, 'God Most High'. It was King Melchizedek, the Canaanite king of Salem, who introduced Abram to 'God Most High'. Old Testament scholars have interpreted the word 'Melchizedek' to be a combination of two Hebrew words – Melchi (king) and Zadok (righteousness). So, in this pagan country to which God sent Abram, there was a righteous king who worshipped 'God Most High'.

Don Richardson calls God's preparation that went ahead of Abram 'the Melchizedek factor'. That is, God had preceded Abram. Even among a people associated with heretical beliefs, notorious for such grievous sins as idolatry, cannibalism, child sacrifice, prostitution and greed, God was present there as well, and there was a priest of God Most High. And the God that Abram was there to proclaim to Melchizedek and the Canaanites was Yahweh.

We would expect that Abram would direct the attention of Melchizedek to Yahweh, the true God he was there to proclaim. The name, El Elyon, was not the name for God with which Abram was familiar. But it is a name closely related to Elohim. Can El Elyon be a valid name for God? Is it possible for God to be known by other names? Does God answer those who use other languages to address God? In this interaction between Abram and Melchizedek, the 'king of righteousness' blessed Abram, saying, 'Blessed be Abram by El Elyon, Creator of Heaven and Earth, and blessed be El Elyon, who delivered Abram's enemies into his hand' (Gen. 14.19–20).

Abram, in relation to Melchizedek, did not insist that the correct name for God was Yahweh and not El Elyon? 'Why did Abram not reject a blessing offered in a foreign name for God?' Should he have said,

One moment, your royal highness! The correct name for the Almighty is Yahweh, not El Elyon! Furthermore, I cannot accept a blessing offered under this Canaanite name, El Elyon, since your Canaanite concept of the Almighty undoubtedly has been tainted by pagan notions. In any case, Yahweh has told me that I am the one who is supposed to bless you, and not you me.

Contrary to all expectations, the response of Abram was to give Melchizedek a tenth of everything he had. This transfer of a gift from Abram to Melchizedek is the 'Abram factor'. So, someone was already acclaiming the true God among the Canaanites before the arrival of Abram, the missionary from God. Melchizedek shared his bread and wine with Abram, who received them without jealousy, arrogance, or a spirit of competition. Melchizedek and Abram became allies, or as some theologians might say, the Melchizedek factor meets the Abram factor, or the general revelation meets the special revelation.

In my view, today's contemporary missionaries should take a closer look at the concept of God they proclaim. Many limitations of the God-concept that are found in modern societies have also been recorded in the Scriptures, but with important modifications that modern missionaries have often filtered out. We need to examine ourselves so that modern missionaries can become aware of the limitations which one's culture imposes on one's concept of God. Understanding this limitation will help missionaries to be more effective today.

What God did Baptist missionaries proclaim to Lawal's grandparents?

The fundamental difficulty with the mission of the Church in the modern world is not in what missionaries have affirmed, but in what they have omitted or denied. In some instances, the Western Church has become monolithic or one-sided. Perhaps, the stance of the Church in the Western world has been fundamentally and unapologetically nationalistic. The Church has not recognized the presence of God in the lives and spirituality of others as Abram did. Whether it is in the expressiveness of the spirituality of Native Americans, or of the Aborigines of Australia, or of the Mayans in Guatemala, or of the over 800 different ethnic groups in Africa, we have not recognized the El Elyon in indigenous peoples, and what these peoples can teach us about the God who has always preceded the missionaries.

The mission of God (*Missio Dei*) and the development of the concept of one God

One of the persistent deceptions that migrated from cultural anthropology to theology in the nineteenth century is the concept of the evolutionary development of God (singular) from gods (plural). This idea created the misperception that a mature concept of the one God who created the universe was the result of long evolutionary development from a primitive culture of polytheism – a view that has long since been discarded. For over fifty years, Edward Tylor's theory of the religious evolution from polytheism to monotheism was regarded as 'gospel' in the Western world. Tylor was also a proponent of the primitive idea of belief of many gods among Africans, but contemporary anthropologists have now discredited his evolutionary theory. Rejecting his ideas, however, did not occur before they had already entered the missionary literature, gaining a foothold in their vocabulary. Tylor's intermediate idea was popular for another fifty years in the West. In the Southern Hemisphere, especially in Africa, Christians continue to carry the lingering wounds inflicted by this idea.

Wilhelm Schmidt, the early Catholic missionary-anthropologist of the early twentieth century, as well as other anthropologists, has argued that monotheism scares those in the West and that polytheism is projected on non-Westerners. Defending Tylor's long career and reputation, young anthropologists who began to see evidence of the concept of One God in the non-Western world conjectured that the presence of monotheism in Africa, for example, was due to Western missionary influence. But contemporary anthropologists such as Franz Boas have admitted that it is wrong to classify any culture as primitive and more diminishing of such cultures to attribute the belief in One Supreme Being in the non-Western world to missionary influence.[5]

Western missionaries have been too slow to realize that other people already worship and praise the God they were sent to proclaim. Should such missionaries acknowledge that monotheism exists outside the Western world, with indigenous peoples affirming God Most High, Elohim or El Elyon – their version of the God the missionaries have come to 'modern Canaan' to proclaim – it would have a deleterious effect on their efforts to enlarge the narrow boundaries of their kind of Christianity.

Theologians and religions: A personal story

In May 2002, approximately 150 theologians from different parts of the world gathered in the heart of Denmark for a major conference. The goal was to answer one fundamental question: 'What is the relationship between the God of "non-Christian" religions and the God of Christianity? What relationship exists between the view of God in missionary-producing regions of the world and the concept of God among the peoples who are the targets of this Gospel message? In other words, how can religion correspond to theology?' In the end, I believe we failed to realize that the problem of humanity is not theological but doxological. Our goal at that conference in Denmark was to foster a harmonious relationship in our theological differences by examining the merits of religious diversity.

In 2003, the Eerdmans Publishing Company published our various papers under the title, *Theology and the Religions: A Dialogue.*

Viggo Mortensen, the Danish theologian who organized the conference, summarized our conclusions by appropriately quoting Raimundo Panikkar, who said, 'I left as a Christian, I "found" myself a Hindu, and I "return" a Buddhist, without having ceased to be a Christian.'[6]

In my estimation, however, as we gathered at Aarhus University looking for the confluence of monotheism among all religions and spiritual groups in the world, we did not find what we were looking for. It needs to be understood that our mission is not to find theological confluence among religions. Theological harmony is not essential. I believe that the purpose of humanity is to be doxological, worshipping and praising God. As Christians, we must realize we should not attempt to replace the natural eloquence in the worship and praise of God among those indigenous groups encountered on the mission fields. The Abram factors can enhance the Melchizedek factor but not eradicate them. Abram can describe Melchizedek, but Abram will not know what it means to be a Melchizedek.

When we invite others to come to Jesus Christ, we are not inviting them to become Christians but to enter a doxological community. Our specific brand of Christianity is only incidental to becoming a redeemed and restored humanity, constituted by Jesus, purchased through the blood of his perfected Passover and launched in the age of God's Kingdom through his resurrection. We are inviting humanity to join and worship together as part of all God's creation. Mark, in his Gospel, recorded a greater commission in ch. 16, v. 15, when he said, 'Go into all the world and proclaim the good news to the whole creation.'

The mission of the church is not Christology only, considering only the nature and deeds of Christ, as the famous Dutch theologian Hendrik Kraemer concluded in *The Christian Message in a Non-Christian World* published in 1938. Nor is it exclusively theological, as John Hick argued in his *God and the Universe of Faiths* published in 1973. Nor do I think that the fundamental problem is essentially ecclesiological or the doctrine of church membership as the famous theologian Karl Rahner maintained in his twenty-volume work, *Theological Investigation*, published in English in 1984.

More recently, Judith Berling, professor of Chinese and comparative religions at the Graduate Theological Union, Berkeley, California, argued that religion is more personal and the understanding of God more pluralistic than it is structural and ideological. Therefore, the human dilemma we face is more anthropological and psychological than it is theological.

After conducting a series of interviews among Christians in Lagos for three consecutive months, I am convinced that our Christian mission should be the same as *Missio Dei*, God's mission; our problems arise when we attempt to force conformity in our doxological worship of God. This does not mean that once human beings agree on how to worship God, our problems will disappear. But we need to see through the eyes of Abram and Melchizedek, who were able to see beyond their specific religions. They became aware that their mission in life was all about God and that they were honoured to participate in *Missio Dei,* the mission of God for the transformation of the world.

We can draw at least three conclusions from the encounter between Abram and Melchizedek, between Yahweh and El Elyon, between North and South. First, we must be more critical of the flaws in our concepts of God and ask, What God do we proclaim in our missional efforts? We are too confident that we have the right idea when deciding about how God is to be worshipped. As witnesses to God, we must realize that we too have idols of our own in our midst, a fact that calls for our repentance and a rededication of our own selves to the one God. It is not easy to embrace the God-concept of others. (It takes time for Abram to accept Melchizedek.) Even Paul insisted that 'God will give to the Jews first and also to the Gentiles' (Rom. 2.10). But we also remember what he wrote to the Gal. 3.28. 'So, there is no difference between Jews and Gentiles, between slaves and free, between male and females, for you are all one in Jesus Christ.'

Except in times of national catastrophe or times of war, when we suddenly see God as national and exclusive, Western Christians perceive God as being beyond topographical, regional or tribal limitations. Generally, missionaries to the Majority World feel they represent a truly universal and non-specialized tribal God. It is probably accurate to say that European and American missional Christians have largely shed the topographical and regional limitations in their concepts of God. However, if I can use the word 'tribe' broadly, stretching it to include all denominations within Christendom, it is their 'favourite God' that missionaries from the Western world continue to proclaim. Perhaps we cannot ever get past this specialization of deity.

Second, a more positive orientation of those in the Majority World is now crucial for global Christian renewal. The concept of God in the Majority World and in the lives of those Christians I encountered in Lagos is more like that in the Bible (especially the Old Testament) than it is in the Northern Hemisphere. Therefore, the tendency of the Majority World in the Northern Hemisphere is to strengthen and renew already existing concepts of God. We must learn that our humanity is not complete if we are not humbled by the mysteries of God and the realization that God loves others as much as God loves us, resulting in forgiveness, acceptance, tolerance, compassion, peace, understanding and the promotion of human dignity.

Third and finally, we learn from this that God has always preceded the missionaries in every part of the world. Melchizedek is always in front of Abram. Therefore, our methods of Christian mission must always be dialogical and not monolithic. No one group and no one faith can adequately and decisively speak for God or of God as we are not God's incarnation. Only Jesus is the incarnation of God. The risk we take (as well as the benefit) in a dialogical approach to mission is finding that mutual transformation becomes a real possibility in the worship and praise of God. Western missionaries can worship like their African Christian brothers and sisters with their liturgical liveliness.

Christians in Lagos are teaching us in the modern world that our faith transcends any division of ourselves into Christian and non-Christian worlds, or the Western and non-Western worlds. We are also all people of both North and South, as the oceans have not only divided us into East and West but have also united us, even as we claim to be from the Northern Hemisphere and Southern Hemisphere. In missiological terms, this means that when we cross the ocean, we become instruments of doxology. Christian mission, therefore, can be an instrument that helps strengthen the worship of God in diverse particularity of tongues and enormous multiplicity. A Christian maturity that values other people and their concepts of God has the advantage of encouraging the roles of recipient cultures as decisive for the final appropriation of the message of redemption.

As our various circles overlap, we continue to discover that the Christian faith can transcend both the scepticism of liberalism and the dogmatic precision of fundamentalism. It is a faith that praises a widow who gave only 100 Naira (a pittance in Nigerian currency) but who gave more than the greedy politicians who became wealthy by appropriating public funds. Our faith in God celebrates life because death cannot suffocate life in Christ, and our faith negates any fear of death because it is not the cessation of life.

What I learned on the streets of Lagos

In Lagos, it was impressed upon me anew that monotheism predates most faith and spiritual traditions, and whether in ancient times or now, God will always precede any missionaries. Melchizedek will always exist before Abram. This is partly because human spirituality predates any organized religions, including Christianity. When we read, 'Thou shall not worship other gods before me', we are being reminded that there is only one God, who is called by many names, including Elohim, Olódùmarè, Allah, Deus, Unkulunkulu and Onyame. Monotheism is a universal concept because 'God' has not been without a witness. This is the way Frithjof Schuon saw it when he wrote, 'The monotheistic religion belonged originally to the entire nomadic branch of Semitic group, a branch that, having issued from Abraham, was subdivided into two secondary branches, one issuing from Isaac and the other from Ishmael, and it was not until the time of Moses that monotheism took a Judaic form.'[7] In other words, it was Moses, the lawgiver, who led the Israelites out of slavery in Egypt and who also gave a distinctly Jewish definition to monotheism. Schuon concluded that

> it was Moses who, at a time when the religion of Abraham was growing dim among the Ishmaelites, was called upon to give monotheism a powerful support by linking it in a certain manner with the people of Israel, who thus became its guardians; but this adaptation, however necessary and providential it may have been, was also bound to lead to a restriction of the outward form, owing to the 'particularist' tendency inherent in each people.[8]

Judaism 'annexed monotheistic belief and made it the sole possession of Israel, with the result that under this form the heritage of Abraham was henceforth inseparable from all the secondary adaptations and all the rituals and social consequences implicit in the Mosaic Law'.[9]

How is monotheism popularized in the historical development of Judaism as we see it in the New Testament, especially in the life of Jesus? It was through Judaism that the idea of monotheism, as Christians understand it today, entered the annals of the New Testament. But it acquired a new revelatory character in the New Testament because of Jesus Christ. While Judaism is a covenantal monotheism, Christianity is a trinitarian monotheism.

It was through the channel of Judaism that monotheism acquired its historical significance. What Judaism contributed to the universal concept of monotheism was that it went further by making monotheism distinct in messianic ideas.

Were Africans worshipping the true God before the arrival of Western missionaries? Before the church in the West began to send missionaries to Africa in the modern era, it was common for African Christians to see their faith through the prism of the ancient Ethiopian church. In Acts 8.25-40, we read the story of an Ethiopian believer who was returning from Jerusalem, where he had gone to worship the one and only true God. Then Philip, also travelling that way, noticed this faithful believer on a desert road sitting on his chariot, reciting the book of Isaiah, the prophet. Was he not worshipping the true God before this encounter with Philip and his subsequent baptism? What is the difference between this Ethiopian man before meeting Philip and him after meeting Philip? It is reminiscent of the difference between Melchizedek before Abram and Melchizedek after his encounter with Abram.

How are we then to define 'mission'? Is there a need for missionaries? As we have seen in the life of Lawal's grandparents, their presence facilitated the delivery of Lawal's father. The primary role of Christian missions is to preserve and respect the indigenous spirituality that has always been at the root of any people's faith. As Christopher J. H. Wright wrote, 'Mission means our committed participation as God's people, at God's invitation and command, in God's own mission within the history of God's world for the redemption of God's creation.'[10]

But I submit that the Christian mission has always been the opportunity to lead others to choose the God who has already chosen them; we are to collaborate with and partner with nationals as we find divine initiative at the root of their faith. The most effective missionaries, therefore, will be those who go to the mission field and, by God's grace, enter creatively and respectfully into the existing worship and praise of indigenous people. Mission, therefore, is a call to doxology – the worship and praise of God.

Our mission is not only to convert others to Christianity but also to bring them to an awareness of the God who has already chosen them, that they should praise this God with all their beings, worshipping God with the eloquence of the local assembly. The Christian faith should be presented and interpreted so that those receiving it can hear God in Jesus Christ addressing them directly and immediately in their own contexts and circumstances, without any insistence on non-native acculturation. Those to whom we bear our witness cannot arrive at full spiritual maturity unless it is through their own languages and existential realities, especially when those who are exercising judgement and making decisions over ecclesiastical and theological matters are Christians from different cultural and ancestral backgrounds.

Cornelius, a Gentile, and his family worshipped the same God as Peter, a Jew.

'In Caesarea there was a man named Cornelius, a centurion of the Italian Cohort, as it was called. He was a devout man who feared God with all his household; he gave alms generously to the people and prayed constantly to God' (Acts 10.1-2). This opening statement in chapter 10 of Acts is illustrative of natural Christian education, proving that one's own home can be an altar.

We see in the rest of the chapter that God, in a vision, asked Cornelius to send some men to Joppa and to bring Peter back with them. When they found Peter, they informed him that Cornelius wanted to see him in Caesarea. Although Jews and Gentiles were not usually in relationship, God had prepared the way for both to meet. When Peter arrived at Cornelius's house, Cornelius fell at Peter's feet and worshipped him. Peter told him to rise as he (Peter) too was only a mortal. After that, Peter preached to the household of Cornelius, and these Gentiles entered the redemptive narrative. Then Peter asked, 'Can anyone withhold the water for baptizing these people who have received the Holy Spirit just as we have? So, he ordered them to be baptized in the name of Jesus Christ. Then they invited him to stay for several days.'

Summary

I see a parallel between the story of Cornelius and the story of Okandiji Babajide Lawal. In Acts, we understand clearly that God shows no partiality, favouring a Jew over a Gentile, with both treated the same way in the extended household of God. Cornelius and his household believed in God and then the leader of that household led his family to God. Perhaps the members of the household of Cornelius did not know when they were converted, but Peter's instruction to baptize everyone in the household was final.

This story further demonstrates that through nurture itself and people other than Jesus, we may be led to God. Those who seek God with all their hearts, just as Cornelius did and as the grandparents of Babajide Okandiji Lawal did when his grandmother was nurtured by Baptist missionaries, are already on their way to God and meet Jesus on the way.[11]

10

God's faithfulness has never failed

Edwin and Christianah Nwaeze live on the outskirts of Lagos with their four children. Edwin studied agricultural science before venturing into the business of buying and selling car tyres. When I met Edwin, it was easy to see that he was very passionate and enthusiastic about God's continued direction in his life.

The couple's devotion to Jesus Christ is reflected in the names they gave to their four children: Favor (girl), David (boy), Success (boy) and Adoration (girl).

Edwin took courses at the Day Star Christian Centre, a megachurch fellowship with over 10,000 worshippers, which also offers training in leadership in various areas. Edwin enrolled in a programme related to agricultural science. It was at the centre that he developed the desire to lead a life totally committed to Christ.

Nwaeze (meaning 'son of a king' in his native tongue) sees a difference between religion and Christianity. He defines religion as a creation of humanity in our futile efforts to reach out to God. Christianity, however, is the internal transformation that occurs when one surrenders one's life to the sacred urging of the Holy Spirit to accept the God who has already accepted us and to worship that God alone. The difference between religion and Christianity is that, in the former, human beings take the initiative, but in the latter, it is God that does it. Nwaeze believes that God the Father, God the Son and God the Holy Spirit dwell in every Christian. Religion may introduce humanity to God, but it is true Christianity that introduces God to humanity through the incarnation of Jesus Christ in his life, death and resurrection.

Edwin Nwaeze conveyed to me the personal testimony of his commitment to this God of redemption and why he would never depart from God because of God's gracious overture and faithfulness to him.

Despite having scarce financial resources, in 2004, Nwaeze took a leap of faith and purchased a piece of property he had seen along a road he travelled. He had earlier heard a word from God saying that he would own a property. As the owner and Nwaeze walked the property together, the owner assured Nwaeze that he would sell the land to him. That was eighteen years ago and, as Nwaeze told me, he and his wife are happy where God has put them and have never been in want since then. When asked whether most Lagosian Christians live in poverty, Nwaeze remarked that we misunderstand poverty as lack of money. Instead, he thinks that it is the outlook of one's heart that determines whether a person is rich or poor. Those who are arrogant and bent on making money at all costs, and those who are greedy are denounced by God, according to the Bible. The Nigerian politicians that make money by embezzling public funds are not rich because they do not have treasures in heaven where it really matters. They are denounced by God, and they will never have peace of mind. On the other hand, those who are humble, and look forward to the coming of the Kingdom of God, experience an abundance of joy and contentment. Because to be rich in life is to have peace of mind that passes all understanding. 'Blessed are the poor in spirit' who reflect the Kingdom of God to come. Nwaeze sees only a life without Jesus Christ that is a life of poverty. Although one may not have money or material possessions, if one is humble and has peace in one's heart and joy in one's family, one is wealthy because God abides in one's heart. Poverty is not defined by one's earthly possessions; a person who has millions of dollars but is arrogant, greedy and exploitative is a poor person.

Nwaeze insists only God can give us peace and joy, and no one can be truly happy in life unless he knows God, who took the initiative for human redemption. He reiterates that Christ made a difference in his life, and he will continue to trust God. It is not a theoretical idea for one to follow Christ, but a practical endeavour through life experiences. He said he would not recoil from God as the Old Testament Israelites did when they complained and expressed the desire to return to Egypt even as Moses was leading them out of slavery. The life he now lives is directed by the Holy Spirit. Life in Egypt must have been 'monotonous, dangerous, reckless and unsustainable', he stated. He cannot derive joy, or peace of mind, contentment and sustainability in a figurative 'Egypt', and there is no going back there, meaning he will follow Christ all the days of his life.

Nwaeze sees his business of selling tyres as a form of ministry because it puts him in contact with customers, thus providing him with endless opportunities to share the Gospel. He feels that through the business, he can touch the hearts of those whose lives have been broken, helping transform them for the glory of God.

As we talked, Nwaeze spoke of the raven, regarded as a distant and selfish bird. Yet God commanded that ravens feed the prophet Elijah, and the birds obeyed God. He sees those who only turn to their fellow mortals for help and security, be it financial or emotional, as really wasting their time and energy. Only the God who created us can heal us and help us unconditionally. We are all wounded and fragile and only God can provide the security we need. It has been a great gain for him to know Christ.

Before I left his home the evening we met, Edwin Nwaeze made one final point describing his faith in Christ as a businessman in Lagos. He had once promised his children that by Christmas Eve 2022, he would give each a monetary gift that would surprise them.[1] This promise was made totally in faith as he did not know where these gifts would come from. He had in mind the designated amount he would give to each of his four children. On December 23, someone called him with a lucrative business deal and the profit of that transaction was equal to the amount he had decided to give his children on Christmas Day.

In telling me this, Nwaeze reiterated that the Christian life is by faith, and not by sight. He reminded me of the encounter Jesus had with Mary and Martha when Lazarus had died. Mary and Martha were sorrowful, but Jesus told them that 'if you believe, you will see'.

I left Edwin Nwaeze's home with the knowledge that in our contemporary culture of 'seeing is believing', the faith of Christians transcends that, and God is more than what our eyes can see. Faith in God can rise above the culture of greed, exploitation and blindness. Perhaps, it is not only our eyes that can be blind, but also our hearts. Nwaeze would not return to the 'Egypt' he had left because he had seen the light of God through Jesus Christ.

Jesus Christ, the Lamb of God

One of the unexpected moments in Lagos was when I encountered an octogenarian who was originally from Ogbomoso and studied at the Nigerian Baptist Theological Seminary. He lives in Lagos and was visiting Yaba Baptist Church when I ran into him. He was openhanded and generous with his time after the worship service, and he was excited that I was writing a book about Christians in the city of Lagos. He desired to share with me a story about the Lamb of God and wanted me to know why Jesus Christ is that Lamb of God that took away the sins of the world at Christmas. I asked if I could include his name in the narrative, but he was modest and desired to be anonymous. Initially I thought his story about the Lamb of God was speculative, but later decided that the 89-year-old man was creative in his imagination, and his story needed to be included in this chapter because of his wealth of experience.

According to him, creation and redemption are linked biblical concepts, and they are the two sides of the same coin of God's love for the world. After God finished the work of creation in six days, using as agents of creation the heavenly hosts, God rested on the seventh day. The agents approached God and requested to see the new world that God had created. Their request, however, was denied. A few months later, the heavenly hosts approached God a second time to grant them the permission to visit the world. God discouraged the agents of creation from visiting the world they co-created with God. But they insisted that it would be a quick visit to the world, and they would return to God. After this repeated request to see the world that God had created, the permission was granted but not without a condition. The agents of God's creation were eager to visit and they told God that they will meet all of God's conditions. God then stated that they will be permitted to go and see the world if they could unseal successfully the four calabash containers in God's possession. The agents of creation gleefully welcomed God's conditionality and were delighted that their humble request was granted at long last. It would be a journey of destiny, and their experience in the world would mean that they knew heaven and the earth by experience.

On the day God handed the first sealed calabash, the angels were delighted as one of them took the sealed calabash from God's hands, trembling as he did so. When the angel opened the container, there was a big and dangerous ram, and he looked scary and pompous. He was arrogant, showing his masculinity with his threatening horns. Some of the archangels in heaven closed their eyes, and some retreated to their camps in heaven. Then God stated to the scanty angels that were present that the world had become scary and dangerous just like the ram, and they would encounter some men and women in the world, as well as other created beings, that would be just like the ram. God then asked if they were still interested in going to visit the world. 'Are you still interested in going?' God asked.

The agents of God's creation were still interested but no one was interested in opening the other three sealed calabash containers that God had prepared for the heavenly hosts. God handed over the second sealed calabash container to an angel, who took it as his hands shook and trembled. When the angel opened it, a big goat appeared, and it was more threatening than the animal that appeared in the first container. The goat started talking down to the angels and was showing off its power and pseudo-might to the heavenly hosts. The angel that opened the calabash was frightened and attempted to release the container but failed. God then warned that the world they desired to visit was full of people who were like the goat in the second sealed calabash container. They believe that they own the world and everything in it. They have gone too far, and they will impose their will and selfish desires on other creatures in their habitation. 'Do you still want to visit the world?' God asked.

The angels complained bitterly that the conditionality God imposed was too harsh for them, but it would still be important for them to visit the world. God then handed over the third sealed calabash container and the archangel opened it and encountered a dangerous rooster with flying wings and an arrogant display of its capacity. The look on its face was threatening and the rooster showed its anger without justification. It was extremely proud simply because it could fly and dominate the surroundings of other creaturely beings. God looked intently and asked the heavenly hosts one more time if they desired to visit the world. No one showed interest or temerity to open the fourth sealed calabash. The desire to visit the universe, however, was undiminished. As the agents kept quiet, God asked again if anyone wanted to open the fourth sealed calabash, but no one volunteered. At that time, the archangel pleaded before God to still grant them the opportunity to see the world although no one would open the sealed container.

After a long silence, God took the sealed calabash and opened it. In the fourth calabash was a little lamb. The lamb was gentle, humble and remained in God's loving hands and without moving.

The man who narrated the story told me that in the past whenever a motorist accidentally ran over a lamb in Lagos, he must stop to pay a respect to the lamb by placing a coin in its mouth or trace the home of the owner to pay compensation. The man did not tell me the interpretation of this story but was excited that he was able to share with me this story with excitement. The last statement the octogenarian made was, 'who can detect or discern God's error, and who can master the wisdom of God?'

We can learn at least three lessons from this story.

First, life on earth is an extension of life beyond this physical realm. When we realize this linkage, we can truly live fully and with a purpose. Second, humility is one of the keys to unlocking the mystery of God's creation. The truth that transforms us is covered with wonder and awe, and to be in sync with that truth is the essence of human existence. Thirdly, the Kingdom of God is not localized and is always within us and around us. When our spiritual eyes and ears become open, we would see and hear the mystery of God in ordinary things. Humanity is trapped for lack of knowledge that God's Kingdom is not localized. The divine nature and connection with the Lamb of God is the essence of life, and he invites us to seek our identity beyond this world. The wisdom of God comes from unexpected places and always in the ordinariness of life. When God's Kingdom is manifested, social and political ranking lose their significance because they are the illusion that trap humanity, and human beings are disillusioned, and they are stuck in a worldly race to be first and the best. But in God's Kingdom and in God's mathematics, the divine truth is that we are all connected, and all the division and comparison we have made are all illusion, separating us from other creaturely beings and our true self and identity with God, and the depth of God's love. The depth of God's love is found in the invitation of the Lamb of God, leading to a personal transformation.

An important Christmas day story: The supremacy of Jesus

One day on the street of Lagos, a young man stopped me to talk about the significance of a particular piece of art in strengthening his Christian faith. We met in front of Yaba Baptist Church at Sabo, and he spoke directly about the power of Jesus Christ in his life and in the life of others. I explained that I came to Lagos to interview Christians in the city for a book, and that I would be delighted to hear what he desired to share with me. He related the following story:

Some years ago, there was a wealthy man who, with his devoted son, shared a passion for collecting art. They had travelled extensively within Nigeria and later around the world, buying only the finest works of art to add to their already impressive collection. Eventually, their collection grew to include pieces that were priceless, including some works of Picasso, Van Gogh, Monet and others. They adorned the walls of the family mansion in Lagos. The widowed father looked on in satisfaction as his beloved son also became an experienced art collector. The son's trained eyes and sharp business mind made the father beam with pride as they dealt with collectors from different parts of the world.

But one year, as the rainy season approached, the region was engulfed by tribal wars, causing the young man's departure to serve his beloved people.

After he had been gone about two-and-a-half years, his father received a telegram that his son was missing in action. The father anxiously awaited more news, fearing that he might never see his son again. Within days, his worst fears were confirmed. The young man had died while rushing a fellow soldier to a nearby hospital for medical attention. Distraught and lonely, the elderly man now faced the upcoming Christmas holidays with anguish and sadness. As he was grieving the death of his son, he was also reminiscing with great sadness how he and his son used to look forward to the joyful season in previous years. But he now knew that his son would never again come into the house. On Christmas morning, the depressed old man was awakened by a knock at his door. As he walked to the door, even the masterpieces of art he saw on the walls reminded him of the son he had lost. He opened the door and was greeted by a soldier with a large package in his hand. Introducing himself to the elderly man, he said, 'Sir, I was a friend of your son's. I was the one he was rescuing when he died. May I come in for a few moments? I have something to show you.' 'I am an artist', the soldier continued, handing him the package. 'And I want to give you this.' As the old man unwrapped the package, the paper gave way to a portrait of the man's son. While the art world would have never considered it the work of a genius, the painting featured the beloved younger man's face in striking detail.

Overcome with emotion, the man thanked the soldier, promising to hang the picture above the fireplace in the living room. A few hours after the soldier had departed, the old man set about his task. True to his words, the painting went above the fireplace, pushing aside several of the most valuable paintings known to humanity. The father sat in his chair, spending his Christmas Day gazing at this gift given by the friend of his beloved son who had saved his comrade in battle. It was only later on that the father learned about the full extent of his son's impact in the world when he found out his son had rescued dozens of wounded soldiers before a bullet from the enemy entered his loving heart.

During the weeks and months that followed, the painting was a constant reminder that although his son was no longer alive, his memory would continue to live on in the minds of those who had known him because he had lived a purposeful life that redeemed others. He had inspired those who knew him to live the kind of life that could transform the lives of others.

As the story of his son's gallantry continued to spread, the father's pride in his son began to ease his pangs of grief. The painting became his most prized possession, far eclipsing any interest in the pieces for which museums around Africa and the world clamoured. He told his neighbours it was the greatest gift he had ever received from anyone.

The following rainy season came, and the old man fell ill and passed away. The art world was filled with anticipation. According to the old man's will, all the artworks would be auctioned on Christmas Day, which was also the birthday of his beloved son. When the day arrived, art collectors from around the world gathered to bid on some of the world's most spectacular paintings.

The auction began with a painting that was not originally on any museum's list. It was the portrait of the man's son. The auctioneer asked, 'Who will open the bidding with one thousand naira?' The room was silent. Minutes passed and no one spoke. Finally, from the back of the room came a sneering voice, 'Who cares about that painting? It is just a picture of his son. Let's forget about that and go to the good stuff.'

Other voices in the room echoed in agreement.

'No', replied the auctioneer. 'We have to sell this one first.'

'Now who will take this painting?'

Finally, a friend of the old man spoke, 'Will you take 100 naira for the painting?' he said. 'That is all that I have. But I knew the boy, so I would like to have it.'

'Will anyone bid higher?' called out the auctioneer in desperation. After a deafening silence, the auctioneer said, 'Going once, going twice, gone.' The gavel fell as cheer filled the room, and someone exclaimed, 'Now we can get on with it and bid on these treasures!'

But the auctioneer looked at the audience and announced that the auction was over. Stunned disbelief quieted the room.

Someone spoke up and asked, 'What do you mean it's over? We didn't come here for a picture of some old man's son! What about all these paintings? There are pieces of art here worth millions of naira of art here! I demand that you explain what is going on here!'

The auctioneer replied firmly, 'It is very simple. According to the father's will, the person who buys the painting of his son, gets the entire collection.'

Summary

Those who are committed Christians tend to see the miraculous results of living for Jesus Christ day by day. Nothing seems to separate them or deter them from trusting God, whose unconditional love they have experienced in many circumstances.

11

My relationship with God is covenantal, not transactional

In the chapter, Toyin Sylvester Sawyerr opined that traditional religions are often transactional – a belief that has crept insidiously into the understanding of Christianity in Lagos. Sawyerr also maintains in the chapter that a person who knows the unconditional love of God would not reject God's divine call. The call of God is not about hell, but heaven; it is not about doing, but being, and it is not about the God who was, but about the God who is yet to come.

Introduction

Toyin Sylvester Sawyerr lives near Lagos with his family and was eager to give me an analysis of his experience as a devoted Christian in Lagos. He maintains that there have been three identifiable stages of his covenantal relationship with God. His opinion is like that of many Christians I encountered on the streets of Lagos.

In the first place, Sawyerr believes that Jesus came not to begin a religion, but to give abundant life to those who follow him faithfully. Jesus came to introduce God to humanity, and this is why Sawyerr says he is a follower of Jesus Christ.

Sawyerr is a church historian in his own right and one of the intellectuals I met in Lagos. He shared with me that the history of Christianity in Lagos has many overlapping stages of development and that it is now experiencing a period of transition. The church, he believes, is between the past and the future. He believes that after the African experience, it would be difficult to see Christianity the same way. Christianity has had a profound influence on Lagosian culture, but the culture has also transformed how Christianity is expressed and practised. The Christian intellectual framework that shaped theology in former times has been challenged, with non-Western Christian church historians and scholars questioning the doctrinal certainties of the past.

Historical developments of contemporary Christians in Lagos

Sawyerr sees the transformation of Christianity as most evident in Lagos. Since the Second World War (1939–45), one can identify three overlapping stages of Christian development in the city. The first stage is emotional, characterized by an uncritical acceptance of the Western understanding of the Gospel in the cultural accoutrements of European missionaries. This stage is also marked by a 'donor versus receptor' paradigm. Earlier African theologians viewed Christianity as a 'weapon' rather than a 'tool', because, under colonialism, it was associated with certain benefits available only to those who embraced it but not to those who chose not to convert. Few of the people I interviewed in Lagos framed their Christian experience in such categorical terms as Sawyerr did. He maintained that the period between 1960 and 1975 was 'the most remarkable years' of Christian success and expansion in Nigeria because of the overwhelming response of young Lagosian to its advocates. This resulted in church growth in Lagos and the surrounding boroughs. Most other Nigerians, however, merely added the new faith to the already existing structures of their traditional religions, giving little thought to their inevitable reframing of Christianity's essential teachings according to the familial traditional religious idioms.

There was a strong desire to replace the existing traditional religions with Christianity, often causing a rote acceptance of Western theological categories to follow. This raises the question of how successful Nigerian Christians were in dealing with the coexistence of their Christian and traditional African identities. How were they supposed to express their new Christianity in the particularities of their cultural contexts? Could the free and translatable Gospel be incorporated into their cultural traditions? These questions were never completely answered.

The second stage, according to Sawyerr, is characterized by an intense examination, not only of Christianity but also of African traditional religious practices and spiritual beliefs. Africans came face-to-face with one dilemma: how to affirm the eloquence of their indigenous religious heritage while practising Christianity at the same time. Outsiders and observers of Christians in Lagos often fail to recognize the tension existing between traditional African Christian expression and the practice of Western Christianity over their own indigenous paradigms. At the same time, Nigerian believers, especially those in Lagos, affirmed the transformational character of the Gospel. According to Sawyerr, the Church in Africa produced some of the most brilliant theologians of the modern era. The list includes John S. Mbiti, E. Bolaji Idowu, Jean-Marc Ela, Bénézet Bujo, Osadolor Imasogie, Mercy Amba Oduyoye, Charles Nyamiti, Ogbu Kalu, Kwame Bediako, Canaan Banana, Charles Villa-Vicencio, Aylward Shorter, Byang Kato, Tokunbo Adeyemo, Kwame Anthony Appiah and Gabriel M. Setiloane.

Many of these theologians began to raise one fundamental question: 'How can the Christian faith be presented and reinterpreted so that we can hear God in Jesus Christ addressing us in our own particular contexts and circumstances without going through the intermediary of non-African acculturation?' The assumption behind this question is that Africans could not achieve the full depth of their spiritual maturity unless their faith was directed by the influence and eloquence of their own existential realities. Today's Lagosian Christians are a product of this theological direction, discarding the ideas of European acculturation. They claimed that final judgement and decision-making regarding ecclesiastical and spiritual or theological matters in Africa should not be handed down by arbiters from different cultural and ancestral backgrounds.

In January 1966, a consultation of African theologians was held at Immanuel College in Ibadan, Nigeria, under the auspices of the All-African Conference of Churches (AACC), and there were participants from different parts of the continent, including Roman Catholic priests from African universities and representatives of the World Council of Churches, with a clearly defined goal:

> [To express] a deep longing that the Churches of Africa might have an opportunity of thinking together of the Christian faith which had come to them from the older Churches of the West and through missionaries of a different cultural background who, in the nature of things, could not fully appreciate the reactions of their converts to their faith in light of their own traditional beliefs and practices.[1]

They made a declaration that gave a signal for the second stage of theological development in Africa:

> We believe that the God and father of our Lord Jesus Christ, Creator of heaven and earth, Lord of History, has been dealing with [hu]mankind at all times and in all parts of the world. It is with this conviction that we study the rich heritage of our African peoples, and we have evidence that they know of Him and worshiped Him. We recognized the radical quality of God's self-revelation in Jesus Christ; and yet it is because of this revelation we can

discern what is truly of God in our pre-Christian heritage; this knowledge of God is not totally discontinuous with our people's previous traditional knowledge of Him.[2]

Approximately two decades later, Jean-Marc Ela echoed these African theologians in *My Faith as an African* (1985):

> If the faith of Africans is not to die, it must become a vision of the world that they can feel is theirs: European cultural orientations must be stripped away. There is an urgent need to reject present foreign models of [Christian] expression if we are to breathe new life into the spoken Word. Our church must experience a Passover of language, or the meaning of the Christian message will not be understood.
>
> One of the primary tasks of Christian reflection in black Africa is to totally reformulate our basic faith through the mediation of African culture.[3]

We learn a fundamental truth about the developments of Christianity in Africa from these two stages. There was a strong desire of Africans to 'indigenize' their faith and make it a 'place to feel at home'. While scholars in this field of studies have seen African Independent Churches as a movement 'founded in Africa, by Africans, and primarily for Africans' (Harold W. Turner), Sawyerr sees it differently and provides a theological modification to this view. He states that Christians who live in Lagos are experiencing a third stage of Christian rebirth, which demonstrates that the Christian faith has developed a firmer footing when it is infused with African idioms and ethos, and I found this to be quite evident during my time in Lagos.

The autonomy of the Church in Lagos

Sawyerr remains one of the leading voices in the third stage of Christian development in Lagos. In his opinion, the distinction Christians have drawn between the African world view and God's revelation in Christ during the formative years of Christianity is not as sharply delineated as we have been led to believe. God's revelation is carried out through concrete human religious or spiritual experiences. Through his service as a church leader in Lagos, he has determined that the Christian faith has developed firm roots within African idioms and an African ethos, with Christians in Lagos to stay.

When we were initially introduced, I thought of Toyin Sylvester Sawyerr as belonging to the second stage of the historical development of Christianity in Lagos. But further conversation suggested that he does not belong to the second or even the third stage of that development. He believes Christian teachings will continue to build upon and be nurtured continuously by the elements of the 'pre-Christian' African spiritual environment and cultural context. There are few African scholars who fall into this category. Sawyerr, with his unique perspective, should be regarded as a pioneer of a new interpretation of Christianity in Lagos. While contemporary scholars often consider that European missionaries 'Christianized' Africans, Sawyerr believes that in his own life and in that of many other believers that Christianity in Lagos has been 'Africanized'. Lagosian Christians are the main actors in the life and mission of the church today, and they take seriously the African cosmological vision as they craft an authentic relationship with God.

If one sees this as the third stage, Sawyerr belongs to it; but he does not like Christians to be categorized in such a chronological light. The Christian faith often creates its own landing space in the hearts of the faithful, unlike an aeroplane with a predetermined place to land. The coming of Christ to the heart of the faithful is more like a bomb that makes its own landing place through the Holy Spirit.

Before I left his residence that afternoon, Sawyerr had raised some fundamental questions about the development of Christianity in Africa: How can Africans become full-fledged partners in theological discussions? How can they make uniquely African contributions to the greater stream of Christian tradition, without simply regurgitating the positions of Western Christian theology or patterns of Christian knowledge?

These questions have dominated his life as a church leader in Lagos. He uses the term *Christianities* to describe the Christian phenomenon in Lagos, which he sees as a microcosm of the early church itself. He sees Christianity as a multicultural world religion, which has blossomed in many cultures, unadulterated by any subversive hegemonic control and galvanized by new missionary impulses crisscrossing the globe in exciting new ways.[4] Christianity in the twenty-first century, therefore, is a multi-dimensional and 'multi-centred reality', comprised of interconnecting networks and communities. One of the most insightful comments Sawyerr made about contemporary Christianity is that 'Christians should feel at home everywhere because of the mystery of the incarnation, but they should not feel comfortable anywhere because of the eschatological emphasis which is geared towards the longing for Christ's return.' Accordingly, one cannot fully understand Christianity today apart from the experience of Christians from a variety of different cultures, especially those of the Global South. He maintains that 'the currents flowing from Asia, Africa and Latin America are the font of the Christian mainstream of the 21st century. A smug neglect or blatant disregard of the Christian movements of the Global

South underestimates the rising tide of the various movements within contemporary World Christianity.'

The autonomy of the Church in Lagos emanates from Sawyerr's philosophy that no one church can represent the whole of Christendom, no matter how great and grandiose it is in historical origin and proclamation. Lagosian Christians represent, therefore, an indirect protest of the assumed superiority or infallibility of the Church in the Global North, especially in the projection of universality. He quotes from the historical Church of Armenia that 'no Church, however great in herself, represents the whole of Christendom; that each one, taken singly, can be mistaken, and that to the Universal Church alone belongs the privilege of infallibility in dogmatic decisions.'[5]

Christians in Lagos are a fraternity in a conglomeration of other churches in the world, such as the Church of England or Armenia. All are a part of Christendom and only when all the churches are in unity, can it be said that the Church represents the Glory of God. Indeed, to the Universal Church alone belongs the privilege of infallibility in teaching, worship and dogmatic character. The Church of the future will continue to develop as a collective of separate entities along cultural and historical ecclesiastical lines, yet be knit together by characteristics that include the common rituals of baptism by water, holy communion, reading of the Scriptures and an emphasis on the ultimate significance of the Lord Jesus Christ.

Sawyerr sees the transformation of the world as the highest purpose of the Christian life and that of the Church. While life in the church often focusses on heaven and how to get there, Jesus talked more frequently about the transformation of *this* world. This is because human beings are not only estranged and disconnected from God, but they are also alienated from each other. Jesus placed greater value on turning towards God than he did on human religion understood as a doctrine. Religions can be useful as catalysts when they are leading human beings to God. Jesus's emphasis was on having faith in God and demonstrating extravagant love to people created in God's image. Sawyerr contends that Christ challenges the world to reflect the Kingdom of God he came to proclaim. The Luke's Gospel recorded a story in Chapter 15. The story highlights the significance of making peace between God and humanity. Such a peace is an actual present human possibility for all humanity. Many Christians have labelled this story as 'the Parable of the Prodigal Son' (and the elder brother), but Sawyerr believes that it can be more accurately seen as a parable of a tenacious and loving father.

In our conversations, Toyin Sylvester Sawyerr frequently cited Luke 15, which records the story of the two brothers and their loving father, often called the Parable of the Prodigal Son, stating that what the two brothers did not realize was that the father was vigilant and constantly looking over his children. While the elder brother did not realize the value of being at home with his father, the younger son took the father for granted. To the older son, the father showed his embracing hand, while never abandoning the younger son, even while he was away.

The Gospel of Jesus Christ transcends any limits that we have imposed upon it. The Good News of Jesus Christ stands above any ancient thoughts and modern visions for the world. While fulfilling the promise and the vision of the Old Testament, it transcends the Hebrew Bible and its prophetic tradition at the same time. That which was a dream, a promise and an aspiration in the Hebrew Bible becomes an achievable gift to humanity through Jesus Christ. What the ancients never thought possible became a gift and an actual possession for humanity through the life and ministry of Jesus Christ. The parables of Jesus Christ were replete with examples from the culture of his days to show humanity a new way, providing a new vision from God, which is good for the world. This new vision proclaimed by Jesus means that all forms of prejudice will be abandoned. The *Kerygma* or proclamation in this story is the message perexcellence of Jesus Christ, transcending religious rules and human logic. Thus, prejudice and discrimination are inconsistent and antithetical to the *Kerygma* of love and redemption. Discrimination is inconsistent with God's vision of love and unity and will not be a part of the Messianic Age. The Kingdom of God as portrayed by Jesus Christ will welcome home God's children, whether Jew or Gentile, male or female, black or white, slave or free.

One of the best parables in the Gospels and Lagos Christians

Sawyerr perceives this story in Luke's Gospel as one of the best parables of Jesus in the Gospels. When I asked him to tell me why he thought so, he was excited, saying that the young son behaved like a typical Lagosian or a teenager, no longer interested in living with his father.

In fact, the young boy behaved like a typical Lagosian or a teenager nowadays. It can be said that many people in Lagos could identify with this younger son leaving his home and becoming a sojourner. He was no longer interested in living with his father. He was likely handsome, ambitious, impatient, prone to risk-taking and reckless. He was also arrogant and overconfident, selfishly clinging to his demands. He was ready to challenge the authority of his caring father, and he was not going to take 'no' for an answer. He wanted his father to release him from the family obligations he had known from birth. He wanted to explore the territory beyond the confines of his present environment. He could not wait. The goal of this younger son was summed up neatly in a single request: 'Father, give me the share of the property that will belong to me when you die.' It was obvious that he wanted his father out of the way so that he could enjoy his life without constraints. The father did not argue with his younger son but gave in to his reckless demands. So, the younger son, now free to live as he wished, left home and went to a distant place where no one knew his name or his family origins. There was no one to see him or tell him that his father was looking for him. He spent everything as if his resources were unlimited. His preparation for the future was sketchy, and his hedonistic lifestyle soon left him wanting and he was trapped. Even in his recklessness, he still never lost sight of what it had been like at home. He did not forget the values of his father. Although he had left home, his home never left him. Coming to his senses, he rued his choices and decided to return home.

It must have been a difficult decision to swallow his pride and decide to ask his father's forgiveness. So, he shifted into a gear he never knew he possessed. He rehearsed ahead of time what he would say upon his return, hoping for reconciliation with his father. His humility was impressive and, perhaps, countercultural.

Sawyerr insisted one of the greatest virtues in this life is humility. This younger son had a strong conviction to leave home. But he also later had the courage to admit the mistake of that conviction. Courage is the archetype of all virtues and the mother of all the rest. Courage cannot exist in isolation as a single trait without related traits such as patience, humility, perseverance, endurance and confidence. The younger son was probably anticipating that he would be rejected. And in his humility, he said, 'Father, I have sinned against heaven and before you. I am no longer worthy to be called your son; treat me like one of your hired hands.'

Where he had expected justice, he received mercy as his father welcomed his return with open arms. He had anticipated rebuke but received a joyous welcome in a warm embrace. While probably thinking he would never be loved again, he received royal treatment.

Sawyerr's interpretation of this parable of a loving father is profound. He sees our father in heaven as not a God of reward and punishment; he is not a God in the business of rejecting those who have failed. There is always the joy of homecoming when we come to God through Jesus Christ. Where we are coming from is not as important to God as where we are heading. We might perhaps imagine that when this younger son became an adult in his forties or fifties, and his father was looking for one of the two boys to send back into the world to proclaim the enduring values of humility and forgiveness, the father would be more inclined to send this same younger son who had rebelled against the father when he was a teenager. After all, this younger son would know the language and ways of the world. He would be more effective because he knew the defining characteristics of those who are homeless. One of the greatest reminders Sawyerr taught me that afternoon is that in God's Garden of grace, even crooked trees can bear good fruits.

We can also learn from the example of the older son, who was unlike his younger brother. They did not share the same values. The older son was constantly at home complaining, seeing his father as a superior he must obey and then be rewarded. While he was loyal to his father, he was just as arrogant as the younger son because he took his reward for granted. He pretended to be at home, but in many ways, he was far away from home. His relationship with his father was transactional. He honoured the requirements of his duty, but only for what he could gain in return.

Summary

Sawyerr posed several hypothetical questions: Why do Christians go to church every day in Lagos? Why do Christians pray without season? Why do Christians sing in the choir? Why are Christians at home with God? His answer: We do the work of ministry because God deserves it, and it has intrinsic value to worship the redeemer faithfully as is the result of obedience to God's command. The older son wanted to please the father at all costs. He loved his father, but not his younger brother, whom his father loved. How can we love God, but be indifferent towards those whom God loves? We do not read in the story that the older son pleaded with his younger brother not to leave home. Perhaps, he was happy that he would no longer have a rival at home. He was just as selfish as his younger brother. While he did not want to go away, the older son wanted to have all that remained to himself. When his younger brother returned home, the elder brother did not participate in the joy of his father but was sad and deflated. Sibling rivalry would resume. In his self-righteous arrogance, he refused to join in the welcome-home celebration, using the disdainful term 'your son' when speaking to his father about his brother. His self-righteousness and anger caused him to boycott the party.

Sawyerr believes that the story is not only about these two sons but also a story about a loving father. It is in fact a picture of our heavenly Father who never gives up seeking his lost sons and daughters in the world.

The two sons were both guilty of arrogance, but the father forgave their sins and offered them a second chance. In this parable, we see in God a capacity for reconciliation, redemption and restoration that has no equal. We also see that any form of prejudice is inconsistent with God's redemptive love.

It is God's grace that redeems our sinful natures. The sins of the two sons in the story were different, but a loving father forgave them both. God accepts us as His sinful children into His heavenly kingdom, even with all our weaknesses. God's love and forgiveness do not discriminate – just as the father in the story loved both his sons unconditionally thus securing their future happiness, which shows us that forgiveness is not about the past but about the future.

Toyin Sylvester Sawyerr opined that traditional religions are often transactional – a belief that has crept insidiously into the understanding of Christianity in Lagos. The message of Luke in telling this parable is that the God who loves also has incessant desires for the return of his children. If a person knows the unconditional love of God, it would be difficult to reject God's divine call. The call of God is not about hell, but heaven; it is not about doing, but being, and it is not about the God who was, but about the God who is yet to come.

12

My Lagos experience of God's faithfulness

Introduction

Samson Abolade Alabi and his wife, Victoria Oluwabunmi Alabi, are some of the most dedicated Christians whom I came to know in Lagos. Any story that deals with how Christians live and work in this most populous of Nigerian cities would be incomplete without their story. Although I had known the family for a long time, this book project brought us even closer. During my frequent trips to Lagos to conduct the ethnographic interviews and research leading to the writing of this book, the couple opened their home to me, and I often stayed with their young family, including Samson, Victoria and their three children. When Samson shared with me the story of his family, I marvelled at what God was doing in the life of this young couple.

At the beginning of our conversation, he told me, 'I'm that little boy from Ikirun, Osun State, who has been helped by God.'

In early 2003, when already in Lagos, Samson met his future wife while shopping in a supermarket owned by Victoria's aunt, Dayo. Although their first meeting was simple, it was unforgettable because of the way Victoria assisted Samson at the supermarket. She was friendly and confident and treated Samson as though he were the only customer there. Suspecting that Victoria was probably living with her aunt, Dayo, Samson quietly asked the aunt if the girl was dating anyone at the time. When Dayo confirmed that Victoria was not only free to date, but that she was also a hard-working and respectable young lady, loved by all of Dayo's customers, Samson quickly became interested in her.

Men in Lagos are hard-working and often like to impress their girlfriends with material goods. And if they have the means, they might choose to lavish their girlfriends with gifts, such as nice cars. As Samson's relationship with Victoria was beginning to flourish, his landlord approached him and asked if he was interested in purchasing a plot of land at Magboro, on the outskirts of Lagos. Apparently, the landlord had been watching Samson and saw him as a dedicated and serious-minded Christian with ambition unlike any of his other tenants. He was so impressed by Samson that he decided to invest in the young man's future.

Samson went to see the piece of land that was being offered to him and was quite impressed. By that time, he had saved enough money to buy a car and solve his transportation problem in Lagos. His desire to impress Victoria by buying a nice car with the money that could be used to purchase the land, however, nagged at him. Taking public transportation or carpooling to work each day was common among workers in Lagos. Distances could be up to 40 miles, which might be a journey of three hours or more because of the traffic jams or 'go slows' as slow traffic is called in Lagos. So, what should Samson do as a man in love with Victoria? It occurred to him to discuss his dilemma with Victoria, who suggested that it would be better to buy the land, a decision shared with his landlord. In no time, Samson had paid for the plot but continued to use public transportation to and from work. What sweetened the pill, though, was the thought that Victoria was not a 'gold digger' but a farsighted, prudent and serious young woman, perfect as his wife.

When Samson had asked Victoria her surname, he was pleasantly surprised to find it was the same as his own, although Victoria was originally from Issua-Akoko in Ondo State. Not too long after that, Samson proposed to Victoria and the two became engaged. The wedding day was set for 11 September 2004, at Foursquare Gospel Church at Soluyi in Gbagada, Lagos.

Christian wedding ceremonies in Lagos

Weddings in Lagos are often a mix of traditional customs and elements of a Christian ceremony. The Western way of celebrating weddings has not been successfully exported to Lagos in its entirety. In fact, some of the wedding traditions among the Yoruba people, for example, have now been exported to the Western world with modifications. One example is the common practice of showering the newlyweds with money as they are dancing. This is a popular custom in Lagos, meant to bless the new couple on their wedding day. In Western cities where there is a large population of Nigerians, such as Houston, Atlanta, New York City, Los Angeles, Chicago or London, it is a common practice at wedding ceremonies to shower the newlyweds with US dollars or British pounds. Also, at wedding celebrations, it is common to serve food that includes jollof rice, akara, chin-chin, puff-puff, moin-moin, egusi soup and pounded yam and amala and ewedu soup, as the bride and groom dance at the occasion to the delight of their guests.

The ancient custom of polygyny, in which one man is married to several women, is prevalent in Africa in general, and among the Yoruba people in particular, and has survived a long time.[1] There is little in African culture, however, that promotes the institution of polygyny. Monogamy is seen not so much as a purer alternative to polygyny, as it is according to the interpretation by the Protestant Church in the Western world, where it is regarded as a form of spirituality among priests because it more closely approximates celibacy.[2]

While in Lagos, I listened to a story by an elderly man about the origin of polygyny in an African agrarian culture, which is identical to the nomadic patriarchal society of the Old Testament. He told me that tsetse flies had decimated the herds, making it difficult to keep cattle. Thus, mothers had resorted to feeding their infants exclusively with their own breast milk, rather than routinely feeding the infants with the milk of cows and goats – continuing for three years, or until the baby could walk. This then resulted in serious demands on breast milk which led to a postpartum sex taboo that mandated that mothers were not to have sex with their husbands for three years while breastfeeding. Consequently, lactating mothers had to find additional wives for their husbands to keep them from going to prostitutes and that led to polygyny. While this cultural interpretation continues to dominate societal norms among Lagosians, the Christian interpretation of a monogamous relationship has prevailed among Christians, as in the case of Samson and Victoria.[3]

Most men in Lagos look for women of marriageable age who are attractive, humble, compassionate, dexterous and intelligent. Christian women are often attracted to men who demonstrate generosity, a protective, caring nature and who are God-fearing. The average age for marriage for women is twenty-two, and most begin to get anxious if they remain single at age twenty-eight. For men, on the other hand, the age of twenty-seven is considered ideal, but nowadays, economic stability has become a major factor for marriage for both men and women considering marriage.

Additionally, most Lagosians live under the shadow of their parents before they get married, and males are considered mature enough to live on their own when they have a steady job with adequate income to take care of their wives. Parents take interest in possible marriage candidates for their unmarried children, often preferring that their children marry within the same ethnic group. But today's young Christians see Christianity, rather than tribal connections, as a bond that transcends cultural boundaries or ethnic particularities.

Wedding negotiations

Christian weddings in Lagos require a complex negotiation between the two extended families. Unlike in the Western world, marriage is not considered to be merely a union between the two individuals but an alliance of two extended families. Often the marriage ceremony means blending of Christian and traditional wedding rituals. Most Christians in Lagos see both as important, feeling that Christianity does not negate the customary demands of traditional wedding negotiations. Weddings among Christians are incomplete without a combination of traditional ceremonies and church service, and 'bride price', or dowry, is paid by the groom's family to the family of the bride.

On the wedding day, many in Lagos sing and dance, waving their hands in joyful celebration. As I stayed in various hotels in Lagos, I often had the opportunity to witness some amazing wedding parties. Parents often prefer traditional wedding celebrations, as they honour time-worn customs, such as blessing their sons and daughters by laying hands upon them. When a mother blesses her daughter, her words might include elements of advice, as the bride is about to make her home with the bridegroom:

- Choose your future destination with determination.

- Do not hurry to get to your destination.

- You will arrive soon enough because destiny will follow you.

- Every now and then, allow yourself to wander the back roads and forgotten paths.

- Keep your destination in your heart like the fixed point of a compass.

- Be a godly and virtuous woman and a caring mother.

- Accept what you can do in your new home.

- Be content with what you can't do.

- Accept the past as past and see the future as future.

- Let love guide your presence.

- Do not measure your worth by what you possess.

- Measure your success by what you can do without.

- Always remember that life is more than the number of cars you have parked on the main street.

- Measure life by how high you can rise after you hit rock bottom.

- Learn to receive God's forgiveness.

- Learn to forgive others and learn to forgive yourself.

- Forgiveness will demand all of you; it will require faith, hope and love.

- When you understand everything, you can forgive others.

- Forgiveness is not about discarding the past, but about enlarging the future.

- Ignore the abuse and let go of yesterday.

- When two elephants fight, the only thing that suffers is the grass.

Before the end of the wedding ceremony, the bride often requests the blessing of the elders of the family. The elders now use Christian vocabulary to do so, since Christian symbolism has been incorporated into traditional wedding ceremonies in Lagos. Quite often, the bride's requests may go as follows:

- Bless me before I depart to my husband.

- Pray that I may be prosperous and fruitful with children.

- Pray that I may be blessed with kind helpers and dependents.

- Pray that my wardrobe is well-fitted.

- Pray the burglars will never rob me of my earthly possessions.

- If you were to ask a masquerader to accompany me,

- The masquerader will, in due course, return to the ancestors.

- If you were to ask Orisa to escort and accompany me,

- Orisa will, in due course, go back to the shrines of the gods.

- But pray that destiny will escort and accompany me as

- Destiny is the only genuine and worthy companion.

- Let destiny follow me to my inner chambers and be my partner.

- Destiny will remain with me forever!

The blessings of the elder in marriage

Nothing is more important than the blessings of the most senior member of the family. It is something that all the wedding guests look forward to. I vividly recall the one I heard at a Lagos wedding ceremony. It took the form of a story told by the elder in the family of the bride and was as follows:

There are many attractive calabash gourds in the garden of life. On entering the garden, you are going to see some that will beckon to you, 'Pluck me; iyawo, please pluck me.' But there would also be other gourds that would be perfectly calm and remarkably peaceful. They will be silent. You will be wise and successful in life if you discipline yourself to ignore the alluring invitation of the clamorous gourds. For in them is deceit and hatred, as well as everything that can cause you suffering and grief. The noisy and boisterous gourds could cause you embarrassment and harm you even though they appear attractive and want you to pluck them. In the quiet ones are all that rejoices the heart and will bring you happiness and delight. For you to be victorious in life, you must listen to the inner voices of the quiet gourds. In them is your destiny, your kadara.

Those who tell lies often do so loudly and forcefully. Remember the song: 'A o merin joba, eweku ewele'.[4] The voice of truth, however, is often weak but consistent.

Samson and Victoria cherish their Yoruba culture, and they, too, incorporated some aspects of it into their wedding in Lagos. The early stage of their marriage demonstrates how God was with them and helped the newlyweds in the challenges common to a new couple.

Early stages of marriage and first pregnancy

The faith of Samson and Victoria in God is strong and life-giving. When Victoria was pregnant with their first child, the pregnancy was fraught with challenges because of fibroids she developed. They are benign tumours made up of fibrous and muscular tissue that exist especially in the uterine wall. When the stomach pains caused by fibrosis[5] would not subside, the couple sought medical attention. Their first healthcare provider examined Victoria and determined that the fibroid had grown big, affecting the healthy development of the fetus in her uterus . He stated that little could be done and perhaps the alternative was termination of the pregnancy. When they got home that day, Victoria continued to have serious pains, and the couple decided to seek a second opinion. Dr Gabriel Akindele Akilo, their second physician, is an obstetrician and gynaecologist and the medical director at Good Tidings Specialist Hospital at Surulere, Lagos. When he was first acquainted with Victoria's condition, he offered prayers and examined her thoroughly. He gave them a word of assurance that God would help her carry the pregnancy to full term and that everything would work out fine. In their native tongue, he asked, 'Se iyen naa l'o wa fa ekun?' Is that why you are crying?

This second physician attended to the couple faithfully throughout the pregnancy. On the day of delivery, Victoria was at the Good Tidings Specialist Hospital at Surulere, after having travelled a long distance. A short time after they arrived at the clinic, a baby girl was born. She was named Moyosore, meaning 'I rejoice in the gift of God'. The birth of Moyosore Adenike Alabi is a testimony confirming what the Lord can do through the hands of a Christian physician with strong faith. While doctors can care for their patients, it is God alone who heals. Moyosore, who was born in December 2005, grew up to study law at Bowen University, one of the top Nigerian Christian universities.

In August 2008, Samson and Victoria had another baby girl who was born at Redeemed Hospital in Lagos. When the couple arrived, it was late at night, and there was a moment of anxiety. Samson called in Dr Gabriel Akindele Akilo, who had delivered their first daughter. He told him that Victoria was in labour. Knowing Victoria's medical history, the doctor did not hesitate to make the night-time drive alone to meet the couple at Redeemed Hospital in Ikeja, fully gowned, with a stethoscope hanging around his neck, as if he were on call. Although the baby was safely delivered before his arrival, his coming was meaningful. It demonstrated that he was a Christian doctor with a passion for the well-being of his patients. The physician often goes the extra mile to care for his patients wherever they might be admitted in need of medical care. The family named this baby Mojola Adeola Alabi. She would later study nursing at Trinity University in Lagos.

After the birth of their two daughters, Victoria tried to have more children for several years without success. She started praying fervently for a male child as her third. Samson shared with me that although she desired to have a male child, he kept reminding Victoria that all children are from God and that the family had been blessed with two beautiful girls. He further stated that he was unconcerned with the gender of the babies that God has given them, unlike many Nigerian fathers.

Victoria did get pregnant again, but it was a difficult pregnancy because of Victoria's recurring health challenges, and there was doubt that she would carry it to full term. But the birth proved to be quite a miracle. Although they had been seeing an obstetrician near them, Victoria preferred the elderly physician who had once prayed with her during the pregnancy of Moyosore. So, after the water broke, the couple travelled to the same experienced doctor, now elderly, at Surulere. In the labour room, when their baby boy was born, the infant did not move or cry. The couple started to panic, and Victoria especially became anxious, but the doctor told them not to worry. As he massaged the baby's back, the child began to cry. Tears of joy ran down Victoria's cheeks. The boy was named Momore, meaning 'I know the gift of God'.

Traditional naming ceremonies for infants in Lagos

Among the various ethnic groups in Lagos, nothing is as important as the birth of new babies and the naming ceremonies that follow. When a baby is born, the infant is not given a name until it is a week old. It is believed that children originate as the ideas of God, which are then passed to the ancestors before they become plans or designs in the minds of their parents, requiring that they be named according to the rules of tradition. Nigerians, and especially the Yoruba people, have a historically high rate of multiple births in the world before the age of fertility pills, and special names are given to twins – Taiwo and Kehinde (first born and second born respectively).

In the naming ceremony, the mother places the baby in the hands of the most senior member of the extended family. An array of natural substances will have been prepared ahead of time. These usually include water, honey, bitter kola, kola nuts, salt and pepper. As the ceremony begins, the leader in the family takes a bowl of water and blesses it, saying, 'This is water, which we drink because our bodies function better when we do. Water is essential to life.' May the body of this new baby function well. In a similar fashion, the leader takes the next substance, perhaps the honey, and blesses it, saying, 'This is honey – the only food that never goes bad.' He then blesses the baby, placing a drop of honey into the mouth of the new baby as he did with the water. He breaks the bitter kola, saying, 'Our ancestors broke the bitter kola, ate it, and lived long, settling disputes as they chewed the bitter kola.' He then blesses the child, praying that the child would also live long. Taking a grain of salt, he would say, 'Salt is a preservative, giving good taste in foods.' He then blesses the child with the wish that his or her life would be pleasant to everyone. And so the ceremony continues as he invokes the names of the family ancestors. Once he has pronounced the baby blessed, he then announces for the first time in public the official name of the baby chosen by the parents. There is no naming ceremony, when done according to the rules and customs of the elders in Yorubaland decorum, that is without the spiritual presence of God in the room. Is this a Christian or a traditional mandate? Many Christians in Lagos would probably say it is both, because there is no contradiction between what is a Christian ritual and what is a traditional ritual in Lagos when one conducts the naming ceremony. It is both religious and traditional simultaneously.

While the tradition of the naming ceremony is fading away in Nigerian cities, this custom is still respected and cherished among many Yoruba people. In some areas of Lagos, the naming ceremony is attended by pastors with some families inviting them to serve as the elder in performing the related rituals, thereby 'Christianizing' the traditional rituals.

Baby outing celebration

It is customary among Lagosian Christians that a month or two after the birth of the baby, the father would approach his pastor to set a date for the church dedication and Christian outing for the baby. The baby outing is significant because it is a time when the parents will begin to share the baby with the community as a member with the potential to make a difference in the life for the glory of God. At this time, the baby would be cared for and nurtured by everyone, young and old, and hence, 'it takes a village to raise a child'.

Summary

Samson and Victoria Alabi met in Lagos, fell in love and got married in 2004. Their marriage was providential and can be seen as a demonstration of God's presence among Christians in Nigeria's most populous city. With the birth of their children and how they have met and overcome the challenges in their lives, we see an inspiring example of how faithful human beings can cooperate with destiny for the glory of God.

Conclusion

A summation of what I have seen and heard in Lagos

Introduction

What I saw and heard from Christians in Lagos

The world is living through an important period in the history of Christianity. With the Church between the past and the future, Christians in Lagos are aware of their unique contributions to the life of the Church in this generation. The map of Christianity has been redrawn; the centre of gravity for the Church is now shifting to Christians in the Global South. The force of this gravitational pull has surprised Christian missionaries, demonstrating that the centre is no longer limited to the cities of Rome, London, Berlin or Belfast. The centre of the Christian faith now includes locales such as Addis Ababa, Manila, Seoul, Shanghai, Hong Kong, Mumbai, Nairobi, Johannesburg, Kinshasa and Lagos. We are experiencing an important period of political, economic and spiritual transition.[1] It is a period of rebirth of the Christian faith that requires 'drinking from our own well' for sustenance. One cannot *act* Christian; we can only *be* Christians. In Lagos, Christians possess the pneuma – the Spirit at the core of who they are as Christians.

The reality of the spiritual world as the source of Christian rebirth in Lagos

The main source of vitality for Christians in Lagos is, perhaps, what Huston Smith called the 'primordial tradition'.[2] We might look at it slightly differently as the first world of non-material reality. While not visible, images abound about the reality of this non-material world that sustains the Christian experience in Lagos. The physical and the invisible primordial worlds are not unconnected, and their relationship is broad and comprehensive.

Osadolor Imasogie (1928–2022) was a highly respected Nigerian scholar and church leader who served as the first indigenous president of the prestigious Nigerian Baptist Theological Seminary at Ogbomosho, a historic Yoruba city approximately 250 kilometres northwest of Lagos. He was greatly admired by Baptists and others worldwide. In his book, *Guidelines for Christian Theology: Theological Perspectives in Africa* (1983, 1993), Imasogie articulated the fusion and complementarity of the relationship between the spiritual and the physical worlds, claiming that they are not disjointed but congruent. The spiritual world enlightens and illuminates the physical world of human habitation. He labelled the European missionary vision of the world proclaimed to Africans as the 'quasi-scientific worldview',[3] maintaining that the African world is akin to the spiritual world of the Hebrew Bible. European missionaries could talk about God, heaven, angels, evil forces and the spiritual world, but those concepts lacked the substance and existential dynamism of both the authentic biblical understanding and of the African belief. Biblical references to demon possession, angels, Satan, all operating actively in the physical world, might be mentioned, but they are diminished in gravity. They are weak in substance because they lack the emotional tones that would grant them legitimacy and reverence.[4] Theologians in the Western world interpreted the relationship between the spiritual and the physical worlds as best they could, seeing them as symbols without ontic content or as figments of imagination created in premodern times, reflecting the ancient world view.[5] When Paul wrote in his letter to the Ephesians, chapter six, verse 12, that 'our struggle is not against enemies of blood and flesh, but against the rulers, against the authorities, against the cosmic powers of this present darkness, against the spiritual forces of evil in the heavenly places', he was speaking in a language familiar to African Christians. In verse 13, Paul continues, 'Therefore take up the whole armor of God, so that you may be able to withstand on that evil day, and having done everything, to stand firm.'

Osadolor Imasogie concluded that

> the earth for the typical African is not just a physical reality on which he lives. It is interpenetrated by spiritual forces and, like an onion, has many layers hidden by the outer layer which is open to immediate casual observation. The earth is, therefore, not only mysterious but [also] sacred and impregnated with both good and evil as well as neutral spiritual forces which can be exploited by man.[6]

For Imasogie, 'there is no event without corresponding spiritual or metaphysical cause. Therefore, humanity must look beyond the physical events to their spiritual etiology.'[7]

The reality of the spiritual world, this first world of non-material reality, runs through both the Bible and African existence. The open lines of the Hebrew Bible state, 'In the beginning when God created the heavens and the earth, the earth was a formless void and darkness covered the face of the deep, while a wind from God swept over the face of the waters.'[8]

It is from this pneuma – this breath – that God brings forth the physical world into existence. The physical world has no independent meaning apart from the first frontier of this primordial universe. The world of the spirit is neither abstract nor far remote, nor even a hypothetical first cause, but it is very much alive, and God is at its centre, its depth, and height.[9] This world of primordial tradition is populated by various beings, including angels, archangels, the ancestors, the cherubim, the seraphim and many other non-material beings. For Christian thinkers in Lagos, there is no solid line of demarcation between the sacred and the secular, the physical and the spiritual. While humanity seems to see the past as the past, the present as the present and the future as the future, it is possible that no such division exists for God who sees everything at once in its entirety. The spiritual interpenetrates the material world. Humanity is, therefore, vulnerable and open to spiritual forces for ill or for good.[10] The human being lives in the presence of metaphysical danger and is constantly needing the help of expertise to guide him so that he does not fall into the danger unprepared or unaware. This is the nature of our reality, and Christians in Lagos understand the metaphysical forces which surround them. Protection against evil forces is seen as one of the leading roles of the Christian minister and is understood by traditional diviners as one of the key aspects of Christian consciousness.

God is at the centre of African consciousness because of the intense awareness of the spiritual world in which Africans find themselves. The Spirit is felt by the average Christian who knows God in the spirit as well as in the flesh. Marcus Borg points out: 'In the Jewish tradition, the prohibition against the graven images of God makes the same point. It is not simply that one should not make a statue or physical image of God. Rather, it means that God is beyond all images, physical and mental.'[11] The Yoruba people in Lagos use Olorun or Olodumare (also Eledumare), while the Zulu in South Africa use the word Unkulunkulu for God. Like the ancient Jewish tradition, these African languages stress the impossibility of naming God definitively.

The perceptions of God among Christians in Lagos

Christians exhibit neither a Eurocentric nor an Afrocentric perspective. Their faith in Christ must be evaluated based on the veracity of the Bible as God's revelation. In his book, *The Church Confidence,* Leander E. Keck argues that the church is imperfect, but the imperfection is not an excuse to stop the proclamation of Jesus Christ. He quotes Janet Martin Soskice, who wrote that the language about God has limitations, and 'to speak of God without claiming to define him, and to do so by means of metaphor',[12] is all that Christians can do. The 'language about God is referential without being tied to unreviewable description'.[13] In other words, human language does not perfectly describe God without distortion in one's efforts to characterize the Divine. What is important to note, therefore, is that 'Tradition is the living faith of the dead; traditionalism is the dead faith of the living.'[14] The veracity of Christianity is evaluated based on the social or political milieus and cultures of the Christian origin, and the vitality of the Church will always depend on the adjustments the Church makes between the past and the future, and between tradition and traditionalism.[15]

When I first read the works of Martin Buber, especially his most mature book, *I and Thou* (1958), and his lesser-known work, *The Prophetic Faith* (1949), I was struck by the similarities between the Jewish understanding of God and the Yoruba and Igbo definition of God. Buber was a Jewish intellectual and one of the most sublime minds of his time. He expressed a view of God that drew my attention to the origin of Yahweh in Judaism, arguing that the divine name originated as an exclamation drawn forth by ecstatic religious experience. This exclamation means roughly, 'the exalted One' or 'O the One'.[16] The same could be said about Olodumare, God in traditional Yoruba religion and spiritual beliefs, and Chukwu (the Most High or Almighty), the name for God in Igbo spiritual beliefs. Among the Yoruba people in Lagos, it was clear that God could not be named. The term *Olodumare,* used by them, means a gift that defends and protects justice, mending lives broken or twisted by oppression and life circumstances. Therefore, in both Judaism and in Yoruba as well as in Igbo spiritual belief, the name of God is an exclamatory utterance spoken in a moment of religious ecstasy, distress, or amid family struggles, when God cannot be named, but is exclaimed.[17] The Christians I met in Lagos were not so much interested in seeking evidence of the existence of God as in the active participation of God in their lives. They did not engage in metaphysics, that branch of philosophy that ponders the issue of God's existence. Most of them stated that God was a gift whose presence is constantly interwoven in their lives. Humanity will always need the God they can neither prove nor disprove; hence, saying that God *exists* diminishes God in human language and dims the light of the glory of God. One can only say, 'God is'. This is also part of the argument in the Hebrew Bible. The whole earth is full of the glory of God, and God does not *exist*, God *is*.

To Lagosian Christians, God is at the centre of Christian consciousness. I observed among them an intense awareness of the *pneuma* of God and an openness to the spiritual world. Perhaps, this is one of the contributions they make to our understanding of their Christian experience – a practice of walking closely in the spiritual world which leads them to encounter the guiding light of the Divine in their lives. A confluence of faith enshrined in their traditional beliefs and the spiritual world is one of the key characteristics of Lagosian Christianity. It gives them a unique identity; their faith cannot be fully understood without referring to the spiritual world, which endows it with meaning and potency, and a more mystical understanding of Christian truth. They live in a large universe with open frontiers into the spiritual world. One can reiterate that 'in the African vision of the world, the frontiers between the empirical world and the spiritual world are being crossed and re-crossed every day in both directions.'[18]

The months I spent in Lagos left me with a lasting image of a people who are energized, focused and united, carried by the Spirit of God as water carries fish in the ocean. They do not attribute their successes in ministry to their own strengths and competence or expertise, but to God. And just as fish do not swim but are carried, Christians do not perform their ministry on their own but are enabled by the Spirit of God.

What do Lagos and New York Christians have in common during moments of calamity?

The northeastern coastlines of the United States have experienced calamities similar to those often experienced by Christians in Lagos during the rainy seasons. Hurricane Sandy in October 2012 is a case in point, with the devastation it brought. At the time, it was estimated that the cost of the damage was more than $60 billion. The New York LaGuardia Airport experienced more than 1,800 flight cancellations during the first few days of the hurricane. It was estimated that more than 100 homes burned to the ground in New York's Breezy Point or were washed away by the hurricane; eight million citizens were without electricity.

I have seen comparable devastation during the rainy seasons in Lagos. I was able to observe how people in Lagos reacted when several boroughs of Lagos, including Maroko, Surulere, and the Lekki peninsula, were severely affected by floods. Citizens of the United States are pragmatic amid calamity, often joining together to solve common problems. Americans respond by facing such challenges together, processing relief efforts speedily. Incidents of heroism and the way in which American people come to the aid of each other in times of natural disaster are one of the best examples of 'American exceptionalism'.

Although I have seen people in Lagos come together to help one another, it is particularly heartwarming to see this kind of unity in the United States, a culture characterized by individualism. Perhaps Americans have a strong sense of belonging to one another that is not as recognized and celebrated elsewhere as could be expected. Perhaps it is a part of the belief that God will not do for us that which we can do for ourselves. In a positive sense, when we face natural disasters and misfortune, we do not wait for destiny, but shape it.

Examining events such as Hurricane Sandy in 2012, many analysts and commentators in the United States, including economists, insurance adjusters, politicians, meteorologists and climate scientists, discussed the resulting damage in purely rational terms. But in the floods which occur in Lagos during rainy seasons, the people who often appear in the media are not limited to scientists and experts but often include religious figures who assess natural catastrophes on the basis of religious or theological grounds, focussing on what such events might be telling the people.

One can say that in the American part of the world, an analysis of such disasters and related economic and ecological concerns outweighs and submerge any theological explanations. In America, we do not hear religious leaders expounding on what God might be saying to us in the midst of the devastation; nor are we reminded of the teachings of Jesus of Nazareth – the Jesus who healed the sick, who walked on water and who stilled the storms – which could lead us to care more responsibly and effectively for the environment.

In contrast, the Christians of Lagos would have asked: 'Are our resources so infinite that we no longer need God or those who could interpret God's words for us during times of such vulnerability?'

It is perplexing and disturbing to note how effectively we have relegated the 'God talk' to the periphery, as if God were irrelevant or inconsequential in the face of major natural disasters. Why are we so readily dismissive of the opinions of pastors or religious leaders when we face such challenges? It does not mean that we do not have faith since a large majority of people all over the world claim that they do believe in God. It does not even mean that the opinions of religious leaders or experts do not count. What can it mean then?

It could simply mean our differing perceptions of God and of God's participation in our life. Lagosian Christians approach God as a more integral part of their lives, seeing God as part of their existential condition. When faced with such challenges, their first line of interpretation is to look for what God might be saying to them. When tragedy occurs, members of the local churches consult with religious leaders at every opportunity. Thus, God often takes centre stage in discussions related to misfortune or catastrophe. These tendencies, however, often relegate human relief efforts to the background, claiming that God is in control and will watch over believers and guide them during moments of misfortune or natural disasters.

The belief of many Christians in Lagos is that everything comes from God and to God it will return. Human beings are, therefore, only coincidental in the plans of the Divine. God is like the invisible third party in all of life, the holy fragrance in the orbit of every life, the one who is in control. Thus, God is a third party in the midst of every raging superstorm and flood, and so human beings should not worry because there is little they can do about it. In some parts of Lagos, the Kiswahili phrase is used in such circumstances: *Asante ndugu. Tuko salama. Hakuna matata.* (Thank you, brother. We are all well. No problem).

While many in the Western world often focus on what humanity can do, those in Lagos tend to look with the eyes of faith or predestination for what God will do. So, in examining the relationship between God and the catastrophes of life, it perhaps comes down to a question of whether we believe God controls human destiny, or whether humanity creates destiny when suddenly faced with natural misfortune. In other words, do human beings believe in God, or can God believe in humanity?

Yet, a passive faith in God is hardly sufficient in itself to shape the future in a positive way without the active participation of human agencies. While our human relief efforts are consistent with our faith in God, those on the streets of Lagos remind us of the fact that human efforts and resources are still finite when compared to God's all-sufficient abundance in the face of challenges and misfortune.

Under the circumstances of poverty, we tend to acknowledge God while still depending on external resources when faced with difficulties. But as we become more prosperous, resourceful and technologically advanced, we tend to depend less and less on God and more and more on our own capacities to fight existential challenges on our own terms. It then seems rather irresponsible and immature to hold God accountable for natural catastrophes or to wait for God to act when nature threatens us with calamity. But it is also not enough to rely entirely on the self-sufficiency of humanity when we are faced with natural tragedies of the scale and frequency which the people in Lagos – Christian and non-Christian alike – often encounter. What one can affirm in a theistic culture is that there is no mountain too high to climb when God is with us – or better yet, when we are with God.

Conceptual claim of living by faith in Lagos

One of the most common food items found on the streets of Lagos is bread, with sellers carrying loaves of bread on their heads as they fearlessly solicit potential consumers among fast-moving cars. It goes without saying that bread-baking is a popular occupation. There is a metaphorical connection between bread-baking and the faith of Christians in Lagos.

Let us imagine a baker who wants to bake banana bread. There will be at least five steps that must occur before those loaves reach the hands of the street sellers in Lagos. A philosopher might see these steps as a reflection of the Aristotelian theory of causality,[19] which includes: (1) the material cause, (2) the causality of efficiency or the efficient cause, (3) the formal cause, (4) the final cause and (5) the 'so-what' or teleological cause – the goal – of the baking of bread.

The material cause

The material cause includes the ingredients needed to make the bread – bananas, eggs, flour, walnuts, baking soda, sugar, butter, water and loaf pans. They are the physical materials necessary to bake bread; without them, there will be no bread, no matter how much the baker tries to implement the concept of baking.

The efficient cause

The efficient cause is even more important, though not as visible as the material cause. The efficient cause is the baker, who gathers the 'raw materials'. The idea of baking bread first occurs in the imagination of the baker. If it did not occur to the baker, there would be no bread in the first place. Therefore, the efficient cause is the baker himself and his inspiration that has led to action. It is the most fundamental cause of the resulting loaf of bread.

The formal cause

The formal cause of baking bread is the creative mind of the baker, who must have some knowledge about what the bread should look like when it comes out of the oven to become a commodity fit for sale on the streets of Lagos.

How big will the bread be? What is going to be its moisture content? Is it going to be soft and fluffy? Will the baker be proud to have that bread identified as his product? What is going to be the label on the bread? These are some of the questions the baker must answer before embarking on the bread-baking business. In other words, the mind must first create bread before it actually becomes bread.

The final cause

The final cause is the resulting product – the bread itself. The baker is either satisfied or unsatisfied, proud or disappointed, when the bread comes out of the oven. The final cause calls for an assessment or evaluation of the baker himself. If the bread is edible and good, he should be congratulated. If, on the other hand, the bread did not come out well, he must assess where things went wrong and how he might correct his errors. Did he use too much flour, or not enough baking soda, or too few eggs? The evaluation, however, does not completely depend on the baker. It also is a product of whether the people for whom the bread is intended like it. If they are satisfied, they will likely purchase more of the same bread; but if they are not satisfied, they will go elsewhere for bread.

Teleological cause or the purpose and goal

The teleological cause is the 'so-what' of the whole process of baking bread. The bread is not baked solely for the baker himself. It is baked for others to enjoy and tell others about the bread. The commercial baker does not say, 'I will bake the bread for myself to entertain myself and to see my worth.' The teleological goal is to spread the reputation of the competence and expertise of the baker and his skills to profit from the sale of the bread.

Summary: God as the grand causality with human beings as coincidental

Let us now look at those who live in Lagos from the conceptual claim of their Christian faith. God's overall plans for the world are beyond human imagination. The material cause for making banana bread is analogous to the abundance in nature created by God. Africa in general, and Nigeria in particular, is replete with rich natural resources. This abundance can lead to faith in God, the Creator. Some Christians in Lagos affirm that everything comes from God, as they 'praise God from whom all their blessings flow'.[20] Perhaps some have taken nature for granted by not cultivating and becoming co-creators with God; but the underlying concept among Christians in Lagos is that God is generous to them. However, one of the greatest needs in Lagos is replenishing the Earth by afforestation and managing the natural resources more proactively.[21]

In our analogy, Christians in Lagos consider the efforts of the baker to provide an adequate oven, purchase good loaf pans and gather enough wood for his oven. The interpretation of many Christians in Lagos is that the baker is strategic and knows where he is going in his master plan and process, knowing that nature's resources are abundant.

Also, in this analogy, the efficient cause is God, the creative force and originator of faith itself. God is the source of the materials and the creator of human beings. They would even say that before any human being becomes an idea in the minds of his parents, he is an idea in the mind of God. The efficient cause has no equal or duplication.

The formal cause is the shape of the world as God intends. Lagosian Christians know with certitude that what God intends for them will come to fruition. It is beyond free will and determinism or predestination for them. It is the design of a loving God. When Christians are oblivious to God's plan, they call that predestination. It becomes an exercise of free will when God's intention is revealed. One of the responsibilities of Christians is to know the will of God and to follow it passionately.

The final cause in our analogy is how Christians are perceived and how they see themselves as agents of transformation in the city of Lagos. It is believed that a Christian is as a Christian does. Are they attractive to others? What are their desirable qualities? The abstract nouns that describe the fruits associated with Christianity in Lagos include humility, gentleness, love, reliability, joy, peace, long-suffering, patience, kindness, generosity, faithfulness, self-control and the ability to listen. This also seems to be their philosophy of Christian mission. The living proclamation of the life of a Christian is its own mission and evangelism. It is hardly necessary to preach to the world when the life of a Christian is such that it becomes attractive and desirable to the outside. This underscores Jehu Hanciles's argument in *Migration and the Making of Global Christianity* (2021) that every Christian is a potential missionary.

The teleological goal is the multiplication of the final cause so that Christians become agents of transformation in the world, beginning in Lagos. It is from this fountainhead that I see my own experience as a Christian from Lagos. Where, then, is the source of the vitality of Christians in Lagos? My response will be one word – God.

This means that no one can take God from one geographical location to another because God is spirit and cannot be localized. Therefore, it needs to be reiterated that Western missionaries have not taken God to Lagos or to Africa. The Lagosian Christians themselves have crafted their faith in Christ with their own cultural lens and African spiritual beliefs and wealth of traditions. The presence of European missionaries, however, was instrumental in the resurrection of African church life and creativity. It is a decisive victory for Christianity, therefore, that it is now grafted in the African spiritual beliefs and creativity. Perhaps, Christianity is not only a religion but also a spiritual map that translates itself into every culture and language with its enduring values to find new homes where it becomes the way of life.

Epilogue

Abstract from Ps. 44.17-26 (NRSV)

All this has come upon us,
Yet we have not forgotten you,
Or been false to your covenant.
Our heart has not turned back,
Nor have our steps departed
From your way,
Yet you have broken us in the
Haunt of jackals,
And covered us with deep
Darkness.
If we had forgotten the name of
Our God,
Or spread out our hands to a
Strange god,
Would not God discover this?
For he knows the secrets of the
Heart.
Because of you we are being killed
All day long,
And accounted as sheep for the
Slaughter.
Rouse yourself! Why do you
Sleep, O Lord?
Awake, do not cast us off
Forever!
Why do you hide your face?
Why do you forget our
Affliction and oppression?
For we sink down to the dust;
Our bodies cling to the ground.
Rise up, come to our help.
Redeem us for the sake of your
Steadfast love.

Introduction

As I write this volume detailing life among Christians in the City of Lagos, I am deeply grateful that these stories will have the capacity to reach a larger audience of contemporary readers and church leaders from different parts of the world. I am fortunate to have learned my ABCs of theological education in Lagos, gleaning inspiration and having been taught and mentored by Baptist church leaders and non-Christian clerics, all of whom played dominant roles in my academic and theological journey. The resulting Christian scholarship has defined my identity and spiritual heritage.

My journey of faith in Christ began in Lagos

In 1972, when I came to Lagos from my hometown in Osun State to visit my uncle, I wished to attend a Sunday church service. So, I took a bus from Itire-Surulere to Yaba.

When I stepped off the bus, unsure of exactly where to go, I saw a number of people walking in different directions with their Bibles and hymn books in hand. I followed one of them, certain that he must be heading to a church.

Following him, I entered Yaba Baptist Church, which I later discovered had been planted by Baptist missionaries in 1942. I found myself in a spirited and inspiring Sunday school class with Baptists who were talking openly about the Word of God, which moved me greatly. Having grown up in the African church tradition where opportunities to read the Bible and interpret it freely were absent then, I was inspired.

A revival service was announced during the service that Sunday. I did not know what that meant, but I decided I would attend all the services at this church that November. The Reverend Emmanuel A. Agboola from Ogbomosho, the city of the first indigenous Baptist seminary, was the preacher that week. It was during that revival service that the most significant event of my life took place: I accepted Christ as my Lord and Saviour. Subsequently, in February 1975, I became a baptized believer at the Yaba Baptist Church in Lagos.

In 1978, I felt that God was calling me into Christian ministry, and I shared my sense of call with a missionary at the church from Georgia (in the United States), whose name was Anita Roper. She affirmed my calling and suggested a ministerial training path in the United States.

In 1980, I enrolled at Wayland Baptist University in Plainview, Texas, where my love and appreciation for the Bible and its interpretation grew stronger. I began to sense my life unfolding with deeper meaning. I started reading the Bible with great devotion and a deep sense of the truth of the promises of God.

Upon my graduation in 1984, I enrolled at Southeastern Baptist Theological Seminary in Wake Forest, North Carolina. There, I met Anne Neil, another missionary who had served in Nigeria and Ghana; I often sought her spiritual guidance during my student days in North Carolina. In one of our many conversations, she stated that 'God might be calling me to serve as a missionary from Africa to America – entirely possible as God had created only one world'.

Upon completion of the Master of Divinity degree in 1987, with the assistance of Glenn T. Miller and Thomas H. Graves, two of my professors, and seminary president, Dr W. Randall Lolley, I entered the divinity school at Yale University where I earned a Master of Sacred Theology degree. It was the personal investment of these saints that enabled me to continue my journey of destiny. I then went on to Baylor University where I received advanced theological training leading to a PhD in theological studies. It was at Baylor that I became convinced in an epiphany that God had called me into a teaching ministry in the United States.

An unforgettable event in 2003

I spent 2003 in South Africa at the University of Cape Town, studying the effects of apartheid on the life and ministry of the church. There, I became acquainted with a local congregation in Cape Town. In November of that year, as I was returning to the United States, the congregation insisted on giving me a gift. The pastor explained that the gift the congregation wanted to give me was the gift of ordination. Even though I informed them that I had already been ordained, following my graduation from Wayland Baptist University in 1984, I soon learned that no one wins an argument with an African congregation! So, I participated in my second ordination as a gift of God's grace. I rejoiced when the congregation ordained me to serve as a missionary from Africa to the United States. Since that time, I have seen my teaching ministry as that of a missionary from Africa to America.

The third stage of my journey
of faith in Jesus Christ

The third stage of this journey of faith in Jesus Christ began as I started to realize the deep impact of the missionary life as a professor in American classrooms. I feel very strongly that a theologian's training and teaching ministry should bridge the gap between faith and reason, and between theology and biblical studies. Without the leadership of ministers who are biblically informed and theologically engaged, the church suffers.

In the writing of this book, I have sensed it to be my 'homecoming' to Lagos. As I conducted numerous interviews there with Lagosian Christians who shared with me stories of their faith, I witnessed the beauty of their diverse takes on Christianity, although they were often messy and complicated. I saw a confluence of identities under the shadow of Islamic faith as well as under the influence of traditional African spiritual beliefs. I did not see any urge to demonize those who are different because of some theological dispute. By not vilifying other religious traditions, they showed the authenticity of their own faith in God. If one looks with heart and mind at others – whether in Lagos or elsewhere – one can see that there is a stamp of God's divine love on every human being.

At Yaba Baptist Church, I learned early on that the term 'mission' is not to be understood exclusively as merely the self-expansion of the Church, but rather as participation in the primary activity of God in redeeming humanity through Jesus Christ. The Christians I encountered in Lagos showed me that there is only one single mission – God's Mission – and that the Church and its individuals have all been invited to participate in the mission of God for the world.

As we are liberated from the artificial walls of division and fences of hostility that are often a product of diversity, we are also freed from any perceived separation from God. It is only through Christ that we can successfully cross the barriers that separate us from one another, including the denominational lines we have drawn ourselves.

I was gratified by the level of openness characterizing the Christians whom I met in Lagos. This allows those who are non-Christian in the city the ability to fully disclose and embrace their own African and religious heritages through faith in Jesus Christ.

My own experience as a missionary from Africa to America began without any language training, without referring to political maps and without hindrance of any denominational creed or even any theological completeness. My life has always been a journey – a journey of one commissioned by God to transform the world, one person at a time. My footprints on that journey can now be found on five continents. Perhaps others are waiting for me and for other readers of this volume to help them experience what these Lagosian Christians taught me through the gift I was given in Lagos in 1972.

I have come to see myself as a global citizen, a missionary for Christ and a conduit between the African Christian world and the Western world. As a child of God, I am a bridge builder among nations in the name of Christ. My destiny, my history and my very life bear the eternal blessed marks of the impact these

Christians made on me, with their prayers and their dedication to the mission of God in the world.

For over thirty years now, I have been teaching in Baptist institutions that train ministerial students. The opportunity to teach future Christian missionaries and to direct mission immersion experience programmes, designed to expose American students to the church in the Global South, has given me the benefit of a rich exposure to the world of faith that I did not know or could have imagined before. Being directly involved in such visionary projects has provided me with the opportunity to learn firsthand how Christians in other lands pray, how they sing, how they read and interpret the Holy Scriptures and how they navigate problems associated with their Christian ministries and callings in extraordinary times. I have seen how Christians in other lands cry and laugh together, which opened my eyes to our shared common humanity through faith in Jesus Christ. In this way, I have learned the importance of seeing that American students are provided with an intimate knowledge of the lives of other Christians in the world during their formative years. I would not trade these opportunities for anything in this world.

In fact, it was through such mission immersion experiences that I became, without realizing it, a bridge builder between the North and the South, the East and the West and between historically and culturally influenced iterations of the Christian faith.

As such, I have had the opportunity to teach at Baylor University's George W. Truett Theological Seminary, the Baptist Theological Seminary at Richmond and Campbell University Divinity School, where I continue to serve as the Snellings Chair of mission and Christian evangelism and the director of the George and Joan Braswell World Religions and Global Cultures centre. Through these experiences, I came to realize it is by living fully in this world under the Lordship of Jesus Christ that we can have a more genuine faith. It is in such faith that true happiness in the world lies, and no one can be truly free without knowing God.

Christianity is best proclaimed through a lens of dignifying what is different. One does not 'perform' being a Christian; one can only be Christian based on how we live and relate to others, especially those who are different from us. I am grateful that, under my leadership, many students in America have been to the continent of my origin and have visited many great cities, including Lagos. We have worshipped and participated together in the Lord's Supper with some of the most respected church leaders in the world, including the late Archbishop of Cape Town, Desmond M. Tutu.

My American students have challenged me to consider all the facets and sides of any given theological issue. I have been profoundly influenced by Western scholarship and have infused and permeated this scholarship with the wisdom of my own African Christian heritage. I have been impacted by the theological openness of the nature of Christianity itself, as I have realized our faith in Christ is dynamic. There is something profound and genuine that occurs when we exercise constructive clarity in our explanation of the Divine because of our unique Christian experience. I have found it more difficult to choose any finite particular interpretative framework that might diminish me and prevent me from participating fully in the lives and contexts of others. Everyone created in God's image has the potential to inspire and transform me in my inconclusive spiritual dimension.

I have had the privilege of serving beside Christians of diverse backgrounds in the United States, Asia, Latin America, Africa and Europe. These places of service became holy ground for me as my colleagues have allowed me to be a missionary to them as they were to me. Every place we find ourselves can be a mission field, and writing this book itself was a personal missionary journey for me. The interviews I conducted in Lagos gave me the opportunity to see my own Christianity as a channel through which I can safely make full revelation of my African identity as well as use my American experience in the classroom. As I listen to Christians in Lagos tell their stories of how they live, work and play, I was able to see myself as they allowed me to tell my own stories of faith without any need to domesticate them, without the need to evangelize others and without censure.

As I saw these Christians dancing and celebrating during worship services, I embraced the freedom to dance as well. Like my Lagosian Christian friends, I dance to the tune of salvation – a salvation that more closely resembles the flight of a butterfly than the path of a bullet. Such love and acceptance allowed me to say the name of Jesus Christ to the world in a way that only my life can say it. And I have not yet finished saying it!

In January 2018, I led a group of divinity school students to South Africa – the most developed African nation state. The two weeks we spent in Cape Town were some of the happiest and most fruitful of my teaching career as I saw my students growing in their global awareness.

This mission immersion experience provided a first-hand experience of the life and mission of the Church in post-apartheid South Africa. We were in South Africa to expand our Christian thinking beyond the Western intellectual and cultural traditions and the familiar ecclesiological life to which we were accustomed. At the University of Cape Town summer housing unit where we stayed, since it was in the middle of the dry season, students learned to ration water. The experience of such cross-cultural hardships engendered good-humoured jokes about our perspectives on the culture of South Africa.

Our wonderful and affectionate South African hosts did everything in their power to make us feel at home. Through our Western eyes, we saw South Africa at times as accommodating, frustrating, amusing, congested, exciting, hospitable, polluted and with a deep spirituality. We experienced the tender kindness of the 'Cape Coloured', as the apartheid era characterized our hosts. We also experienced the beautiful rhythms of nature. We saw non-Africans on business in Cape Town, wandering like the Moabites in Bethlehem – foreigners who felt no less at home than the natives, as God has created one world and only one Africa. We could see that the Africans in South Africa were intensely religious, hospitable and full of joy. We participated in liturgical liveliness of African worship services as we danced and sang.

Our visit to Table Mountain was especially meaningful. The forest there is a botanical paradise. While it is a peaceful place, beneath its surface is a teeming world of small creatures functioning in symbiotic partnerships as they work together peacefully as a team. I was fascinated by how the propagation of some plants is dependent on small ants burying their seeds, protecting them from fire or inclement weather. In an invisible exchange, the ants are rewarded with sweet, delectable snacks beneath the surface. The beautiful birds on Table Mountain might not survive save for the company of the butterflies. The beautiful flowers would not exist without the pollination of the long, juice-seeking beaks of the birds. Many plants on Table Mountain offer specialized protection to their 'fellow' mountain dwellers, like the flies who enjoy haven from the blistering sun on a bush, which is toxic and irritating to larger predators. Many less visible inhabitants on this mountain include rodents and a staggering diversity of insect species – each one a small but vital part of the complex tapestry of the environment that sustains their lives.

I was struck by the beauty of the place and the necessity for the peaceful coexistence of the living organisms on the mountain when all the visitors had gone home. My experience on the Table Mountain imbued me with an awareness related to our pursuit of peace in the world. Peacemaking must be a way of life – not what modern politicians can achieve with a stroke of a pen at a peace accord. Peacemaking is not a dramatic event. Peacemaking efforts can be rewarded in the very rhythm of our existence, expressed by how we live. Lasting peace is achieved by our becoming intentional peacemakers in our families, in our communities, in our states and in the world. If we fail to pursue peace in the world, we lose our heritage and our hope.

'When will there be peace in the world', I often ask myself. 'When will there be shalom?'

There will be peace in the world when the hearts of the people are my nationality, not my land. There will be peace in the world when nations begin to learn to love their children more than they hate their enemies. There will be peace in the world when the leaders of nations realize that no person should live in fear.

There will be peace when we realize it is our grandchildren who will pay the price for the poor choices we make each day. There will be peace in the world when we attempt to understand before we act so swiftly. There will be peace in the world when teachers are students and students are sustained in the habit of learning. There will be peace in the world when devotees of every religion are challenged to think new thoughts and dream new dreams. There will be peace in the world when Christians begin to realize that practising religion like Jesus is not the same as practising the religion of Jesus. There will be peace in the world when leaders of every nation not only have the courage of their convictions, but when they have the courage to challenge those convictions when appropriate to do so. There will be peace in the world when political leaders realize that there is more to leadership than getting one's way, and there is more to cooperation than convincing others that we are right.

There will be peace in the world when Christians insist on the common connections among the Jewish temples, the Christian churches and the Muslim mosques. There will be peace in the world when the gatekeepers of the mosque, of the church and of the temple embrace suffering children as the sons and daughters of Abraham. There will be peace in the world when we protect and nurture the children of our neighbours as our own children.

When military experts recognize that there is more to victory than not losing, there will be peace. Peace will reign when we no longer label ourselves as blacks and whites, Jews and Gentiles, rich and poor, heaven-bound and hell-bound, slave and free, male and female. There will be peace when citizens of every nation begin to realize that the ruin of any nation begins in the very homes of its people. There will be peace in the world when it is just as easy to cross the street to meet our new neighbours as it is to go to the moon and back.

There will be peace in the world when Israeli children and Palestinian children hold each other's hands and walk together in Jerusalem, in Ramallah, in the West Bank and in Gaza – all as children of God's promise. When husbands realize that the greatest gift they can give to their sons is to love their mothers, peace will follow. There will be peace in the world when wives realize that the greatest gift they can give to their daughters is to love their fathers. Then there will be peace in the world.

Peacemaking must be a way of life. It is not achieved through wars or conflicts. It is not achieved through exhibitions of strength. Peace is achieved through the exercise of humility. Peacemaking efforts must be a part of the rhythm of how we live.

A personal story

When I was fifteen years old, I was the leader of the football (soccer) club in my high school. We ordered special shirts, but I could not pay the 200 naira to get my own special shirt, as my family had nothing! I was very sad. On the day the order was to be placed at school, my mother came into our classroom and knelt right in front of me. She had run for four miles to bring me the 200 naira she had managed to gather. She arrived tired, crying and broken. I told her, 'Mom, stop because you are embarrassing me in front of my classmates. There was no need for you to work and run so hard just for me.' She addressed me by both my middle name and my birth name. 'You don't understand; this money is not for you; this money is for your destiny!'

I did not fully understand what she meant that day until I arrived in Lagos in 1972 and was baptized at Yaba Baptist Church, and later went to the United States, where I became a member of the American Theological Society. My story continues in the writing of this book, as I have reflected on the depth of the stories of the Christians I interviewed in Lagos. In this experience, their destinies have become intertwined with mine.

More than a religion: Christians as catalyst for unity in Lagos

The burgeoning Christian faith in Africa has become a catalyst for unity among different ethnic groups. While the missionary Church in the West has communicated its own ineffable stories, the indigenous Christians in Africa have crafted their faith with the infusion of their local idioms and traditions. Christianity is now a catalyst for unity, equally benefiting rival ethnic groups among the younger generation of believers. This is not the pattern of Christianity of Western missionary faith vying for African souls, where it is not uncommon for rivalries among competing Christian missionaries from the West.

We have heard the stories of the bloody conflicts between Muslims and Christians in Northern Nigeria, and between Hausas/Fulanis and Igbos. But the religious conflicts of the last two decades of the twentieth century do not tell all the stories of the growth of Christianity in Nigeria – the most populous African nation state. With over half a million people, Nigeria now has the largest number of students in the International Fellowship of Evangelical Students (IFES) in the world. The vibrant and hope-filled faith of these men and women, mostly high school and university students, transcends the tribal particularity that characterized Nigeria for more than six decades since its independence from Great Britain.

Christianity has always been a motivating force for progress among Africans, often acting as a gateway for understanding new life – social and political as well as cultural. In the 1980s and 1990s, religious paths that some Nigerians followed brought sufferings that were spawned by intolerance. Evangelical Christians in Nigeria knew they were facing new challenges as they sought ways to enlarge the boundaries of Christian proclamation and build upon the distinctive truths of Christian convictions. One of these still-existing challenges revolves around how to determine what aspects of religion are oppressive or abusive, and what aspects foster unity among the more than 250 ethnic groups in Nigeria. Many evangelical students in Nigeria have witnessed the decisive and distinctive power of their relationship with God. Aspects of their witnesses are obvious, if not prolific. But their desire was to promote participation among non-traditional members of the Church – a testimony that through Christ, humanity encounters possibilities of unity that are available in no other way. Hence, whether Yoruba Christians and Hausa or Igbo, they can find common unifying ground through the testimony of their faith and through prayers and service.

Evangelical Christians in Lagos have now started to see religion not as an obstacle on the path to godly living, but to celebrate ethnic identity and what different groups can accomplish together. In defining other faith traditions in Nigeria, evangelical students no longer cling to the premodern categories of division, as these concrete categories between Muslims and Christians, or between ethnic groups, have started to break down. Christians in Nigeria now face an unprecedented exposure to the reality and goodness of Islam, as well as to the values of ethnic diversity.

Evangelical students and the quest for relating to Muslims in Lagos

Christians began to experience religious persecution in the late 1980s and early 1990s for their assertion that non-Christian faiths (especially Islam) are the result of human error in need of redemption. Such assertions often betrayed the universal transparent goodness of ordinary cultured and devoted Nigerians. The pull of ethnic and family loyalty is often stronger than that of religious identity; Christian-Muslim relations are more amicable than the benign contempt displayed by certain evangelical Christians in Lagos in post-independent era. The exclusivist assumptions of Christian superiority, therefore, are now on shaky grounds. And taking other religions more seriously has been a part of

Lagos Evangelical culture. However, the kidnappings, persecutions and killings of Christians in their thousands by the radical Boko Haram in Northern Nigeria have opened new wounds and old atavistic hatred between Christians and Muslims. The religious tension is often exacerbated by opportunistic politicians. This is not without the polarities of what political scentists have identified as a result of an unyielding attempt by certain Northern Nigerian Muslims to islamize the country. Respected religious leaders have estimated that there can be no lasting peace in Nigeria unless the Fulani political elites in Northern Nigeria renounce violence and the insidious agenda to islamize the country. The Christians have been kind but not blind to the agenda of the silent enemies of progress in the country who have inflitrated themselves across Nigeria, playing a protracted and long game of islamization. Christians have realized that the soul is always dyed with the colour and tone of its environment. The Fulani Muslim elites, who continue to trace their steps back to the dark days of Shehu Usman dan Fodio (1754–1817), the founder in 1804 of Sokoto Caliphate, and whose desire was to islamize Nigeria, often collected religious details from Southern Nigerian Christians. The collection is not out of cooperation to build Nigeria and strengthen cooperations among Christians and Muslims, but out of preparation to islamize the country. The Catholic bishops in Northern Nigeria have stated again and again that it is better to trust the patterns of islamization since 1960 by the Fulani elites than to have faith in their words. Christians in Lagos are open-minded, but not exposed to the venom of islamization by the Fulani Muslim elites in Northern Nigeria. A free and fear election was annuled in 1993, for example, partly because the winner, M. K. O. Abiola, a Muslim from the South, was not a Fulani Muslim. Therefore, he was imprisoned for four years and died under mysterious and baffling circumstances. It was speculated that he was not prepared to carry out the agenda of islamization. Islamic religion has been highjacked by the Fulani herdsmen and bandits, who continue to rape Christian women, and killing their husbands. The world was outraged in April 2014, when the Boko Haram bandits in Northern Nigeria abducted 276 high school Chibok girls in their sleep, and many still remain in captivity. The Muslim political elites who continue to sponsor Boko Haram banditry and Fulani herdsmen have contaminated a fragile democratic political process with a permanent agenda to continue killing Christians in their hundreds during church worship services, instilling fears in the Nigerian Christian population with the hope in the grand illusion that Nigeria, a secular state, exclusively belongs to them as a gift from Allah.

Pluralistic assumptions about the interchangeability of various faiths are seamlessly woven into the concrete and unique textures of Lagos' religious traditions. Devotees of non-Christian religions are often united elsewhere in African urban cities for a common cause. Allan Boesak of South Africa, for example, who was not invited by his own Dutch Reformed Church to preach in the white congregations under apartheid, was welcomed to preach at Muslim mosques in Cape Town in the 1980s and 1990s, evidence that Muslims and Christians could set aside doctrinal differences to work together for a common cause and develop a common plan for action against injustice. Whether this open cross-fertilization between people of differing religions was a mark of the future in all of Africa is difficult to determine. There is no question, however, that such cross-fertilization among living faiths is indicative of the inadequacies of the past frozen religious silos with little interaction between people of different religions.

Finding echoes of Christianity in Islam, however, cannot be dealt with by the assertion of general revelation alone, and many Lagosian Christians I interviewed are pragmatic about their faiths, affirming that there is something substantive in the Christian religious tradition on its own. Likewise, Islam has validity not despite its differences from Christianity, but because of these differences. On the other hand, one cannot explain a tradition's power by simply appealing to the common truth behind its specific doctrinal teachings. The distinctive convictions that believers in Lagos use to define the truth of their religious traditions are crucial. Evangelical Christians who find much that is appealing in other religious traditions have raised conscientious doubts about the need for a universal Christian witness and about the uniqueness of Christianity.

Evangelical Christians in Lagos are not necessarily those who have found a better way to be saved, but the people who have accepted their responsibilities to serve God in this life and promote God's reign in all its forms in their own unique ways. Christians have seen this mark in the people professing to be Muslims in Lagos, thus calling their attention to an exercise of religious tolerance.

An epistemological defence of evangelical tolerance in Lagos

The average evangelical Christian never considers that 'mere accident' determined which religious view he has adopted and that the same causes that made him a Christian in Lagos might have made him a Muslim in Kano. In 99 per cent of cases, the religion to which one adheres depends upon an accident of birth, with a decisive effect upon the culture and the religion one would likely favour.

The experience of adopting Christianity is partially internal to the evangelical tradition itself. Therefore, there is no justification for rejecting the epistemological reliability of the experience of God in Islamic religious traditions in Northern Nigeria.

Evangelical Christians in Lagos, however, have often assumed the epistemological reliability of the Gospel with indigenous methods of Christian proclamation. When Yoruba Christians faced persecution for building churches in Northern Nigeria in the 1950s and were charged in court for illegally converting Muslims to Christianity, they articulated their actions in ways that were consistent with a diverse ethnicity in Nigeria. In a popular court case in Northern Nigeria in the 1950s, Christians were charged for erecting an illegal structure called a 'church'. When the court asked Reverend A. A. Adegoke how he would plead and knowing that it was a severe offence carrying a penalty of five years imprisonment, Adegoke changed the signpost bearing 'Nasarawa Baptist Church' to read 'Nasarawa Christian Mosque' the night before the court proceeding. The following morning when court representatives went back to the church location, the court was taken aback upon seeing 'Nasarawa Christian Mosque' on the sign. Adegoke pleaded 'not guilty' defending his fellow Christians by declaring they had only erected a Christian Mosque.[1]

The indigenous underpinnings of the Christian faith in Nigeria have contributed to its remarkable success and rapid growth. While Christians in the Western world often assume that indigenous Christians in Africa were blind to 'proper' methods of evangelism, native Christians themselves have been surprised by their effectiveness because of the tolerance engendered by their complex perceptions of God. I personally believe that Christianity in certain areas of Africa is more constructive when expressed through the lives of the devoted in personal settings rather than in public forum. Believers live a life of dignity and purpose in the transparent, but non-invasive, practice of their spirituality. This stance has been an effective tool for evangelism in Nigeria.

Post-colonial Christian writers in Nigeria have affirmed attempts by Christianity in Africa to give structure and power to the universality of that which is ultimately desirable for all human beings – love. The essence of Christianity is to affirm and guide the universal human urge to live a meaningful and purposeful life. This is a phenomenon to which evangelical Christians in Nigeria are most sensitive. Thus, the Christian faith is seen as more than just an assortment of cultic activities, but rather as an indivisible entity unified by the efforts to grasp the totality of one's existence. Evangelical Christians must not measure the faith or spirituality of others by comparing it to Christianity. To do so would be comparable to trying to measure human intelligence by measuring the size of one's skull.

When adherents of a religion concede that their faith is relative to a more ultimate and greater reality, they often become more honest, which in turn makes their brand of religion more universally attractive. An openness to the possibility of that 'greater reality' effectively negates any exclusive and proprietary claims on ultimate truth. This acknowledgement renders Christianity plausible, when it recognized the possibility that other religions can legitimately put forth their own distinctive dimensions of God. When a particular faith or religion surrenders exclusive and proprietary claims on ultimate reality, it validates itself by making credible the possibility of authenticity in the perspectives of other faith groups.

To affirm Christianity unapologetically, evangelical Christians need not seek out conflicts associated with non-Christian religions but should recognize the validity of what those faiths might have to offer.

The common typology of views, such as exclusivist, inclusivism and pluralism,[2] presumes there is religious fulfillment, or what evangelical Christians call 'salvation'. This typology has been developed with painstaking thoroughness within the circles of evangelical Christianity in the West but applied analogously to other faiths. Many evangelical Christians believe that the Christian tradition alone possesses religious truth, thus offering the only path to salvation. There are those Christian inclusivists who affirm that salvation is available through other religious traditions because the God most fully revealed in Christ is also present within or through those other faith traditions. Leaders of Christian pluralism maintain that various religious traditions are independently valid paths to salvation and Christ can be considered irrelevant to those in other traditions, although for Christians, Christ serves the same end.

This typology is irrelevant in a Nigerian context because the principal categories of Christianity are often immeasurable, being too personal and intimate. Separating people according to their convictions about how to attain salvation is now on shaky grounds.[3] Believers are drawn to share in innovative ways about their tribalism, sharing and caring for the whole person. Most have made it their goal to be on a spiritual pilgrimage with their fellow Nigerians, whether they are Yoruba or Hausa or Fulani or Igbo, responding to a universal need for love and dignity. I see this as a reason for real hope in Nigeria and in the world. This cross-tribal Christianity demonstrates that what we teach others about God with words has influence; but what we teach with our lives and our relationships, all emerging from the wealth of a caring heart, has much greater influence. The non-verbal influence coming out of how one lives gives testimony to God that no words can match.

The Nigerian evangelical Christianity and salvation

Theologian S. Mark Heim has pointed out that salvation is not only a matter of external reward and hell a matter of punishment. If someone overeats and consequently has a stomachache, it is entirely his or her fault. The situation is the product of his or her choice, the distress resulting from that choice; it is not something 'enforced' by someone else from the outside.[4] Paradoxically, the person who overeats chooses to overindulge but does not intentionally choose the suffering. However, the suffering is already factored into the overeating. In a way, the overeater does not really regret the behaviour but focuses his or her regret elsewhere. It becomes, for instance, a reason to reproach God for mixing this vexing concomitant with the pleasure of overindulgence, and the reproach itself becomes a pleasure the person does not wish to give up.

God gives and honours radical freedom in God's creatures. To take away that freedom of choice from the lost, Heim continues, would be the last, absolute destruction of their worth and dignity. Thus, in matters pertaining to salvation, there is no dichotomy created between the freedom of the human will and the determinism of God.

Jesus on religious tolerance: Lessons from Lagos for evangelical Christians

What can we learn from Jesus on religious tolerance? In the gospels, the two passages where Jesus comes the closest to addressing this question are (1) Mk 9.40: 'Whoever is not against us is for us', and (2) Mt. 12.30: 'Whoever is not with me is against me, and whoever does not gather with me, scatters.'

In the first passage, the Gospel of Mark records that it was John who said to Jesus: 'Teacher, we saw someone casting out demons in your name, and we tried to stop him, because he was not following us.' But Jesus said: 'Do not stop him; for no one who does a deed of power in my name will be able soon afterward to speak evil of me.'

Both passages occur in the context of a discussion about casting out demons. There is no doubt that casting out demons was an important religious activity. The incident in Mark's Gospel involves a person who does not belong to the group of followers of Jesus but is casting out demons in the name of Jesus. This unknown exorcist is using the name of Jesus religiously but does not join him directly as a disciple. In Matthew's gospel, it is the exorcism of demons by Jesus that was challenged by people who claimed that he did this work by the power of the devil.

When both passages are taken together, it appears that in a case where someone associates the true works of the spirit with Jesus's name (though with no explicit contact with or authorization from Jesus), the principle is 'whoever is not against us is for us'. This is the case in the situation recorded in the Gospel of Mark. But in the case of someone who attributed the actual acts of Jesus and the presence of the Holy Spirit to Satan, as in the Gospel of Matthew, the principle is 'whoever is not for us is against us'. S. Mark Heim observed the difference with great insight, stating that what is most severely rejected is any claim that the spirit and power of God are not associated with Christ. Jesus exercised a broad religious tolerance for the 'unauthorized' association of his name with real works of God's spirit. In the gospel account, and in these two examples specifically, what is at issue is the way those of 'other religions' treat Jesus, the person. Neither text, for example, really addresses the question of religious practice that simply ignores Jesus. What the passages affirm is the integrative tolerance of religious principle. A human being reaches the lowest level of religious arrogance when thinking that other human beings do not merit God's favour because they do not believe in God the same way he does. The teachings of Jesus provide no license for speculation about the religious practices of others in the way many evangelical Christians have done.

Jesus makes at least three important points in these passages that are crucial in thinking about religious tolerance. First, Jesus cautions that there are more than one way of casting out demons. Could this mean that there is far more than one way to God and that belief in God can be fulfilled in many ways? Is it not a fearful thing for any faith group to think that it has a monopoly on the path to God? Furthermore, religious thinkers are often too quick to name what they do not understand. The disciples were too quick to pass judgement on the exorcist, excluding the acts of exorcism. By doing so, the disciples cast a shadow on a common ground for religious dialogue – the act of exorcism.

In the same way, early European evangelical Christians lumped together the vast co-ordinated and amorphous mass of new and old religious cults, customs and practices of the people of India and called them 'Hinduism'. Its own adherents never named it Hinduism. They knew it as *Sanatana Dharma*, Eternal Teaching or Eternal Law. The designation *Sanatana Dharma* is broad, drawing on the term 'Dharma' that signifies 'truth', 'practice', 'duty' and 'way of life'. The European and evangelical term 'Hinduism' has diminished the original meaning of *Sanatana Dharma.*

But one should not infer any pluralistic comfort from the criticism invoked by the statement of Jesus. There is no specific reference, for example, to a non-Jewish faith by Jesus, and he remained faithful to Judaism, although disappointed by it and its religious leaders. Jesus was much more interested in the people than in their religions.

Second, we can infer from the passages that Jesus maintains that religious truth is always more comprehensive than any human being's grasp of it, making established theology or doctrines constantly out-of-date because of the inability of the mind to 'catch up' with religious experience. In other words, the basis of tolerance is simply the realization of the magnitude of the sphere of truth about God. We cannot possess the truth about God; we can only be possessed by it. Tolerance means, therefore, reverence for all the variations of truth and an acknowledgement that truth dwells in diversity and speaks in strange tongues. Religious tolerance is a frank respect for freedom of indwelling conscience against mechanical forms, official conventions and social force. It rests upon the love that is greater than faith and hope. Intolerance, on the other hand, is a sign of both arrogance and ignorance; saying there is no truth beyond the circles of truth we ourselves see.

Third, Jesus reminds the disciples to be genuinely open to others by practising an attitude of questioning and searching. The disciples are challenged to always be ready and willing to change and move from where they are and make the attempt to enter into the religious world of others as thoroughly as possible.

With such attitudes and efforts in cross-fertilization, a 'shaky common ground' can begin to take shape. Even though at first it will be fragile and thin, even though it will always be 'breaking down' and need to be 're-examined', it will provide a sufficient footing on which both evangelical Christians in Lagos and devotees of other religions can genuinely hear from, learn from, challenge and be challenged by the other.

Each faith language is distinct and can be judged only by the rules of its own 'game'. The problem with so many efforts to carry on cross-cultural discourse or global religious conversation until recently is that one language 'game' is always hearing and judging the other according to its own rules. In the two passages I have examined above, we see that Jesus constructed bridges of communication over the chasms of diversity by humbly and attentively listening to others.

Conclusion

As the world grows smaller and the interactions with those of different traditions become greater, a positive view of the insights of other religions will be evident. Religious tolerance will increasingly become the most widely held alternative to that which is antithetical to the gospel of faith and reconciliation.

Christians of every era have seen Jesus as a reality to help them in their existential condition. This is what evangelical Christians in Lagos must do today. In interpreting the message of Jesus and the various categories of Christianity, evangelicals must be willing to work under new conditions.

Critical analyses of the Christian traditions have prepared believers to see beyond the documents, and the prevalence of religious diversity is preparing Christians in the modern era.

The disciples of Jesus looked at the reality of what he taught without the constraints of a predefined faith, and Christianity demands a certain kind of preparation. The new vision of evangelical tolerance of other living faiths, especially Islam, will have all its original freshness just as it did when the disciples first perceived it. But the Lagosian Church alone cannot arrive at this new vision. This does not mean, however, that the church is incapable. To encourage a risk-forming picture of the reality before us in Lagos, we must join our critical doubt with a feeling for visionary evangelical tradition. It is then that we will have a sustained and substantiated story of Jesus for our time, and our knowledge of the past and the light through which we see Jesus will be uniquely our own.

I am convinced that religious tolerance can be achieved through this method of cross-fertilization. By following this pattern, the original intentions of those who first called Jesus their Lord take on greater clarity. Without this cross-fertilization with other living faiths, our experiences in the world would be limited, and we would be poorer by ignoring what other faith contexts and the confluence of religious knowledge have to offer.

Meanwhile, this method of cross-fertilization I am proposing is, I believe, consistent with the mind of Jesus Christ, who, with unlimited radicalism, broke through the established worldly orders. Without denying the world, he subjected all things to the condition of the kingdom that will come at the end of the age.

Religion in the sense of church dogma was not essential to Jesus. Religion, rather, was a stimulus to resistance by which one first gained self-awareness. Jesus is not only a model to imitate, but he also delineated a manner of thinking to show us a new way forward.

Most evangelical Christians I encountered in Lagos have not adopted this cross-fertilization approach to understanding modern realities but have continued to understand themselves from within the circle of their own experience and tradition. In this age of religious confluence, we must expand our ways of knowing God. How can we know the truth unless we allow our disparate circles to touch and overlap with the religious circles of others?

That is how I have come to understand my own Christian religious identity and story. Responses to events such as what took place in the United States on 11 September 2001, and the Asian tsunami disaster a decade later, in today's intercommunicated world require such a cross-fertilization of religious and cross-cultural self-understanding. Our interdependence means that if we are to survive on this planet, we will somehow have to embrace one another in celebration and recognition of our common humanity. The spirit of cross-fertilization speaks with a voice that transcends our religious differences and calls us to join hands as we both affirm our own particularities and disallow them at the same time, opening ourselves to the idiosyncrasies and individualism of others in an effort to remove religious intolerance.

But to announce a universal spirit that makes tolerance possible is not to announce a universal foundation that all participants can affirm. In proposing a cross-fertilization method for understanding our religious life, I am not proposing a single truth that we evangelical Christians at home in Nigeria and abroad can all finally come to or a universal foundation on which we can build a new religious world order. Rather, I am suggesting a process – a way of being and being together by which a community of religious thinkers can be structured and maintained, but not necessarily completed. I am proposing a process in which we respond to our common religious problems or to concerns we can all identify as universal. These will then provide us with the inspiration and the data to form a greater community in which we can act and talk together. Our various circles and elements of our religious heritage will then truly overlap. The truths we discover along the way will not be a universal propositional statement that we can all affirm; rather, it will be a way of being in which we find that we can indeed move between one another's worlds in a way that enhances the well-being of one another both individually and collectively.

Notes

Introduction

1 Nigeria is the most populous African country, and Lagos is its commercial capital with striking geographical, religious, ethnic, linguistic, and intra-cultural diversity. See Mario J. Azevedo, 'Nigeria' in Thomas Riggs, ed. *Worldmark Encyclopedia of Religious Practices,* vol. 3 (New York, NY: Thomson Gale, 2006): 149.

2 There are between 250-400 ethnic groups in Nigeria and Lagos has the reputation of been accommodating to most of the Nigerian ethnic groups. Mario J. Azevedo, 'Nigeria' 149.

3 There are many indications that the original name for Lagos was Eko, and there are attempts to resurrect the original name in such names as: Eko Bridge, Eko Hotel & Suites, Isale Eko, Eko Akete, Eko City, Eko Atlantic City, Eko Development Company, Eko Hospital, Eko Beach, Eko Atlantic School, and Eko International Bank, Eko International School, Eko Park, etc.

4 Maria J. Azevedo, 'Nigeria' 151–152.

5 Niels Kastfelt provides an account of how missionaries withdrew creatively while simultaneously training early Nigerian Christian politicians in mission schools to fight for political independence, using the vocabulary they learn in the church. Niels Kastfelt, *Religion and Politics in Nigeria: A Study of Middle Belt Christianity* (London: British Academic Press, 1994): 25ff.

6 Mario J. Azevedo, Nigeria, 151.

7 Ibid. 153.

8 Andrew F. Walls, *The Cross-Cultural Process in Christian History*, (Maryknoll, N. Y.: Orbis, 2002), 155–164.

9 Ibid. 157.

10 Andrew F. Walls, 'Samuel Ajayi Crowther,' in *Eerdmans' Handbook to The History of Christianity,* Tim Dowley, ed. (Grand Rapids, MI. Wm. Eerdmans Publishing Co., 1977): 567.

11 Mario J. Azevedo, Nigeria, 153.

12 Andrew F. Walls proposed two principles that have engaged scholars of Christian mission as the most important insights for our understanding of Christianity in the modern era: the indigenizing and the pilgrims' principles. The indigenizing principle states that God takes us as we are and we can feel at home by making the Christianity our own, growing under the indigenous stimulus. At the same time, we are part of the transformation

of the world through Jesus Christ, because God takes us as we are but also to transform us. Therefore, every Christian has dual nationality – the culture into which we are born and the kingdom of God. Thus, the Gospel is simultaneously a 'Prisoner and Liberator of every Culture.' See Andrew F. Walls, *The Missionary Movement in Christian History* (Maryknoll, N.Y. Orbis, 1996), 3–15.

13 See Tremper Longman, III, How to Read the Psalms(Downers Groves, Ill. Intervarsity Press 1988). The book shows that we learn so much more about the ways of God in the world by reading the Book of Psalms.

14 Many Christians I interviewed in Lagos quoted Proverbs 3:5-6 as their guiding light and favourite passage of the Bible. 'Trust in the Lord with all your heart, and do not rely on your own insight. In all your ways acknowledge him, and he will make straight your paths.' (NRSV).

15 See Tremper Longman, III *How to Read the Psalms* (Downers Grove, Illinois InterVarsity Press, 1988).

16 Isaiah 55:8 'For my thoughts are not your thoughts, nor are your ways my ways, says the Lord.' NRSV.

17 In *Jesus Christ and Mythology* (New York: Charles Scribner's Sons, 1958), Rudolf Bultmann, the German New Testament scholar wrote about this controversial biblical interpretation with an attempt to recover the deeper meaning behind what he thought was a mythological concept of the New Testament. In *Christ without Myth: A Study Based on the Theology of Rudolf Bultman* (Dallas, SMU Press, 1961), Schubert M. Ogden was not critical but constructive in his assessment, attempting to solve the problems Rudolf Bultman posed, and putting forth an existential interpretation of Jesus in the New Testament. Most Christians in Lagos see mythology as a story that is true on the 'inside,' but not on the 'outside.' Objective or scientific verification cannot be applicable, but remythologizing the reader.is essential for proper interpretation of the stories of the Bible.

18 Volker Küster, *The Many Faces of Jesus Christ: Intercultural Christology*, trans. John Bowden (SCM Press 1999): 75.

Chapter 1

1 One of the Christian experiences in the Christian life is grace. An analogy that comes to mind is that of fish in the Atlantic. While one may state that the fish are in the ocean swimming, it is also true to say that fish do not swim but are carried by the ocean water. This is the experience of Aborishade when describing his experience of the grace of God in Lagos. Sometimes, Christians are unaware of the water of grace that carries and sustains them.

2 Jonathan Sacks, *Not in God's Name: Confronting Religious Violence* (New York, N.Y.: Schocken Books, 2015): 41.

3   Jonathan Sacks, *Not in God's Name: Confronting Religious Violence* (New York, N.Y.: Schocken Books, 2015): 41.

Chapter 2

1   Matthew 10:32-33. (NRSV).

2   The parable of the ten bridesmaids in the Gospel of Matthew 25:1-13 underscores this understanding. Verse 13 says, 'Keep awake therefore, for you know neither the day nor the hour.'

3   Now the man who had been healed did not know who it was, for Jesus had disappeared in the crowd that was there. And my God will fully satisfy every need of yours according to his riches in glory in Christ Jesus.

4   Christianity is a catalyst that holds different ethnic groups together and the tendencies to form clannish groups become minimal because of the all-empowering Christian brotherhood.

5   High Religions are laden with doctrinal positions such as beliefs in heaven, baptism, virgin birth and in the resurrection of Jesus Christ in Christianity. See Paul G. Hiebert, *Anthropological Insights for Missionaries* (Grand Rapids, Michigan: Baker Book House, 1985). See also Paul. G. Hiebert, 'Popular Religions' in James M. Phillips and Robert T. Coote, eds. *Towards the 21st Century in Christian Mission* (Grand Rapids, Michigan: Wm B. Eerdmans Publishing Co., 1993): 253-66.

6   All the nations will gather before God at the last days of judgement and, as a shepherd separates the sheep from the goats, God will separate those who have served other fellow human begins from those who have neglected to serve others. God would declare: 'Come, you that are blessed by my Father, inherit the kingdom prepared for you from the foundation of the world; for I was hungry and you gave me food, I was thirsty and you gave me something to drink, I was a stranger and you welcomed me, I was naked and you gave me clothing, I was sick and you took care of me, I was in prison, and you visited me, Matthew 25: 34b-36.' Those who serve others in the name of Jesus Christ are called 'righteous' and this is the most important pronouncement for being a Christian in the Gospel of Matthew.

7   The Acts of the Apostles represents the functions and experiences of the Holy Spirit by early Christians. Their experiences transcend any other experience foundational to the life of the Church, and from the promise of the Holy Spirit to the salvation of the Gentiles, the Acts of the Apostles broke new ecclesiastical grounds and secured Christianity as a religion for all human beings in the world.

8   Kwame Bediako, *Christianity in Africa: The Renewal of a non-Western Religion* (Edinburgh University Press: Orbis Books, 1995), 118.

9   Ibid. 43.

Chapter 3

1 It should be noted that the Hebrew Bible underscores the creativity of God, and the first line in Genesis states: 'In the beginning when God created the heavens and the earth, the earth was a formless void and darkness covered the face of the deep, while a wind from God swept over the face of the waters.' (Genesis 1:1-2, NRSV). God is always the subject of the Hebrew word 'to create' in the Hebrew Bible.

2 In *Migration and the Making of Global Christianity,* the Sierra Leonean theologian at Emory University Jehu J. Hanciles, argues that 'the presentation of religious development in human history in terms of stages inevitably conveys a sense of linearity, or consistent improvement over time. But the notion that each successive development replaced or superseded the previous system, resulting in progressively "superior" forms, is unwarranted and flawed.' In other words, when the Christian faith was introduced by European missionaries, for example, the understanding of God in Igboland was not replaced by the Christian one, and *Chineke* endures but is added to the understanding of God cumulatively. One can even argue that the concept of 'paganism' or 'heathenism' does not exist de facto, but a missionary imposition to bring legitimacy to the concept of God they came to proclaim in Africa. In essence, every pre-Christian faith category was labelled 'paganism' or heathenism. See Jehu J. Hanciles, *Migration and the Making of Global Christianity* (Grand Rapids, Michigan: William B. Eerdmans, Publishing Company, 2023): 46–67.

3 Howard Thurman, *Jesus and the Disinherited* (Boston, MA: Beacon Press, 1976) 1.

4 Luke 11: 1-4; See also Matthew 6:9-13.

5 For a detailed discussion of Imasogie's unique understanding of God in African Traditional Beliefs, see O. Imasogie, *African Traditional Religion* (Ibadan, Nigeria: University Press Limited, 1985): 25.

Chapter 4

1 At the Faith and Freedom Sunday School Class at the First United Methodist Church in Cary, North Carolina, David Mann recalled one Sunday morning that it is, perhaps, more accurate to say about the narrative in Genesis 22 that Abraham did not sacrifice Isaac. Therefore, David proposed that we can say that the story is 'Abraham not Sacrificing Isaac' and I will use this phrase in this chapter. David and Barbara Mann have been instrumental in my own theological development, and I will always owe them a debt of gratitude for introducing me to the Faith and Freedom Sunday class, and the First United Methodist Church in Cary, North Carolina where my twins were baptized in 1985.

2 Daniel 3:16-18. NRSV.

3 See Alasdair MacIntyre, 'Kierkegaard, Søren Aabye' in *The Encyclopedia of Philosophy* Vol. 4 (New York, N.Y.: Macmillan Publishing Co., Inc. & The Free Press, 1967): 337.

4 Søren Kierkegaard, *Fear and Trembling,* trans. Walter Lowrie (Princeton, N.J.: Princeton University Press, 1968), 62.

5 Ibid.

6 Ibid.

7 Christian theologians in the Western world, and from earliest times, understood Isaac as a pre-figuration of Christ, the Beloved Son of God offered as the expiatory sacrifice for the sin of the world. The textual parallels between Isaac and Jesus are striking. Isaac, like Jesus, was miraculously conceived. Isaac carried the wood for his own sacrifice (Genesis 22:6), just like Jesus carried his own wooden cross when he was about to be crucified. The journey to Mt. Moriah took three days, parallel to the three days and three nights Jesus spent in the tomb before his resurrection.

8 In Luke 18:1-8, Jesus told a parable of a widow and the unjust judge. In the parable, Jesus showed that the widow was aware of the injustice of a judge, but her persistency made the judge change his mind and granted the widow justice, saying in 18:4-5 'For a while he refused; but later he said to himself, "Though I have no fear of God and no respect for anyone, yet because this widow keeps bothering me, I will grant her justice, so that she may not wear me out by continually coming."' In Matthew 15:21-28 and Mark 7:24-30, Jesus was unwilling to heal the demon-possessed and a tormented little daughter of a Syrophoenician woman, saying to her that: 'It is not fair to take the children's food and throw it to the dogs.' But the woman retorted: 'Yes, Lord, yet even the dogs eat the crumbs that fall from their masters' table.' The bold statement of faith that Jesus was an internationalist and will not reject his followers wherever their religious or cultural background might be, led Jesus to render a healing hand to the daughter of the Canaanite woman, and she received the benefit that was originally meant for the children of Israel. Jesua commended her, saying 'Woman, great is your faith! Let it be done as you wish.' Therefore, speaking up persistently by faith within one's context is a path to understanding the mind of God. The Kingdom of God requires the persistent and faithful participation of all, including Jews and Gentiles, black and whites, natives and foreigners. The Kingdom of God is dynamic and is an on-going project of faith, requiring the participation of everyone. This is because the eschatological community that Christ came to inaugurate transcends religions and ethnic particularities. Christians and non-Christians are invited to build God's Kingdom because God is beyond any faith tradition of humanity.

9 Ethics, along with Aesthetic, Epistemology, Metaphysics, and Logic, are all branches of philosophical inquiries. Ethics inquires 'what is the purpose of life and the appropriate thing to do to lead a good life?'

10 These attributes of hope, love and justice correspond to the three aspects of emphasis in Judaism, Christianity and Islam respectively.

Chapter 5

1 See Hebrew 13:8 that states, 'Jesus Christ is the same yesterday and today and forever.' NRSV.

2 Ritual killings were associated with the unfounded belief that a person could obtain instant wealth and fortune by murdering a close friend or associate by the means of traditional African voodoo. Ritual killers often take the head of their victims to a diviner and perform certain rituals so that the victim's destiny of fortune can be then transferred to them. In some parts of Africa, this is a cosmic law of cause and effect.

3 In pre-colonial era, the philosophy of imprisonment across Africa was restorative justice. In post-colonial era, however, this philosophy becomes retributive justice. In restorative justice, proponents see the accused people as the victims of the state brutality. Violence has antecedent, including poverty and mismanagement of public funds by the state. The proponents of retributive justice, on the other hand, see the state and the society as the victim. Retributive justice focuses on the past, but restorative justice focuses on the future of the individual victim. For restorative justice, the debt is paid back when the state makes provision to the victim through dialogue, whereas in retributive justice, the debt is paid to the state and society through the imprisonment, using it as punishment with the hope that incarceration will serve as a deterrent. See Nina Rosenstand, *The Moral of the Story: An Introduction to Ethics*. sixth edition. (Boston, MA: McGraw-Hill, 2009): 346-348

4 Like fruit trees, they give to live well and productively. We do not give to be depleted but to serve others and be renewed.

5 Yolanda Pierce, *In My Grandmother's House: Black Women, Faith, and the Stories We Inherit* (Minneapolis, MN: Broadleaf Books, 2021).

Chapter 6

1 'For there is still a vision for the appointed time; it speaks of the end and does not lie. If it seems to tarry, wait for it; it will surely come, it will not delay.' (NRSV).

2 A crossover service is a worship service on New Year's Eve. Most churches in Lagos begin the service at 10:00 PM on December 31st through January 1 at 2:00 AM.

3 This story is regularly referred to as 'the story of a prodigal son.' In Lagos, however, many Christians call it 'The story of a loving father.'

Chapter 7

1 Readers who are interested in knowing more about the historical formation, theological developments, and transformation of faith in Africa would benefit from the exhaustive bibliographical materials I provide in this volume.

2 North Africa has a dual identity – it is both a part of Africa culturally and geographically, and a part of Western Asia culturally and religiously. Egypt shares this dual identity with Ethiopia, and both are mentioned in the Bible frequently.

3 Thomas C. Oden, *The African Memory of Mark: Reassessing Early Church Tradition* (Downers Grove, Ill.: IVP Academic, 2011).

4 This would explain why Mary and Joseph took Jesus to Egypt, for example, when he was an infant. Jesus was born around June 4 B.C.E.

5 Thomas C. Oden, *The African Memory of Mark: Reassessing Early Church Tradition* (Downers Grove, Ill.: IVP Academic, 2011), 21.

6 Thomas C. Oden states that 'This Saint [Mark] was born in Cyrene (one of the Five Western cities), Pentapolis – in North Africa.' *The African Memory of Mark: Reassessing Early Church Tradition* (Downers Grove, Ill.: IVP Academic, 2011), 45. See also Oden's quotation: 'Coptic Synaxarion for Baramouda [Ethiopic-Amharic Miyazia] 30, (Miyazia is one of the months in the Ethiopian Coptic year, like the Egyptian Coptic month of Baramouda; cf. Shenouda III).'

7 Thomas C. Oden, *The African Memory of Mark: Reassessing Early Church Tradition* (Downers Grove, Ill.: IVP Academic, 2011), 33.

8 Ibid. p. 22.

9 Kwane Bediako, *Christianity in Africa: The renewal of a Non-Western Religion* (Edinburgh University Press, 1995): 155–6. The subtitle of the book is the focus.

10 Thomas C. Oden, *The African Memory of Mark,* p. 48.

11 Perhaps what surprised Mark most was the resurrection of Jesus Christ. He was likely a young boy at the resurrection site. Resurrection is the appearance of the living but transformed Jesus who died. Mark believed this (as a pharisaic Jew), and he lived it with his willingness to die proclaiming its credibility in Alexandria, Egypt.

12 In his seminal work, *The Historical Figure of Jesus,* E. P. Sanders states that his preferred title for Jesus was viceroy because Jesus seems to have been quite reluctant to adopt a title for himself. Even the title 'king' is not precisely correct according to Sanders. Sanders's favourite term for Jesus's conception of himself is 'viceroy.' In other words, God was king, but Jesus represented God and would represent God still in the coming kingdom. See E P. Sanders, *The Historical Figure of Jesus* (New York, N.Y.: Allen Lane the Penguin Press, 1993), 248.

13 Thomas C. Oden, *The African Memory of Mark: Reassessing Early Church Tradition* (Downers Grove, Ill.: IVP Academic, 2011), 48.

14 Thomas C. Oden, *The African Memory of Mark*, p. 82.

15 See 1 Peter 5: 13 which reads, 'Your sister church in Babylon, chosen together with you, sends you greetings; and so does my son Mark.' (NRSV). Family ties are often defined sociologically rather than biologically in biblical times. When familiar faces from Nazareth saw Jesus discussing in the Temple in Jerusalem, he responded to those who said that his father and mother have been looking for him by saying, 'these are my fathers and mothers.'

16 It is not impossible that Mary, the mother of Mark, also had a maternal inclination for her son to hear the new Jewish Rabbi Jesus of Nazareth and his ministry. Therefore, Mary planned for the family to return to Jerusalem so that Mark would have the benefit of knowing his Jewish identity in the homeland.

17 Thomas C. Oden, *The African Memory of Mark*, p. 80.

18 Thomas C. Oden, *The African Memory of Mark*, p. 80.

19 Thomas C. Oden, *The African Memory of Mark*, p. 80.

20 The details of this miraculous event are unusual to narrate in the Western world, but Thomas C. Oden was probably writing for Africans in Chapter 5 of his book which he titled, 'A Portrait of Mark.' See Thomas C. Oden, *The African Memory of Mark: Reassessing Early Church Tradition* (Downers Grove, Ill.: IVP Academic, 2011), 80 ff.

21 This means that every Christian is also a missionary in waiting. It is not enough to learn someone else's definition of Christ or project another person's personality for there is a way of saying the name of Jesus Christ to the world that only our lives can say.

Chapter 8

1 The principle of epistemological reciprocity was popularized by N. Ross Reat and Edmund F. Perry in their book, *A World Theology* (1991). In the book, the author, without undermining the identity or integrity of individual faith traditions, points the attention of religious thinkers and philosophers towards integrating the respective messages of the world's living faiths in a comprehensive and systematic manner that constitutes world theology— religious thought that is informed by the faiths of all humankind without dominated by any one of them. See *A World Theology: The Central Spiritual Reality of Humankind* (New York, N.Y.: Cambridge University Press, 1991).

2 See Abraham J. Heschel, *The Prophets* (New York, N.Y.: Harper & Row, Publishers, 1962) See also, Alan Race, *Thinking About Religious Pluralism: Shaping Theology of Religions for Our Times* (Minneapolis, Fortress Press, 2015).

3 This is Pastor Yusuf's understanding of "Jesus did not come to abolish the law of Judaism, but to fulfil it" according to the Gospel.

4 It is not impossible to find a common ground with people of Abrahamic faith traditions, and some scholars have maintained that Prophet Muhammad

as the son of Abraham, can also be seen as the brother of Moses and the successor of Jesus of Nazareth. See *Ekram Haque, Muhammad: Son of Abraham, Brother of Moses, Successor of Jesus: Finding Common Ground with People of the Book* (Murphy, Texas, Inner Traditions International and Bear & Company, 2016; also, in Al-Waqidi's Kitab Al-Maghazi, 2013).

5 Deuteronomy 34:10-12.

6 Hebrews 11:38.

Chapter 9

1 Horace Bushnell, View of Christian Nurture (New York, N.Y. Scribner, Armstrong & Co., 1876), 38.

2 This story is identical to the one written by Jacob A. Loewen, a Mennonite missionary to Columbia. Loewen's article was published in 1986, and it was an insightful story about the disparity of the concept of God missionaries proclaim to the indigenous people when missionaries arrive on the mission field. See Jacob A. Loewen, 'Which God Do Missionaries Preach?' *Missiology: An International Review.* Vol. XIV No. 1 (January 1986). In my conversations with Christians in Lagos, I experienced directly what Loewen described so well in his 1986 article.

3 Apostasy is a fall away from the faith that one initially proclaimed. It is the opposite of evangelism.

4 See E. Bolaji Idowu, *Olódùmarè: God in Yoruba Belief* (London, Longman, 1962). Chapter 4 specifically deals with the name of God among the Yorubas in Nigeria: Olódùmarè.

5 Don Richardson, *Eternity in Their Hearts,* (Ventura, CA.: Reggal Books, 1981), 52.

6 Viggo Mortensen, ed. *Theology and the Religions: A Dialogue* (Grand Rapids, Michigan: Wm B. Eerdmans Publishing Co., 2003), 477.

7 Frithjof Schuon, *The Transcendent Unity of Religions* trans. Peter Townsend, rev. ed. (New York, N.Y.: Harper & Row Publishers, 1975), 91.

8 Ibid.

9 Ibid.

10 Christopher J. H. Wright, *The Mission of God: Unlocking the Bible's Grand Narrative* (Downers Grove, II.: InterVarsity Press, 2006), 22-23.

11 See Howard Thurman, *Jesus and the Disinherited* 1.

Chapter 10

1 Across Lagos, all school children anticipate that their parents would buy them new clothes, and the expectations are often high. Parents who fail to provide monetary gifts or buy new clothes for their children are often ashamed. When the new school years begins, often in January, children often show off their new Christmas clothes their father bought them to celebrate Christmas.

Chapter 11

1 Kwesi A. Dickson and Paul Ellingworth, eds. *Biblical Revelation and African Beliefs* (New York: Orbis Books, 1969), vii.

2 Kwesi A. Dickson and Paul Ellingworth, eds. *Biblical Revelation and African Beliefs*, 16.

3 Jean-Marc Éla, *My Faith as an African* (Maryknoll, New York, N.Y., Orbis Books, 1985), 44.

4 Lamin Sanneh and Joel A. Carpenter, *The Changing Face of Christianity: Africa, the West, and the World* (New York, N.Y.: Oxford University Press, 2005). See also Andrew F. Walls, *The Cross-Cultural Process in Christian History* (Maryknoll, New York, Orbis Books, 2002).

5 See The Introduction by Bishop J. E. C. Welldon to Archbishop Maghakia Ormanian, *The Church of Armenia* (Yerevan, Armenia Ankyunacar, 2011), 7.

Chapter 12

1 Polygyny is the practice of a man marrying more than one wife. It is often misunderstood or confused with polygamy.

2 In Mark 12:25, Jesus stated, for example, 'For when they rise from the dead, they neither marry nor are given in marriage, but are like angels in heaven. (NRSV)'

3 Levirate marriages are not common among the younger generation in Lagos, but the obligation of caring for the wife of a deceased older brother remains. In some instances, the wife of a deceased older brother and her children could move in to live with a younger and more prosperous brother without conjugal rights or sexual relationship, but this is rare. When this occurs, the society automatically assumes that the wife of the deceased brother has practically become the wife of the younger brother. Levirate marriage is also common in the Old and New Testament periods, and many of the patriarchs in biblical times had multiple wives.

4 The story of 'A o merin j'oba, eweku, ewele' is about a group of plotters who were about to put an elephant on the throne. The elephant started rejoicing prematurely, not knowing that it was a plot to destroy him. On the day of his enthronement and coronation, the plotters dug a hole underneath the chair of the new king, covering it with beautiful clothes. As they were singing, the elephant sat on the beautiful throne meant for the king; he fell into the ditch underneath the chair. The moral of this popular story is that one must be careful when everyone is praising him. The only one who truly wants the best for you and be successful in life is God.

5   This is a condition marked by increase of interstitial fibrous tissue. With medication, it could shrink but could affect the foetus severely.

Conclusion

1   Political analysts have examined the past 20 years and concluded, for example, that either democracy will destroy the world as we know it, or the world will destroy democracy. There have been more wars, economic stalemate, and unfulfilled promises of prosperity in many regions of the world, and the Western attempt to babysit democratic governance in west Asia continues to be perplexing. Niall Ferguson, *The War of the World: Twentieth-century Conflict and the Descent of the West* (New York, N.Y. Penguin Books, 2006). Ferguson's book demonstrated that the west has been fighting unending wars since World War II (1939-1945). Many political analysts in Africa believe, however, that the decline of the West started at the Berlin Conference of 1884/85 when 14 European countries scrabbled for Africa and divided the continent and colonized it exclusively for their political and economic gains. Not a singler African was invited, and since Africa was so colonized without a voice of protest, war psychology consumed Adolf Hitler (1889-1945), the dictator of Nazi Germany, who attempted to conquer the world, begining in Europe, but it backfired on him, leading to World War II. See also Hernando De Soto, *The Mystery of Capital: Why Capitalism Triumphs in the West and Fails Everywhere Else.* (New York, N.Y.: Basic Books, 2000). De Soto's argument is convincing, stating that the bedrock of economic prosperity is the rule of law that defends private assets. In the third-world countries, however, there are assets, but they are dead assets, and the citizens cannot use them to acquire bank loans to create wealth.

2   Huston Smith, *The Forgotten Truth* (New York: Crossroad, 1982).

3   Osadolor Imasogie, *Guidelines for Christian Theology in Africa*, 52.

4   Osadolor Imasogie, *Guidelines for Christian Theology in Africa*, p. 52-3.

5   Osadolor Imasogie, *Guidelines for Christian Theology in Africa*, p. 52.

6   Osadolor Imasogie, *Guidelines for Christian Theology in Africa*, p. 56.

7   Osadolor Imasogie, *Guidelines for Christian Theology in Africa*, p. 60.

8   Genesis 1: 1–2.

9   See Marcus J. Borg, *Jesus: A New Vision: Spirit, Culture, and the Life of Discipleship* (New York: HarperCollins, 1987). Although, some non-Western theologians characterize modern theology as 'flat tire' theology, believing

that all the *pneuma* has gone out of it, Marcus Borg disagree with this characterization. The irony of this characterization depended on the double meaning of *pneuma*, a Greek word meaning both air and spirit, according to Borg. According to Borg, modern theology brings joy and insight; it is as challenging as it is liberating. Borg's book celebrates the reality of the Spiritual world, stating that 'a world of Spirit, was the common property of virtually every culture before ours, constituting what has been called the primordial tradition.' Marcus Borg, *Jesus: A New Vision: Spirit Culture, and the Life of Discipleship* (New York: HarperCollins, 1987).

10 Osadolor Imasogie, *Guidelines for Christian Theology in Africa,* 75.

11 Marcus J. Borg, *The God We Never Knew, Beyond Dogmatic Religion to a More Authentic Contemporary Faith* (New York: HarperCollins, 1997), 48.

12 Leander E. Keck, *The Church Confident: Christianity can Repent, but It Must not Whimper* (Nashville, TN.: Abingdon Press, 1995) 52.

13 Leander E. Keck, *The Church Confident: Christianity can Repent, but It Must not Whimper,* 52.

14 Leander E. Keck, *The Church Confident: Christianity can Repent, but It Must not Whimper,* 45.

15 Leander E. Keck, *The Church Confident: Christianity can Repent, but It Must not Whimper,* 45.

16 Martin Buber, *The Prophetic Faith,* 37.

17 See Marcus Borg, *The God We Never Knew: Beyond Dogmatic Religion to a more Authentic Contemporary Faith,* 48.

18 Andrew F. Walls, 'Christian Scholarship and the Demographic Transformation of the Church' in ed. T. I. Okere. *Religion in a World of Change: African Ancestral Religion, Islam and Christianity* (Owerri, Nigeria: Whelan Research Academy, 2002), 158.

19 See Nina Rosenstand, *The Moral of the Story: An Introduction to Ethics* Sixth ed. (New York, N.Y.: 2009 McGraw-Hill Company Inc., 2009), 437.

20 Christians in Lagos often teach their children the lyrics of The Doxology: 'Praise God from Whom all Blessings Flow, Praise him, all Creatures here below, Praise Him above Yee Heavenly Host, Praise Father, Son and Holy Ghost.'

21 The Kenyan Nobel Peace Prize Laureate, Wangari Maathai, consistently advocated for nurturing the environment. She maintained that a utilitarian view and exploitative relationship that humanity has with the environment is inconsistent with bold spirituality, and abusing the covenantal relationship humanity has symbolically with the environment would ultimately destroy humanity. See *Replenishing the Earth: Spiritual Values for Healing Ourselves and the World* (New York: Doubleday, 2010).

Epilogue

1 In his ground-breaking work, *The History of Baptist Work in Northern Nigeria (1901-1975),* Ezekiel A. Bamigboye relates a profound indigenous story of how

Baptist leaders from the South worked with political wisdom and evangelistic sagacity to plant churches in the stronghold of Muslims in Northern Nigeria. I was moved by Bamigboye's story when I first heard it at Ogbomoso in 2013 during my sabbatical leave at the Nigerian Baptist Theological Seminary, there. See Ezekiel A. Bamigboye, The History of Baptist Work in Northern Nigeria 1901-1975 (Ibadan, Nigeria: Powerhouse Press and Publishers, 2000):120-21. See also Caleb O. Oladipo, 'How Indigenous Traders Brought Christianity to Northern Nigeria' in Casely B. Essamuah and David K. Ngaruiya, eds. *Communities of Faith in Africa and the African Diaspora* (Eugene, OR: Pickwick Publications, 2013).

2 See a comprehensive diagnosis and analysis of the relationship between Christianity and other living faith traditions in the Western world by Paul F. Knitter. *One Earth Many Religions: Multifaith Dialogue & Global Responsibility* (Maryknoll, New York, N.Y. Orbis Books, 1995): 23-37.

3 The points of the inadequacies of making salvific determination for others without knowing them have been made with clarity by Judith A Berling in *Understanding Other Religious Worlds: A Guide for Interreligious Education* (Maryknoll, New York: Orbis Books, 2004).

4 See S. Mark Heim, *Salvations: Truth and Difference in Religion* (Maryknoll, New York, Orbis Books, 1995). In this book, perhaps the author gives the Christians in Lagos a rare gift of scholarship by contending that Christ is the revelation of God definitively but not absolutely and exclusively. The unity of religions, according to Heim, stems from participation in a single historical continuum. Therefore, as one participates in one religion, he participates in all the others whether he knows it or not.

Bibliography and Recommended Readings

Achunike, Hilary. 'Catholic Charismatic Movement in Igboland, 1970-1995'. PhD thesis, University of Nigeria, Nsukka, 2001.

Acolatse, Esther E. *Powers, Principalities, and the Spirit: Biblical Realism in Africa and the West*. Grand Rapids, Michigan: Wm. B. Eerdmans Publishing Co., 1918.

Adeogun, Ebenezer O. *A Transplant of the Vine: Forty Years of Foursquare History in Nigeria*. Lagos: Foursquare Gospel Church in Nigeria, 1999.

Adogame, Afe. 'Appropriating Malachi Rhetoric in African Pentecostalism: The Case of the Redeemed Christian Church of God in Nigeria and the USA'. Paper delivered at the African Studies Association Conference, New Orleans, November 11–14, 2004.

Adogame, Afe. 'Politicization of Religion and the Religionization of Politics in Nigeria'. In *Religion, History, and Politics in Nigeria: Essays in Honor of Ogbu U. Kalu,* edited by Chima Korieh and Ugo Nwokeji, 128–139. Lanham, Md.: University Press of America, 2005.

Adogame, Afe. 'A Walk for Africa: Combating the Demon of HIV/AIDS in an African Pentecostal Church: The Case of Redeemed Christian Church of God'. *Scriptura: International Journal of Bible, Religion and Theology in Southern Africa* 89 (2005): 396–405.

Akutto, F. W. B. *The Indigenization of Christianity: A Study of Ghanaian Pentecostalism*. Oxford: Oxford University Press, 1975.

Althouse, Peter. 'Towards a Theological Understanding of Pentecostal Appeal to Experience'. *Journal of Ecumenical Studies* 38, no. 4 (Fall 2001): 399–411.

Anderson, Allan. 'The Prosperity Message in the Eschatology of Some Charismatic Churches'. *Missionalia* 15, no. 2 (1987): 72–83.

Anderson, Allan. 'African Pentecostalism'. *Studia Historiae Ecclesiaticae* 22, no. 1 (1996): 114–148.

Anderson, Allan. *African Reformation*. Trenton, N.J.: Africa World Press, 2000.

Anderson, Allan. 'The Newer Pentecostal and Charismatic Churches: The Shape of Future Christianity in Africa?' *Pneuma: The Journal of Society of Pentecostal Studies* 24, no. 2 (Fall 2002): 167–184.

Anderson, Allan. *An Introduction to Pentecostalism: Global Charismatic Christianity*. Cambridge: Cambridge University Press, 2004.

Anderson, Allan. 'African Independent Churches and Global Pentecostalism: Historical Connections and Common Identities'. In *African Identities and World Christianity in the Twentieth Century,* edited by Klaus Koschorke, 63–76. Wiesbaden: Harrassowitz, 2005.

Anderson, Allan. 'The New Jerusalem: The Role of the Azusa Street Revival in the Global Expansion of Pentecostalism'. Paper delivered at the 35th Annual Meeting of the Society for Pentecostal Studies, Pasadena, CA., March 23–25, 2006.

Archer, K. J. 'Pentecostal Hermeneutics: Retrospect and Prospect'. *Journal of Pentecostal Theology* 8 (1996): 63–81.

Asamoah-Gyadu, J. Kwebena. *African Charismatics: Current Developments Within African Independent Indigenous Pentecostalism in Ghana.* Leiden: Brill, 2005.

Asamoah-Gyadu, J. Kwebena. 'Half a Century of Touching Lives: Nigerian Charismatic Personalities and African (Ghanaian) Christianity, 1953–2003'. In *Religion, History and Politics in Nigeria: Essays in Honour of Ogbu U. Kalu,* edited by Chima J. Korieh and G. Ugo Nwokeji, 230–245. Lanham, Md.: University Press of America, 2005.

Ayegboyin, Deji I. 'A Rethinking of Prosperity Teaching in the New Pentecostal Churches in Nigeria'. *Black Theology: An International Journal* 4, no. 1 (2006): 70–86.

Bamigboye, Ezekiel A. *The History of Baptist Work in Northern Nigeria, 1901 to 1975.* Ibadan, Nigeria: Powerhouse Press & Publishers, 2000.

Barrett, David. 'Twentieth Century Pentecostal/Charismatic Renewal in the Holy Spirit with Its Goal of World Evangelization'. *International Bulletin of Missionary Research* 12 (July 1988): 119–129.

Baur, John. *2000 Years of Christianity in Africa: An African History 62–1992.* Nairobi, Kenya: Paulines Publications Africa, 1994.

Bediako, Kwame. *Christianity in Africa: The Renewal of a non-western Religion.* Edinburgh: Edinburgh University Press, 1995.

Baur, John. *Theology and Identity: The Impact of Culture upon Christian Thought in the Second Century and Modern Africa.* Oxford: Regnum, 1992.

Berling, Judith A. *Understanding Other Religious Worlds: A Guide for Interreligious Education.* Maryknoll, New York, N.Y.: Orbis Books, 2004.

Boesak, Willa. *God's Wrathful Children: Political Oppression & Christian Ethics.* Grand Rapids, Michigan: Wm. B. Eerdmans Publishing Co., 1995. This book was written as a reflection of oppression under apartheid. Allan Boesak's brother argues that God's wrath was reflected in the anger of the oppressed people.

Borer, Tristan Anne. *Challenging the State: Churches as Political Actors in South Africa: 1980-1994.* Notre Dame, Indiana: University of Notre Dame Press, 1998. This book is very brilliant about the creative response of the Church against oppression and that the Church can be an agent of transformation.

Borg, Marcus J. *Conflict, Holiness and Politics in the Teachings of Jesus.* Harrisburg, Pennsylvania: Trinity Press International, 1998. Although written for the audience in the West, it has some good coverage in the teachings of Jesus as a revolutionary leader that are useful in the time of African transition to democracy.

Borg, Marcus. *Jesus: A New Vision: Sprit Culture, and the Life of Discipleship.* (New York: HarperCollins, 1987).

Bosch, David J. *Transforming Mission: Paradigm Shifts in Theology of Mission*. Maryknoll, New York: Orbis Books, 1991. This is a complete and comprehensive study. Divided into three parts, the book covers the biblical, historical and theological aspects of mission that are instructive to the Church anywhere.

Bradwshaw, Bruce. *Change across cultures: A narrative approach to Social transformation*. Grand Rapids, MI: Baker Book House, 2002. This is an excellent study about the cross-cultural approach to social and political transformation.

Bruce, Steve. 'The Charismatic Movement and the Secularization Thesis'. *Religion* 28 (1998): 223–232.

Buber, Martin. *I and Thou*. New York, N.Y.: Charles Scribner's Sons, 1958.

Buber, Martin. *The Prophetic Faith*. New York, N.Y.: Harper & Row, Publishers, 1949.

Bujo, Benezet. *African Theology in Its Social Context*. Maryknoll, New York: Orbis Books, 1992. The approach of Bujo in this work is that the social contexts, such as a strong sense of community and family, are important ingredients for developing African theology.

Bultmann, Rudolf. *Jesus Christ and Mythology*. New York, N.Y.: Charles Scribner's Sons, 1958.

Burgess, G. 'The Calcutta Revival of 1907'. *Asian Journal of Pentecostal Studies* (AJPS) 6, no. 1 (2003): 123–143.

Burgess, Richard H. 'The Civil War Revival and Its Pentecostal Progeny: A Religious Movement among the Igbo People of Eastern Nigeria 1967-2002'. PhD diss., University of Birmingham, 2004.

Burgess, Stanley M., ed. *International Dictionary of Pentecostal and Charismatic Movements*. Grand Rapids, Mich.: Zondervan, 2002.

Callaway, Helen. 'Women in Yoruba Tradition and in the Cherubim and Seraphim Society'. In *The History of Christianity in West Africa*, edited by Ogbu U. Kalu, chap. 18. London: Longman, 1980.

Caygill, Howard. *Levinas & the Political*. London: Routledge, 2002.

Christellow, Allen. 'Islamic Law and Judicial Practice in Nigeria: An Historical Perspectives'. *Journal of Muslim Minority Affairs* 22, no. 1 (2002): 185–204.

Coleman, Simon. 'Charismatic Christianity and the Dilemma of Globalization'. *Religion* 28 (1998): 245–256.

Cone, James H. *The Cross and the Lynching Tree*. Maryknoll, New York, N.Y.: Orbis Books, 2011

Cox, Harvey. *The Secular City: Secularization and Urbanization in Theological Perspective*. New York: The Macmillan Company, 1965. This classic by the Harvard professor shows that theology reflects human beings, and it develops.

Cox, Harvey. *The Future of Faith*. New York: HarperCollins Publishers, 2009. In this relatively recent work of Harvey Cox, he acknowledges the transformation of Christianity in our time and shows appreciation for a de-westernization of the Christian faith.

Cox, Harvey. *Fire From Heaven: The Rise of Pentecostal Spirituality and the Reshaping of Religion in the Twenty-First Century*. Reading, Mass.: Addison-Wesley, 1995.

Dayton, Donald. *Theological Roots of Pentecostalism*. Metuchen: Scarecrow, 1987.

De Gruchy, John W. with Steve de Gruchy. *Christianity and Democracy: A Theology for a just world order.* Cape Town: David Philip Publishers, 1995. This is a well-written book that places Christian principles at the heart of democratic values.

De Gruchy, John W. with Steve de Gruchy. *The Church Struggle in South Africa.* Minneapolis, Minnesota: Fortress Press, 2005. This brilliant work is both a prediction and a challenge for the Church. The father and son authors showed that apartheid was the Church against the Church. Their claim is instructive about the roles of the Church in crafting a steady democracy in other parts of Africa, especially Nigeria.

Delaney, Carol. *Abraham on Trial: The Social Legacy of Biblical Myth.* Princeton, NJ: Princeton University Press, 2000.

Dickson, Kwesi A., and Paul Ellingworth. eds. *Biblical Revelation and African Beliefs.* Maryknoll, New York: Orbis Books, 1969. This book is the result of the first conference of African theologians at Ibadan in 1966. I see the book as the second conversion of Africans to Christianity. Many of the essays were attempts to craft Christianity in the African idioms and cultural contexts.

Ekeh, P. P. *Colonialism and Social Structure.* Ibadan: University of Ibadan Press, 1983.

Ellington, S. A. 'Pentecostalism and the authority of Scripture'. *Journal of Pentecostal Theology* 9 (1996): 16–38.

Ellis, Stephen, and Gerrie ter Haar. *Worlds of Power: Religious Thought and Political Practice in Africa.* New York: Oxford University Press, 2004.

Emeka, Paul. 'Benson Idahosa Factor in Nigerian Pentecostalism,' PhD thesis, University of Nigeria, Nsukka, 2001.

Engelke, Matthew. *A Problem of Presence: Beyond Scripture in an African Church.* Berkeley, California: University of California Press, 2007. This is a bold study about a Church in Zimbabwe that the Bible could be a weapon when used as a book of privilege to prevent others from a direct relationship with God.

Enwerem, I. M. *A Dangerous Awakening: The Politicization of Religion in Nigeria.* Ibadan: IFRA, 1995.

Falola, Toyin. *Violence in Nigeria: The Crisis of Religious Politics and Secular Ideologies.* Rochester: Rochester University Press, 1998.

Falola, Toyin, ed. *Christianity and Social Change in Africa.* Durham, N.C.: Carolina Academic Press, 2005.

Gifford, Paul. *African Christianity: Its Public Roles.* Bloomington: Indiana University Press, 1998.

Gifford, Paul. 'Chiluba's Christian Nation: Christianity as a Factor in Zambian Politics, 1991–1996'. *Journal of Contemporary Religion* 13, no. 3 (1998): 363–381.

Hackett, R. I. J. 'Charismatic/Pentecostal Appropriation of Media Technologies in Nigeria and Ghana'. *Journal of Religion in Africa* 28, no. 3 (1998): 258–277.

Hanciles, Jehu J. *New Religious Movements in Nigeria.* Lewiston, N.Y.: Mellen, 1987.

Hanciles, Jehu J. *Migration and the Making of Global Christianity.* Grand Rapids, MI: Eerdmans Publishing Company, 2021

Hawn, C. Michael. *Gather into One: Praying and Singing Globally.* Grand Rapids, Mich.: Eerdmans, 2003, 104–188.

Heim, S. Mark. *Salvations: Truth and Difference in Religion*. Maryknoll, New York: Orbis Books, 1995.

Heschel, Abraham J. *The Prophets*. New York, N.Y.: Harper & Row, 1962.

Ibe, Basil O. *The Ultimate Christian Generation: The Emergence of the Prophetic Company*. Lagos: Rehoboth, 2001.

Ibrahim, Jibrin. 'Religion and Political Turbulence in Nigeria'. *Journal of African Studies* 29 (1991).

Ilesanmi, Simeon. *Religious Pluralism and the Nigerian State*. Athens: Ohio University Press, 1997.

Imasogie, Osadolor. *Guidelines for Christian Theology in Africa*. Achimota, Ghana: Africa Christian Press, 1983.

Isichei, Elizabeth. 'The Maitasine Rising in Nigeria, 1980–1985: A Revolt of the Disinherited'. *Journal of Religion in Africa* 17, no 3. (October 1987): 194–208.

Jenkins, Philip. *The Next Christendom: The Coming of Global Christianity*. New York: Oxford University Press, 2000.

Kalu, Ogbu. *Divided People of God: Church Union Movement in Nigeria, 1867–1967* New York: NOK, 1978.

Kalu, Ogbu. 'The Practice of Victorious Life: Pentecostal Political Theology and Practice in Nigeria, 1970–1996'. *Mission: Journal of Mission Studies, University of Ottawa* 5, no. 2 (1998): 229–255.

Kalu, Ogbu. 'Sharia and Islam in Nigerian Pentecostal Rhetoric, 1970-2003'. *Pneuma* 26, no. 2 (2004): 242–261.

Kalu, Ogbu. *African Pentecostalism: An Introduction*. New York: Oxford University Press, 2008.

Kato, Byang H. *Theological Pitfalls in Africa*. Nairobi: Evangel Publishing House, 1987. This book has important coverage but embraces the western categories of missionary understanding of Christianity uncritically.

Keck, Leander E. *The Church Confident: Christianity Can Repent, But it Must not Whimper*. Nashville, T.N.: Abingdon Press, 1993.

Kierkegaard, Søren. *Fear and Trembling and The Sickness unto Death*. Trans. Walter Lowrie. Princeton, N.J. Princeton University Press, 1941.

Kirk, J. Andrew. *What is Mission? Theological Explorations*. Minneapolis: Fortress Press, 2000. This is a good book that reflects and criticizes the traditional understanding of Christian mission as well as colonialism.

Knitter, Paul F. *One Earth Many Religions: Multifaith Dialogue & Global Responsibility*. Maryknoll, New York: Orbis Books, 1995.

Kukah, Matthew Hassan. *Religion, Politics and Power in Northern Nigeria*. Ibadan, Nigeria: Spectrum, 1994.

Küster, Volker. *The Many Faces of Jesus Christ*. London: SCM Press, 2001.

Lawson, E. Thomas. *Religions of Africa: Traditions in Transformation*. San Francisco: Harper & Row, Publishers, 1985. There is a good coverage of the Yoruba traditional religions and their existential dimension as they go through transformation.

Loewen, Jacob A. 'Which God Do Missionaries Preach?' *Missiology: An International Review* XIV, no. 1 (January 1986).

Maathai, Wangari. *Replenishing the Earth: Spiritual Values for Healing Ourselves and the World*. New York: Doubleday, 2010.

Mabogunje, Akin. *Urbanization in Nigeria*. London: Oxford University Press, 1968.

Magesa, Laurenti. *African Traditional Religion: The Moral Foundations for Abundant Life*. Maryknoll, N.Y.: Orbis, 1997.

Makhubu, Paul. *Who are the Independent Churches?* Johannesburg: Skotaville Publishers, 1988.

Marshall-Fratani, Ruth. 'Mediating the Global and the Local in Nigerian Pentecostalism'. *Journal of Religion in Africa* 28, no. 3 (1998): 278–315.

Marshall-Fratani, Ruth. 'Power in the Name of Jesus: Social Transformation and Pentecostalism in Western Nigeria Revisited'. In *Legitimacy and State in the Twentieth Century Africa*, edited by T. O. Ranger and Olufemi Vaughn, 213–246. London: Macmillan, 1993.

Martin, David. *Pentecostalism: The World Their Parish*. Oxford: Oxford University Press, 1990.

Mbiti, John S. *Introduction to African Religion*. London: Heinemann, 1975. This book illustrates that African Traditional religion has legitimacy and can serve as precursor for understanding God.

Mbiti, John S. *African Religions and Philosophy*. New York: Doubleday and Co. Inc., 1970.

Meyer, Birgit. 'Christianity in Africa: From African Independent to Pentecostal-Charismatic Churches'. Annual Review of Anthropology 33 (2004): 447–474.

Mudimbe, V. Y. *The Invention of Africa: Gnosis, Philosophy, and the Order of Knowledge*. Bloomington: Indiana University Press, 1988.

Mugambi, J. N. K. *African Christian Theology: An Introduction*. Nairobi, Kenya: East African Educational Publishers, Ltd., 1989.

Muzorewa, Gwinyai H. *The Origins and Development of African Theology*. Maryknoll, New York: Orbis Books, 1985.

Nyamiti, Charles. *Christ as Our Ancestor: Christology from an African Perspective*. Gweru, Zimbabwe: Mambo Press, 1984.

Oden, Thomas C. *How Africa Shaped the Christian Mind: Rediscovering the African Seedbed of Western Christianity*. Downers Grove, Ill.: IVP Books, 2007

Oden, Thomas C. *The African Memory of Mark: Reassessing Early Church Tradition*. Downers Grove, Ill.: IVP Academic, 2011.

Oduyoye, Mercy Amba, and Musimbi R. A. Kanyoro. eds. *The Will to Arise: Women, Tradition, and the Church in Africa*. Maryknoll, New York: Orbis Books, 1992.

Ogden, Schubert M. *Christ Without Myth: A Study Based on the Theology of Rudolf Bultmann*. Dallas, TX.: SMU Press, 1961.

Ojo, Matthew. 'The Dynamics of Indigenous Charismatic Enterprises in West Africa'. *Missionalia* 25, no. 4 (1997): 537–561.

Ojo, Matthew. 'Pentecostalism, Public Accountability and Governance in Nigeria'. Pentecostal-Civil Society Dialogue on Public Accountabilty and Governance Conference, Lagos, Nigeria, October 18, 2004.

Ojo, Matthew. 'Nigerian Pentecostalism and Transnational Religious Networks in the West African Coastal Region'. In *Enterprises Religieuses Transnationales en Afrique de L'Ouest*, edited by Laurent Fourchard et al., 395–438 Paris: Karthala, 2005.

Ojo, Matthew. *The End-Time Army: Charismatic Movements in Modern Nigeria*. Trenton, N.J.: Africa World, 2006.

Olayinka, Bolaji Olukemi. *Female Leaders of New Generation Churches as Change agents in Yorubaland*. PhD thesis, Obafemi Awolowo University, 2000.

Oosthuizen, G. C. et al. *Religion, Intergroup Relations, and Social Change in South Africa.* 1988.

Pauw, C. 'African Independent Churches as a 'People's Response' to Christian Message'. *Journal for the Study of Religion* 8, no. 1 (1995).

Reat, N. Ross, and Edmund F. Perry. *A World Theology: The Central Spiritual Reality of Humankind.* New York, N.Y.: Cambridge University Press, 1991.

Regehr, Ernie. *Perceptions of Apartheid: The Churches and Political Change in South Africa.* 1979.

Rosenstand, Nina. *The Moral of the Story: An Introduction to Ethics.* New York, The McGraw-Hill Companies, Inc., 2009.

Sacks, Jonathan. *Not In God's Name: Confronting Religious Violence.* New York, N.Y.: Schocken Books, 2015.

Sanneh, Lamin. *Translating the Message: The Missionary Impact on Culture.* Maryknoll, New York: Orbis Books, 1989.

Sanneh, Lamin. *Whose Religion is Christianity?* Grand Rapids, Mich.: Eerdmans, 2003.

Sanneh, Lamin, and Joel A. Carpenter. *The Changing Face of Christianity: Africa, the West, and the World.* New York: Oxford University Press, 2005.

Sender, John, and Sheila Smith. *The Development of Capitalism in Africa.* New York: Methuen, 1986.

Setiloane, Gabriel M. *African Theology: An Introduction.* Johannesburg: Skotaville Publishers, 1986.

Shorter, Aylward W. F. *African Culture and the Christian Church.* London: Geoffrey Chapman, 1973.

Smith, Jordan Daniel. 'The Arrow of God: Pentecostalism, Inequality and the Supernatural in Southeastern Nigeria'. *Africa* 71, no. 4 (2001): 587–613.

Sundkler, Bengt, and Christopher Steed. *A History of the Church in Africa.* Cambridge: Cambridge University Press, 2000.

Takya, J. 'The Foundations of Religious Intolerance in Nigeria'. *Bulletin of Ecumenical Research* 2, no. 2 (1989): 31–41.

Tasie, G. O. M. *Thoughts and Voices of an African Church: Christ Army Church, Nigeria.* Jos: Connack Nigeria, 1997.

Ter Haar, Gerrie. *How God Became African: African Spirituality and Western Secular Thought.* Philadelphia, Pennsylvania: University of Pennsylvania Press, 2009.

Thangaraj, M. Thomas. *The Common Task: A Theology of Christian Mission.* Nashville, TN.: Abingdon Press, 1999.

Thurman, Howard. *Jesus and the Disinherited.* Boston: Beacon Press, 1976.

Tinder, Glenn. *The Political Meaning of Christianity: The Prophetic Stance.* New York: HarperSanFrancisco, 1989.

Tinney, J. B. 'The Blackness of Pentecostalism'. *Pneuma* 3, no. 2 (1980): 27–36.

Todd M. Johnson, and Kenneth R. Ross, eds. *Atlas of Global Christianity.* Edinburgh: University of Edinburgh Press, 2010.

Turner, H. W. 'Nigerian Pentecostalism'. *Orita,* University of Ibadan (1971): 7–15.

Tutu, Desmond. *The Rainbow People of God: South Africa's Victory Over Apartheid.* New York: Doubleday, 1994.

Ukah, Asonzeh. 'Advertising God: Nigerian Christian Video-Films and the Power of Consumer Culture'. *Journal of Religion in Africa* 30, no. 2 (2003): 203–231.

Ukah, Asonzeh 'Mobilities, Migration and Multiplication: The Expansion of the Religious Field of the Redeemed Christian Church of God, Nigeria'. In

Religion in the Context of African Migration, edited by A. Adogame and C. Weisskoppel, 317–342. Bayreuth: Bayreuth African Studies 75, 2005.

Ukah, Asonzeh 'Seeing Is More Than Believing: Posters and Proselytization in Nigeria'. In *Proselytization Revisited: Rights Talk, Free Markets and Culture Wars*, edited by R. I. J. Hackett. London: Equinox, 2006.

Usman, Bala. *Manipulation of Religion in Nigeria*. Kaduna, Nigeria: Vanguard, 1987.

Vilakazi, Absolom. *Shembe: The Revitalization of African Society*. Johannesburg: Skotaville, 1986.

Walls, Andrew F. *The Cross-Cultural Process in Christian History*. Maryknoll, New York: Orbis Books, 2002.

Walls, Andrew F. 'Christian Scholarship and the Demographic Transformation of the Church'. In *Religion in a World of Change: Africa Ancestral Religion, Islam and Christianity*, edited by T. I. Okere. Owerri, Nigeria: Whelan Research Academy, 2002.

Wink, Walter. *Unmasking the Powers: The Invisible Forces that Determine Human Existence*. Philadelphia: Fortress Press, 1986.

Yamamori, Tetsunao, and C. René Padilla, eds. *The Local Church, Agent of Transformation: An Ecclesiology for Integral Mission*. Buenos Aires: Kairos Ediciones, 2004.

Yoder, John Howard. *The Politics of Jesus*. Grand Rapids, Michigan: Wm. B. Eerdmans Publishing Company, 1972.

Yong, Amos. *The Spirit Poured Out on All Flesh: Pentecostal and the Possibility of Global Theology*. Grand Rapids, Mich.: Baker, 2005.

Index

Personal Names

Scriptures

Old Testament

New Testament